the ORIENT EXPRESS

The story of the world's most fabulous train

MICHAEL BAR

STEIN AND DAY/*Publishers*/New York

First published in the United States of America by

Stein and Day/*Publishers*/1967

Published in Great Britain in 1966 by

Macdonald & Co. (Publishers) Ltd.

Printed in the United States of America

Stein and Day/*Publishers*/7 East 48 Street, New York, N.Y. 10017

Date Due

AUG -	1983		

DATE DUE

ORIENT EXPRESS

Other Books by Michael Barsley

Autobiography
THE WOLF AT THE DOOR
BEHIND THE SCREEN

Satire
RITZKRIEG
COLONEL BOGUS
COMMON MAN AND COLONEL BOGUS
HOW TO BECOME ARCHBISHOP

Humorous Verse
GRABBERWOCKY
ALICE IN WUNDERGROUND

Anthologies
MODERN AMERICAN HUMOUR 1943
THIS ENGLAND 1940-46
THE PHOENIX BOOK OF WIT AND HUMOUR
THE PHOENIX BOOK OF MODERN AMERICAN HUMOUR
LIFE AND LAUGHTER

Drawings
BROUGHT TO BOOK

To my brother
ANTHONY
with whom I shared our first
model railway

ACKNOWLEDGEMENTS

In a train-and-travel book of this kind, there are many passengers, officials and friends who have made valuable suggestions or given individual reminiscences. These helpers are too numerous to mention individually, but I hope they will accept this general acknowledgement.

For specific co-operation I would like to thank Mr. J. H. Price, Editor of Cook's *Continental Timetable*, for much helpful advice; Mr. Swinglehurst of Thos. Cook & Son, London; M. Réné Desbalnes, Curator of the Railway Museum, Vienna; Capitaine Renon and M. Commault of the *Compagnie Internationale des Wagons-Lits*, Paris; M. Youssef Mardin, of the Turkish Government Tourist Office, London, and Mr. Senih Tugrul and Miss Cevsa Ozil, of the Tourist Office, Istanbul; Mr. Numan Taner, Director of the First Region, Turkish Railways, Haydaparsa; Miss Lilian Medeleva of Sofia, Bulgaria; Mr. A. C. Streatfield, of British Rail, Southern Region; Mr. John East, of the French Government Tourist Office, London; Mr. George Behrend, railway historian extraordinary, of Jersey; the staff of the Library at the United States Information Service, London.

Acknowledgements and thanks are also due to the following for permission to quote copyright material: George Allen and Unwin Ltd. for extracts from *As I Seem to Remember* by Sir Leonard Woolley; George Allen and Unwin Ltd. and Soccer Associates for extracts from *Grand European Expresses* by George Behrend; Arthur Barker Ltd. for extracts from *Express to the East* by A. Den Doolard; for extracts from *The Owl's Watchsong: A Study of Istanbul* by J. A. Cuddon, copyright 1960, reprinted by permission of the publisher of the United States edition, Horizon Press; The Bodley Head Ltd. and M. Maurice Dekobra for extracts from his book *The Madonna of the Sleeping Cars;* S. J. Perelman for extracts from his books *Westward Ha!* and *Swiss Family Perelman;* Jonathan Cape Ltd. for extracts from *Twenty-Five* by Beverley Nichols; Curtis Brown Ltd. for extracts from *No Place Like Home* by Beverley Nichols; Glidrose Productions Limited for extracts from *From Russia with Love* by Ian Fleming; William Collins Sons & Co. Ltd. and Dodd, Mead & Company for extracts from *Murder on the Orient Express* by Agatha Christie, published in the U.S. under the title *Murder on the Calais Coach;* Constable & Co. Ltd. and the Crompton family for extracts from *Reminiscences* by Lt.-Col. R. E. Crompton; Faber & Faber Ltd. for extracts from *High Road to Hunza* by Barbara Mons; for extracts from *Esprit de Corps* by Lawrence Durrell, copyright © 1957 by Lawrence Durrell, reprinted by permission of E. P. Dutton & Co., Inc.; Grayson & Grayson Ltd. for extracts from *The History of the King's Messengers* by Captain Wheeler-Holohan; The Viking Press, Inc. for extracts from *Stamboul Train* by Graham Greene; Holder & Stoughton Ltd. for extracts from *Victoria Four-thirty* by Cecil Roberts; Hutchinson & Co. (Publishers) Ltd. for extracts from *Romance of the Bosphorus* by Dorina Lady Neave; Herbert Jenkins Ltd. for extracts from *Unknown Yugoslavia* by Bernard Newman; Miss Marghanita Laski for extracts from an article which appeared in *The Guardian,* April 19, 1965; Macmillan & Co. Ltd. for extracts from *On The Old Lines* by Peter Allen; Mr. Johnny Morris and Mr. John Orczy-Barstow for extracts from their B.B.C. talks; Laurence Pollinger Ltd. and William Collins Sons & Co. Ltd. for extracts from *The Wheel Spins* by Ethel Lina White; Paul R. Reynolds Inc., 599 Fifth Avenue, New York 17, N.Y., for extracts from Joseph Wechsberg's article "Take the Orient Express," published in the *New Yorker,* April 22, 1950, Copyright © 1950 The New Yorker Magazine Inc.

Every effort has been made by the author and publishers to trace owners of copyright material. If any have been inadvertently overlooked, they beg the indulgence of those concerned, and would be pleased to have the matter brought to their notice, so that the error may be rectified in any future editions.

M.B.

CONTENTS

ix

LIST OF PLATES

xi

Acknowledgements and thanks are due to the following for variously providing and giving permission to reproduce illustrations: The British Film Institute; British Rail (Southern Region) for 29, 30; Collection Commault (Archives of the Compagnie Internationale des Wagons-Lits) for 3, 6, 7, 9, 11, 19, 20, for the menu card on page 28 and for the end-of-chapter drawing of early Orient Express rolling stock; Thomas Cook & Son Ltd. for 14, 15, 16, 17, 23, 40 and for illustration of timetable on page 72; Fontana Books for 36; French Railways for 2, 39, 42; William Heinemann Ltd. for 37; Radio Times Hulton Picture Library for 1, 4, 5, 8, 10, 12, 13, 21, 31, 32, 33; Railway Museum, Vienna, for 22, 25, 26, 41; The Rank Organisation for 38; Editions Standard, Berlin W. for part of the score of "Orient-Express" by Gerhard Mohr on page 98; Turkish State Railways for 18; Turkish Tourism Office for 47; Wagons-Lits/Cook for 24, 27, 28, 44 and for the Wagons-Lits emblem on page 21.

TIME-TABLES

1834   "I know it—I know all—the particulars have been faithfully related to me, and my mind comprehends locomotives. The armies of the English ride upon the vapours of boiling cauldrons, and their horses are flaming coals! Whirr! Whirr! All by wheels! Whizz! Whizz! All by steam!"

The Pasha of Belgrade to Alexander Kinglake. *Eothen*.

1876   "There is no heating apparatus for night travel : above all, if you are worn out and must sleep, you must sit up and do it in naps, with cramped legs and a torturing misery—for behold, they have not that culmination of all charity and human kindness, a sleeping car, in all France. . . ."

Mark Twain. *The Innocents Abroad*.

1881   "Herein, I think, is the chief attraction of railway travel. The speed is so easy, and the train disturbs so little the scenes through which it takes us, that our heart becomes full of the placidity and stillness of the country; and while the body is being borne forward in the flying chain of carriages, the thoughts alight, as the humour moves them, at unfrequented stations. . . ."

Robert Louis Stevenson. *Ordered South*.

1883   "The landscape flies at your feet, the streams seem to flow under the wheels, villages and houses shine like morning stars, and from your Rue de la Paix you can see the minuscule population of a little world. . . ."

Henri Stefan Opper de Blowitz,
of the London *Times,* on the Orient Express.

1884   "The time has now arrived when we may without doubt do everything we possibly can to induce travellers to visit these interesting districts. With Constantinople for a centre may be visited the principal battlefields of the Russo-Turkish War, the Dardanelles, and the reputed site of Troy."

Thomas Cook and Son.
The Excursionist and Tourist Adviser.

xiii

1921 "Let us get straight on to Greece, for it is easier to do that in a book than in the so-called *Train-de-luxe* which totters across Europe, falling over bridges, blundering through ravines, and waiting for a whole day at deadly-looking hamlets in strange countries. . . ."

Beverley Nichols. Twenty-Five.

1924 "I have a ticket for Constantinople. But I may step off at Vienna or Budapest. That depends absolutely on chance or on the colour of the eyes of my neighbour in the compartment. . . ."

Lady Diana Wynham in Maurice Dekobra's
La Madone des Sleepings.

1928 "The old artist always did himself well. Sir Malcolm took berths in the Orient Express, in spite of Connie's dislike of *trains-de-luxe*, and the atmosphere of vulgar depravity there is aboard them nowadays. . . ."

D. H. Lawrence. Lady Chatterley's Lover.

1932   "Waiting at the station,
For a near relation,
Puff, puff, puff, puff—
The Istanbul Train. . . ."

Graham Greene. Stamboul Train.

1934 "The train, it is as dangerous as a sea-voyage. . . ."

Hercule Poirot, in Agatha Christie's
Murder on the Orient Express.

1935 "Lady Kilmichael lived in a world which knew no other way of getting to Venice than to travel by the Orient Express. . . ."

Ann Bridge. Illyrian Spring.

1937 "In imagination, she saw it shooting through Europe. . . . It caught up cities and threaded them on a gleaming whistling string. Illuminated names flashed before her eyes and were gone— Bucharest, Zagreb, Trieste, Milan, Basle, Calais. . . ."

Ethel Lina White. The Wheel Spins.

1957 "James Bond gazed vaguely at one of the most romantic signs in the world. . . . The great trains are going out all over Europe, one by one, but still, three times a week, the Orient Express thunders superbly over the 1400 miles of glittering steel track between Istanbul and Paris. . . ."

Ian Fleming. From Russia With Love.

ORIENT EXPRESS

1

THE WAGONS-LITS MYSTIQUE

A nostalgic glimpse of a fabulous train in its heyday—Pullman and Wagons-Lits—George Mortimer Pullman of New York—Colonel Mann of the Boudoir Sleeping Cars—George Nagelmackers of Liége—The *Compagnie Internationale* is founded.

Once upon a time, a long, luxurious, darkened train stood along the main platform of the Gare de l'Est in Paris. Long, because it was to take travellers across the whole of Europe and to the edge of Asia. Luxurious, because it was an exclusive, all-Pullman, all-Wagons-Lits creation, in livery of royal-blue picked out with gold, and owing no allegiance to any country or company save the *Compagnie Internationale des Wagons-Lits et des Grands Express Européens*, a resounding title which fitted the full length of the coaches. Darkened, because, apart from the pink and gold glory of the dining-car and perhaps two non-sleepers, these coaches were already dedicated to the nightly comfort of the distinguished passengers.

The *Chemin de Fer de l'Est,* most enterprising of the French railway complex of the time, rightly called this Orient Express a train-de-luxe, with *"premier service permanent"*. It left Paris three times a week at one minute past seven in the evening. The baggage allowance was enormous—330 lb. per passenger. The facilities were exceptional : all passports and hand-luggage would be examined on the train, which meant no waiting in a draughty shed in some Balkan outpost. *Haute cuisine* was available throughout the journey. And though there were other Grand Expresses leaving this station, for Vienna, Frankfurt, Carlsbad, Prague and Budapest, there was one magical, compelling name on this destination-board : the word "Orient".

15

It conjured up the atmosphere of the Near East. The five hundred mosques in Constantinople, Asian atmosphere, the clamour of the casbah, the beggars in the streets, the Bosphorus where little ferry-boats ply between Europe and Asia in a matter of minutes, the fantastic treasury of the Sultans in the Palace of Topkapi, the Seraglio, the veiled women, the promise of a new, non-European tempo of life under a cloudless sky. It is all there in that one word "Orient"—the most compelling, come-hither word ever hung on the side of a railway coach.

This was the time when everyone who was anyone went by the Orient Express. A royal archduke travelled on the first trip over the new Danube bridge. A Greek Orthodox patriarch inaugurated the resumption of an Orient Express route, only sixteen years ago. King's Messengers and State Department Couriers, sometimes handcuffed to their diplomatic bags, regarded it as the normal means of travel. You didn't need to go the whole way. As recently as 1965 the Duke of Edinburgh took two of his children on part of the journey of the Arlberg-Orient Express, to reach Liechtenstein. D. H. Lawrence imagined Lady Chatterley on the Simplon-Orient Express from Venice, with her father.

"Sir Malcolm decided to travel with Connie and Duncan would come on with Hilda. The old artist always did himself well : he took berths on the Orient Express, in spite of Connie's dislike of *trains-de-luxe* and the atmosphere of vulgar depravity there is aboard them nowadays. . . ."

In the halcyon days before and between the two world wars, the international express was something to capture the imagination. Imagine yourself as a de-luxe passenger, with an impressive sheaf of first-class tickets made out by Thomas Cook or American Express, arriving at the Gare de l'Est. It is a modest, uncomplicated station. The way to the Orient Express is clearly indicated. You have perhaps twelve minutes in hand to see that your baggage is safely bestowed in your cabin-de-luxe. The conductor of your car leaps around like something from the flea-market, but this is expected, because the Ambassador has arrived in his Rolls-Royce, and an elegant lady in mink, with matching luggage, has to be discreetly but comfortably installed in Cabin No. 3, Voiture No. 7, and there are chauffeurs with rugs, and a few troublesome press-

16

photographers who want to know what she's doing there, and where she's going.

Then the late arrivals turn up. From the *Georges Cinq* comes a last-minute Mercedes with a portly gentleman who must do a lot of business in South America. There is no elaborate ceremony with him, but being, by implication, a descendant of the Aztecs and the Incas, he tends to tip porters and conductors before they have performed any service, and there is brisk competition for his perfunctory favours. The Man in the Dark Glasses follows: alone, aloof, adroit, with one streamlined suitcase which he carries himself, and the unchallenged right to the single *cabine-de-luxe* in No. 7.

This would be enough to start endless speculation if there was time enough, but there isn't. You stroll up the platform (knowing that you, as a Wagons-Lits passenger, are such valuable cargo, they wouldn't let even the Orient Express go without you) to check on the other coaches. There are the day-coaches, packed to the roof with luggage, and with hardy souls who are apparently willing to sit the journey out for three days and nights. Here the only *bonhomie* exists. The top Orient Express traveller is either a snob, a spy, or what is known as "a lady companion" or even "a bit of stuff". You recoil from the humanity of the day-coaches and return to the silent spectral splendour of those reserved for the night-folk so well beloved of the Wagons-Lits Company.

Supreme above all is the *Chef du Train,* in a blue uniform instead of brown. He is the ultimate arbiter of accommodation. He probably speaks six languages and could have been a minor civil servant had he so wished. But here the atmosphere is much more exalted. He can inhale the chypre and Chanel worn by the elegant creatures strolling down the corridors. He knows the meaning of a good tip, whether it be given out of guile or generosity. The same is true, in an appropriately lesser degree, with his conductors. Let other people just catch a train : these clients are being welcomed aboard the Orient Express. Their slightest whims must be condoned, if not necessarily obeyed.

It is many years before the 1960s, so the train is due to leave, not at midnight, but at the hour when dinner can be comfortably served, as a gracious final reminder of French cuisine and viniculture.

17

The Veuve Cliquot is cold upon the ice-block. The Chambertin is *chambré*. Nothing less for the first-class *voyageurs* heading for the Danube and the primitive Balkans. Has not the mighty *Compagnie Internationale*—for the last fifty years—fought to preserve this *cordon sanitaire* around its passengers?

The last flurries of farewell. A trolley trundles by from the area of the day-coaches, but no-one installed in a Wagons-Lits even notices it. Perhaps a rose is exchanged, as a token. Perhaps a stiff white envelope is thrust into a black-gloved hand, at the last moment. Perhaps the conductor realises that, with the lights burning late in the Quai d'Orsay, the Minister may not arrive to claim his cabin. Perhaps ... but for those with a sentimental turn of mind, there are so many twists and turns of fortune at every such departure.

The hiss of steam blurs the image as, prompt to time, this railroad symbol of a sumptuous way of life pulls out into the night, through the suburbs of Paris, heading for those romantic names on the destination-boards.

Fanciful? Not in the great days of the train's long history. There was even a time when the dining-car of the Orient Express took on a touch of fancy-dress, and the rest of the train, according to the researchers of *Time* magazine, was similarly decked out.

"The seats had velvet covers topped by Brussels lace, and lush damask curtains hung from the windows; the fittings were of solid oak and mahogany; hand-cut glass separated the sleeping compartments from the outside aisle. In elegant salon-cars, diners lingered over oysters and chilled glasses of champagne, served by attendants in morning coats, light blue silk breeches, white stockings and buckled shoes. Elegant prostitutes provided companionship for the lonely on the long journey to the Orient. . . ." (*Time* magazine, October 31, 1960).

This, at least, was the legendary Orient Express, the sort of train peopled by the tycoon, the rich eccentric, and the highly-placed courtesan. Joseph Wechsberg in the *New Yorker* (April 22, 1950) relates how one Katharina Schratt, actress at Vienna's Burgtheater and a favourite of the Emperor Franz Joseph, would have her dogs with her on the train, and the chef in the wagon-restaurant would make special dishes for them; their favourite was *schnitzel.* Wechsberg adds: "A Viennese beer magnate, Deber, didn't trust the food in the dining-car, excellent though it was, and had the Hotel Sacher deliver a seven-course meal in a hamper to the Orient Express."

There has always been something very personal about Pullman trains and Wagons-Lits coaches. It was George Mortimer Pullman, born in New York in 1831, who fathered and fostered the cars which still proudly bear his name. Pullman was a mechanic's son, and a cabinet-maker by trade. He first thought up the idea of sleeping carriages in the 1860s, and began by re-modelling coaches on the Chicago-Alton line, providing twenty upper and lower berths per car. His first complete Pullman car, the Pioneer, cost eighteen thousand dollars and took a year to build. For the next year it remained on the sidings, unwanted because it was too big for normal loading gauges. But after the assassination of President Lincoln, the Pullman car was specially hired to take his body, accompanied by his widow, from Chicago to Springfield, Massachusetts. This was the turning point in George Pullman's career.

A rival to Pullman in America arose in the spectacular figure of Colonel William d'Alton Mann. The colonel not only ran a profitable newspaper, but invented and promoted a number of private Boudoir Sleeping Cars. It was Mann who made the first bid for the European market, and in this he was helped by an enterprising Belgian, Georges Nagelmackers of Liége, who as early as 1868 visited the United States to inspect the six-wheeled vehicle at first hand. Europe was at that time in a state of considerable unrest, with massacres in Bulgaria and the Franco-Prussian war on the horizon.

Nagelmackers was fortunate in being Belgian. Since his nation was not involved in the railway struggle for power across Europe, he could mediate as well as operate. Had he been French or German, the war of 1870 might have put paid to his plans for a long time, but soon he was negotiating with the Italians to service the railway to Brindisi, at that time the main embarkation point for the Near and Far East (this was the route taken by Phileas Fogg when he went Around the World in Eighty Days). He also introduced Mann sleeping cars on several local routes.

Subsequently, Colonel Mann sold out to the Belgian, in 1875, and returned to America to resume battle, unsuccessfully, with Pullman. Nagelmackers, with his six-wheeled equipment, now became Pullman's rival in Europe, and was moreover experimenting with German-built sleeping-cars running on bogies, an innovation which changed the whole prospect for comfortable night travel, but which some railway companies at first regarded as unsafe.

From the very first, Pullman had established his right, in America, not only to have his special cars, but to charge a big supplement in addition to the fare. In Europe this vital item had already been agreed. By 1874 Pullman cars were already running in Britain, and in that year the first meal was served on a British train, on the Pullman car "Victoria" between London and Bedford. By 1882 there were Pullmans to Dover on the London, Chatham and Dover Railway. The new era had begun, thanks to George Mortimer Pullman, who envisaged a train not simply as a piece of machinery to haul a pay-load from one place to another, but as a means of travel which could be memorable (and therefore profitable) as an example of gracious living on wheels.

The railway historian C. Hamilton Ellis has summed up Mr. Pullman as "one per cent inventor, nine per cent improver, and ninety per cent businessman". At any rate, he left behind him a name which has passed into history, and into many languages, as a symbol of luxury travel.

By 1876 Nagelmackers & Company had become the International Sleeping Car Company, registered in Brussels. Here was a title, *Compagnie Internationale des Wagons-Lits,* which was to stay and to become famous, embellished later with the additional words *Et des Grands Express Européens.*

In his history of the *Compagnie* (*La Compagnie Internationale des Wagons-Lits.* Marcel Terras, Marseille) Capitaine Pierre Renon, now its Press Officer, describes the double objective : to assure, by using specially-equipped vehicles, continuity of journey, especially on international routes, and to provide maximum comfort to passengers on long journeys, allowing them complete rest, in real beds, throughout the night.

Renon estimates the strength of the new company (with King Leopold II as its active patron) at fifty-eight Wagons-Lits, none of them more than four years old. Nagelmackers was no longer content with local trains. The company had to replace its dependence on individual railway administrations with an international concept. Separate contracts had, of course, to be made with each railway authority, and these varied considerably in duration, from three to twenty years.

The second essential component of the Wagons-Lits service—the restaurant car—was not fully operative until 1883, but by that year Nagelmackers could claim he had all the elements for a "Grand Express". "It was a work of *rapprochement*," writes Renon, "from an economic, political, touristic and cultural point of view." It was also a pioneering effort. No previous attempt had ever been made to obtain co-operation or standardisation between the many individual railway companies of Europe. Nagelmackers conceived the grandiose plan for a through train running as far as the Black Sea, or at least as far as the Danube. His first all Wagons-Lits special had reached Vienna in 1882, but for the extended plan even as far as Bulgaria, where local rolling stock would take the passengers to the coast, and the steamer to the Bosphorus, the company had to negotiate with no less than eight different railway administrations, including three in Germany alone. These negotiations, lasting for two months, were concluded on May 2, 1883. A trial run was made without mishap, and the stage was set for one of the most spectacular inaugural journeys in railway history.

2

"MESSIEURS LES VOYAGEURS, LE DINER EST SERVI!"

The first Orient Express to Constantinople, 1883—Account by the *Times* correspondent de Blowitz and the French novelist Edmond About—Electric lights, bogie-cars and *bonhomie*—Ladies at Vienna—A Hungarian serenade —dancing aboard—Royal interview in Rumania—Misery in Bulgaria—The sea voyage.

On the evening of October 4, 1883, a Sunday, the event took place. Crowds at the Gare de l'Est, brilliantly lit by the new electricity, stared at a magnificent train labelled *Express d'Orient*, gleaming with polish and paint. More than 200 feet in length, it consisted of an outside-cylinder *Est* 2-4-0 locomotive, a *fourgon* (baggage car) laden with mail for the many countries which lay ahead; two of the new bogie sleeping-cars, replacing the old six-wheelers; a glinting, coruscating dining-car, which was to be the scene of so much garrulity, conviviality, and even music and dancing during the next few days, and another *fourgon* bringing up the rear.

All was ready for the much-publicised journey to Constantinople, eighteen hundred miles and ninety hours away. For this trip Nagelmackers and his company had spared no expense, and overlooked no detail. It is said that he arranged for a smaller train to be drawn up—as if by chance, and containing two of the uncomfortable six-wheeled dormitory cars of Mann—alongside the proud, bogie-furnished Orient Express. To overcome all Customs problems for his V.I.P. passengers, Nagelmackers had also provided a special badge, which he called his "talisman". The one hazard for the trip was that of health, i.e., "Cholera permitting". There were, of course, no passports to worry about in those days. (It was a former British Foreign Secretary, Ernest Bevin, many

22

years later who, when asked what his foreign policy was, replied, "I want to be able to go to Victoria Station, buy a ticket, and go where the hell I like !'").

Guests and officials numbered about forty, a convenient group for such an expedition, to allow interchange of ideas and experience, and freedom and individuality for the journalists. Ahead of them lay a route, partly by rail, partly by sea, which had already been tried out and inspected. It was no journey into the unknown. But so much had been laid on for the V.I.P.'s, and there was so much at stake for the company's international reputation, that the atmosphere, to a servant of Wagons-Lits, must have been as electric as the lights under the arches of the Gare de l'Est.

The French and Belgian parties were the largest. The French included the son of the Minister of Posts and Telegraphs, a man from the Finance Ministry called Grimpel, and several French railway officials. Among the Belgians, there was the Minister of Public Works, M. Olin, and naturally some Wagons-Lits directors, to emphasise the Flemish origin of the company. There was one Dutchman, a M. Janszen, who charmed everybody. There were two or three German newspapermen, who charmed nobody, it seems, and who kept themselves to themselves. The First Secretary of the Turkish Embassy, Mishak Effendi, an all-round career diplomat of impeccable experience and grace, represented the Sublime Porte. Other Austrian representatives and, it was hoped, Rumanian officials, were to join the train at Vienna and elsewhere along the line.

The presence also of two distinguished writers, one a novelist, the other a celebrated journalist, made this inaugural run of the *Express d'Orient* one of the most minutely and entertainingly documented railway journeys in history. The novelist and essayist, Edmond About, an Alsatian who had left Alsace after the German occupation of 1871, had his residence near Paris. It seems that he needed a little persuasion to join the party, since his experience of railway sleeping-cars had not been altogether happy in the past.

On his return, Edmond About wrote a complete book about this historic adventure on rails. (*De Pontoise à Stamboul.* Hachette, Paris, 1884).

But the more absorbing and, one can understand, triumphant

account of the trip came from the Paris correspondent of *The Times*, a naturalised Frenchman of Bohemian origin with the resounding name of Henri Stefan Opper de Blowitz. Tiny, rotund, voluble, with an enormous cranium and fantastic garb, his presence must have caused alternate amusement and embarrassment to the other V.I.P.'s, for de Blowitz was a first-rate, fast-working interviewer of international reputation, and seemed more interested in obtaining an "exclusive" with the King of Rumania en route than with the comfort and cuisine offered by the *Compagnie Internationale*. As it happened, he ended by getting one of the most spectacular interviews of the time, with the Sultan of Turkey himself, Abdul Hamid II, a feat never before achieved.

De Blowitz may have been something of a big-head in more ways than one. His biographer, Frank Giles, who called him "The Prince of Journalists" has summed up his unpopularity with the French Press of the time :

"He was accused of being a spy in the pay of England, a German, a Polish Jew, a conceited fellow, a cosmopolitan, an opportunist, of not brushing his hair, of being under five foot high, of being more than five foot round the waist, and of being an agent of Bismarck." (*The Prince of Journalists*. Faber, 1962.)

Professional envy apart, this was a heavy indictment which Henry Stefan Opper de Blowitz bore on his sloping shoulders. At least, he was an obvious choice for an important inaugural trip such as this, as Edmond About admits. The Frenchman described his fellow passenger as *"un homme très particulier, de physiognomie bizarre, et d'une coquetterie originale"*. At first, About did not feel enthusiastic about knowing him but admitted that de Blowitz improved with acquaintance, that he was highly intelligent, well enough informed, quick in repartee, capable of having his leg pulled, and giving good value in return. The one inevitable criticism was that he was too concerned with his own importance, and with getting the rest of the travellers to follow his lead. In the event, the others left him in Constantinople, still pursuing the elusive Abdul Hamid II, and returned without him. But de Blowitz had the last laugh, and returned to Paris with his famous Royal interview, and the Turkish Order of the Medjidie (Second Class).

24

Journalists are a notoriously jealous group. They have to be. If there's a possible "exclusive" in the offing, as an alternative to the group interview, they behave towards each other with all the vicious wariness of the wild cats under the Pantheon in Rome. For they are cats that walk by themselves, cats who will cheat and lie and double-cross and claw and snatch, and sidle away into the darkness, protesting they're only off to buy a packet of cigarettes or go to the toilet, when in reality they have the story in their pockets and are heading for the nearest phone-box.

But this journalist-jealousy, this love-hate relationship which usually accompanies any inaugural trip sponsored by public relations men, does not seem to have affected the first journey of the Orient Express. Edmond About, in any case, was not a journalist, but a well-known author, and de Blowitz had no rival. The *Times* correspondent, moreover, had been curious to meet About. In his own account of the journey (*Une Course à Constantinople*. Librarie Plon, 1884), written in a magnificent but very exaggerated and occasionally purple style, he describes the Frenchman as having "one of the best-known Paris faces". Edmond was handsome, with hair and beard grey before their time. His worldly success had not spoiled his vivacity—his delight in the cut-and-thrust of argument. To talk with Edmond About was to remember the satirical touch in his writing. He was, "a joker, when dealing with an undergraduate type", but when serious talk began, he dropped the light banter, and brought an observant mind and a good memory to the discussion.

There was, alas, no Boswell on the train, to catch the witticisms and the profundities which must have been expressed so often in that favourite restaurant car, after the claret and the cognac (and later, the rare vintages of Rumania) and amid the haze of cigar-smoke. But it is obvious that About and de Blowitz, the two main chroniclers of the journey, ended up with a healthy respect for each other. Looking back, perhaps the most interesting thing is to note where their chronicles agree or disagree, and which aspects of the inaugural journey intrigued or escaped them. There can, at any rate, have been few railway journeys which have combined such different aspects, between the diplomatic and the dietetic, between the sense of history flashing past the windows of the Wagons-Lits amid the ruins of Bulgaria, and the sense of discomfort engendered by certain menus and mannerisms which are apt to afflict the long-distance traveller.

Unless there was deliberate face-saving (and it is difficult to imagine Edmond About and de Blowitz simply as grateful guests willing to write up anything good about Wagons-Lits in return for the hospitality), the V.I.P. travellers seemed to have mingled well together.

Just as the French novelist noted his fellow travellers, so did Opper de Blowitz. He regarded the Turk, Mishak Effendi, as having just that amount of obesity appropriate to an Oriental—a nice solidity, he added, which doesn't belong to the category of nervous or thin men. Big Brother Nagelmackers of Wagons-Lits (who never, it seems wrote his account of the first journey) he described as being "a slightly Arab type". This could readily be understood from a photograph of the time, or from the portrait which looks down to this day on the board room of the company in Paris. But de Blowitz added that he was, by origin, entirely Belgian, and was "*sans bruit, sans trouble et sans défaillance*"—a tribute to inexhaustible qualities as well as to self-effacing ones. He praised M. Olin, the Belgian Minister of Public Works, praised M. Regray, Chief Engineer of the Est Railway, and looked in awe and wonder at the Flying Dutchman, M. Janszen, who brought with him a valise so wonderfully contrived, it contained everything. "A piece of luggage such as a Houdini would have used," he notes. "This Dutchman could have produced a completely equipped bathroom out of it, if he'd wanted to." The Dutchman was obviously a popular colleague, on all sides.

Edmond About agreed that M. Janszen would have received the Orient Express prize for his outstanding bonhomie. He was also very impressed by Belgium's M. Olin—a man, he wrote, without an atom of official arrogance or pride, something remarkable in a Belgian being received by the French.

There were others in this cosmopolitan company, but their names emerged, in the accounts of Edmond About and Stefan Opper de Blowitz, later on the journey. Otherwise, all was set. De Blowitz noted that, of the two Wagons-Lits "*les salons de société*" as he called them, one was set aside for the ladies—and he had to wait till Vienna till that became an actuality and the other for the male company.

He was asked to take his place, by an immaculately garbed and gloved attendant of Wagons-Lits, in Voiture No. 151, bed No. 3. We can imagine that de Blowitz was in a slight state of euphoria, particularly about the restaurant car, which he later described in glowing terms, and where he later enjoyed the first meal served by the Burgundian chef.

Such was the scene as the Orient Express left the platform at the Gare de l'Est, bearing not only M. Nagelmackers' talisman, but all his hopes for a train which would set a new standard of international travel. De Blowitz even had some comments about departures, those embarrassing scenes which are painful on railway stations, impossible at airports, and very harrowing at the quayside. "People should say goodbye at *home*," he noted, "*not* on railway stations." But the *Express d'Orient* went off on time. And within a few minutes of the departure, Stefan Opper de Blowitz noted the welcome call of a Wagons-Lits attendant :

"Messieurs les voyageurs, le dîner est servi!"

Edmond About, being a Frenchman and used to good living, made many observations en route about that varied and often vexed subject—railway food. The party were to taste several unsavoury dishes in the far-off Balkans, but the first meal, cooked by the black-bearded Burgundian, was a great success, and after inspecting the travelling kitchen, the novelist marvelled at the wonders which could be performed in such a tiny space. The trimmings included genuine *Beurre d'Isigny*. De Blowitz, too, was obviously something of a gourmet, but also a florid stylist. To him the meal seemed like a heap of jewels, from the ruby-red of the claret to the sparkling crystal of the water in the carafe.

De Blowitz shared his sleeping compartment with the Dutchman Janszen, and was very happy at the arrangement. After a breath of fresh air on the open platform at the end of the *voiture-lit*, he turned in, to find Janszen unpacking his spectacular valise.

Edmond About had the Turk, Mishak Effendi, as his companion; again a happy partnership, since among other attributes, Mishak turned out to be an exemplary sleeper. The Frenchman

27

Menu au 6. Decembre 1884
Diner

Potage Tapioca
Olive et beurre.
Barde truitee Hollandaise
Pomme au naturel
Gigot mouton Bretonne
Poulet du Mans cresson
Epinards au sucre
Tartre de fruit
Fromage, Fruits.

Vintage fare on board the Orient Express a year after the inaugural journey.

confessed that he wasn't looking forward to three nights on wheels: he had vivid memories of the American-built six-wheel dormitory cars, which obviously went wump in the night. Due perhaps to the first flurry of departure, the service hadn't been all that good, and About wondered if he should have brought some *"dragées pharmaceutiques"* (the 1883 equivalent of the sleeping pill). He needn't have worried. His compartment was as clean as a new *sou,* and to persuade their guests of the smoothness of bogie travel, the Wagons-Lits hosts had previously tried out the familiar glass-of-water experiment, and not a drop had been spilled.

The train roared on at over fifty miles an hour through the night towards Strasbourg, but About didn't sit up to see his native Alsace. The first spectacle laid on for the party was the station, newly lit, like the Gare de l'Est, by electricity. There was a short conducted tour for the wide-awake. Then on through Wurtemberg, past Ulm with its vast church tower, and across the stripling Danube to Munich. At the Bavarian capital a new restaurant car had to be attached to the train: something had gone wrong with the original one, and the Compagnie Internationale could not, above all things, risk their culinary reputation before such a gallery of gourmets. Edmond About noted, somewhat bitterly, that the new station at Munich had been built out of French reparations after the war of 1870. Previously it had been used as a troop station. It is small wonder that the German journalists (who are not named by either author) were vaguely unpopular, but the Wagons-Lits authorities were determined to stress the international aspect of this, the pride of their Grand Expresses.

At Vienna, another *petit tour* allowed passengers to look again at the marvels of electrical illumination, but de Blowitz and About were both more interested in the latest additions to the inaugural party. Female company appeared for the first time in the attractive shape of Frau von Scala, wife of a high functionary of the Royal Austrian State Railways (*"le type anglais animé par la physiognomie Viennoise"*) and her sister, Fraulein Leonie Pohl, not only a classic beauty, but a *"blonde cendre"*. Could M. About have been the first to use the phrase "ash-blonde"?

With their arrival, the whole character of the *vie du rail* changed. In the phrase of the *Times* correspondent, "the men put on their gloves". The club-room atmosphere gave way to compliments and flattery, and the two ladies, from then onwards, figured in all the many toasts along the route. One can imagine that the unattached ash-blonde became the focus of much male attention, but there is no hint that she qualified as the first Madonna of the Sleeping Cars. One of the two *voitures-lits* was exclusively reserved for female travellers, and no James Bond habits would have been permitted.

As soon as they reached Budapest, the passengers became aware that this was, in effect, a peasant country, with little to offer but mounds of grapes sold to the travellers on the platform by dark-skinned Magyars who wore the *csizma*, the long boots which were part of the national costume. Boots, boots, boots, boots, marching over Hungary . . . but for the women in their muddy lanes or on their farms it was—and still is—an entirely practical fashion.

Now the route led across the vast Hungarian plain. There were many labourers in the fields, and those who stopped to watch the train go by wore striking costumes. Edmond About noted much of the detail; the blouses embroidered with flowers and even scenery; the black hat with its ribbons; the cloaks braided in traditional style; the baggy pants which looked like skirts. Several shooting parties were seen—and several obvious poachers.

At Szegedin, one of the brief stops on the plain, a rumbustious festivity began for the passengers on the Orient Express. They were serenaded on the platform by a group of gipsy musicians, complete with *tziganes* and singers. Then the gipsy band climbed aboard the train. It is not quite clear whether this was part of M. Nagelmackers' programme, or a last-minute inspiration on the part of Onody Kahniar, the leader of the band. But whatever the origin, the effect was extraordinary, and developed into something reminiscent of a Marx Brothers' film.

The dining-car was cleared (the chairs being dumped in the luggage-van), and Onody, with a happy, sunburned face decorated with a big black moustache, led his musicians into a non-stop session which lasted until the train reached Temeswar, about a hundred miles down the line. It was a tight squeeze in the *voiture-restaurant,* but Onody and his band offered a complete repertoire, including special waltzes for the ash-blonde Viennese girl and the other ladies, Oriental music for the Turkish diplomat Mishak Effendi, which was played as soon as he made his appearance, and finally a tribute to the French—their own version of the national anthem. This, the climax, brought the Burgundian chef out of his kitchen, and we must rely on de Blowitz's original French to describe his remarkable appearance : *"Le main sur le coeur, l'oeil en flammes, le tête en extase, d'une voix rougie par le feu, il accompagne d'une façon sonore et profonde—le chant de la Marseillaise!"*

The *Times* man joined in the dancing; certainly the first time any correspondent of that staid and venerable paper had done such a thing. But though this was an impromptu entertainment, there were subsequent attempts to revive dancing on the Orient Express in the 1930s. A converted kitchen car was used, but it was only large enough to permit four couples to dance simultaneously. The Trans-Siberian Express, before the first world war, also made provision for discreet dancing during its eight-day journey. Such gaiety disappeared long ago : it is hardly in keeping with the regimes of either the Soviet Union or The Chinese Republic.

It may seem odd to many people that there has not been more dancing on trains. Given a straight route and good rolling-stock, it is an admirable way of passing the time. In recent years an enterprising British travel agency under a Major Ingham pioneered a "Snowsports Special" to the Austrian Alps from Calais to Innsbruck. This train has a control box which pipes continuous music to all compartments throughout the night (mercifully, it can be individually switched off) and particularly to the dance-coach, where students and secretaries and other youngsters twist and jive and drink beer and coke till dawn. Then, at breakfast time, those who have survived, twist again, until the Tyrol and the ski-slopes are reached. Enthusiasm is the primary requirement and stamina a close second.

The departure of the lively group at Temeswar was a matter of great regret. The farewells echoed down the platform. Onody Kahniar, indeed, invited de Blowitz to leave the Orient Express forthwith, and join him in a concert he was giving at a small town near by. "When do you start playing ?" asked the journalist.

"Oh, in about twenty minutes," said Onody. "We'll just turn

up at lunch time." He added "We shall still be playing at eleven o'clock tonight. Ten hours? Fourteen hours—that's nothing. We play as you breathe, and with intervals only for drinks." Onody Kahniar fixed de Blowitz with his big dark eyes and if the correspondent had succumbed, there would have been no interviews with King and Sultan along the line. But he regretfully refused. "*Ils ont le diable au corps*," remarked Edmund About, as he waved goodbye.

Things became rather flat after this interlude. The passengers took to reading books, playing games, and writing letters. On the last stage of the journey through Hungary, groups of peasants waved as the train went by. Rumania was reached, and to signify the occasion, Nagelmackers had provided a special Rumanian wine for dinner that night in the voiture-restaurant—a white vintage made and signed on the label by none other than the famous Liberal leader and President of the Council of Ministers, M. Bratianu. "The Rumanians," remarked Edmond About, as he approved the wine, "are really Turkish Christians, and they needn't blush at that. Turkey is a noble and proud nation. . . ."

Bucharest, the Rumanian capital, had been chosen as the taking-off place for an excursion into the Transylvanian mountains, to see the new summer Palace of the King at Sinai—and perhaps, with a bit of luck, since it was the first day the Peles Palace was open, to meet Charles of Hohenzollern himself.

Breakfast was served at the station buffet, with tea and fresh caviare sandwiches—at six in the morning! There followed a short tour of the town in elegant victorias drawn by ponies. Everyone admired the modern buildings, and nearly everyone bought an astrakhan hat as a souvenir. De Blowitz, however, refused to abandon his own outlandish headgear and continued to look, in his colleague's phrase, like a Calabrian bandit.

There is a tragi-comic quality about the visit to the royal Palace. The transit passengers, looking a bit dishevelled, were to be thrust into an alien atmosphere of patrician good living. Sinai was the show-place of Rumania, set among picturesque woods and streams, and the sumptuous villas of the well-to-do, with the peasants kept out of sight.

The party was first conducted to the Nouls Hotel, with a view

1. *"Votre billet, Monsieur?"* The *chef du train* makes his rounds on the Orient Express.

2. The Gare de l'Est, point of departure for the first Orient Express on October 4, 1883.

3. Georges Nagelmackers of Liége, founder of the Compagnie Internationale des Wagons-Lits.

4. The company's royal patron, King Leopold II of the Belgians.

Henri Stefan Opper de Blowitz, *The Times* correspondent in Paris, travelled
n the first Orient Express and gave a spirited account of his journey. His
:clusive interviews with two heads of state were a notable journalistic coup.

The inaugural train en route from Paris to Constantinople.

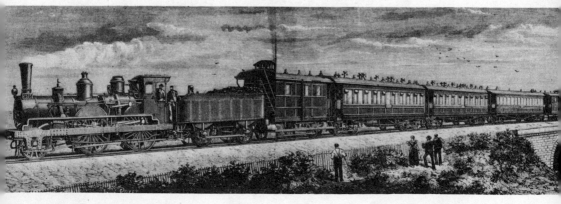

7. "*Messieurs les voyageurs, le dîner est servi!*" The *wagon-restaurant*, scene of much conviviality on the inaugural train. De Blowitz compared the first dinner served to a heap of jewels, from the ruby-red of the claret to the sparkling crystal of the water in the carafe.

8. Novelist Edmond About from Alsace, a fellow traveller of de Blowitz, was inspired to write a whole book about the historic journey, complete with observations en route about that varied and often vexed subject, railway food.

9. Exterior of the *wagon-restaurant*: the Orient Express was the first train to have cars with bogies, a notable improvement on the previous six-wheelers.

COMPAGNIE INTERNATIONALE DES WAGONS LITS

N° 151 D   DINING CAR   WAGON RESTAURANT

10. In terms of fiction, this artist's impression of the smoking lounge and library of an Orient Express of the 1880's could be fraught with sinister undertones. Is the reclining Turk in a drugged sleep? Is the angle of that cheroot a secret signal to the couple on the left who, just a few years later, might well have been Holmes and Watson on the track of a master criminal?

11. Early
Wagons-Lits
sleeping car
arrangements in
France, as seen by
L'Illustration in
1875. The line is
the pioneer
Chemin de Fer de
l'Est.

12 and 13. The two crowned heads interviewed by de Blowitz on the inaugural journey. On the left, Sultan Abdul Hamid II of Turkey, "The Shadow of God on Earth", dubbed by Anatole France "*Le grand saigneur*". In conversation he proved mild enough and invested de Blowitz with the Order of Medjidie (second class). On the right, Charles of Rumania who played host to the travellers at his new summer palace while the train waited.

across to the mountain (Sinai had been named after a monastery) and the new palace. The hotel's *tzigane* band seemed dull compared with Onody's group on the train. There the Orient excursionists sat while the organisers tried to lay on introductions to the royal family. Carpet-sellers began to pester them, and Edmond About was outraged by the hideous dyed colours. De Blowitz was told, to his extreme annoyance, that he couldn't be received by King Charles for an interview, since he hadn't got a black suit. Then, suddenly, all their doubts and difficulties were solved. At the royal request, protocol had been abandoned, and in view of the interest obviously aroused by the Orient Express trip, they were to be received as they were.

By now, it was raining hard, and the party had to squelch their way across the fields to arrive, in disarray, with dripping umbrellas, at a lordly mansion which had taken ten years to build and cost a fortune. Boots and brollies were left in the hall, and the motley group shuffled towards the Royal presence. A handsome officer received them ("I've only seen handsome ones in Rumania," remarked Edmond About) and put them at their ease. The Hohenzollern King and Queen greeted them in the music room, and invited them to tea. The monarch, wearing his gleaming Star of Rumania, and his wife, with her celebrated Grecian beauty, obviously made a great impression on the visitors. De Blowitz, thinking up his opening questions over tea, was gratified to have his cup replenished by "a ravishing dark-haired lady of the Court, Miss Theodori".

There was a tour of the rooms, with their magnificent mountain views and their elaborate panelling, and a recital in the music room, with its wooden stalls which made it look like a church. A young Rumanian tenor sang, and de Blowitz swears that the Queen accompanied him herself, and that the King came in later, and turned the pages of music for her, throwing aside all etiquette. Who can tell how much of this is pardonable exaggeration due to a slight state of euphoria, or the result of the sudden success of the visit? The opening exchanges between the Queen and the *Times* man are also rather fanciful, but worth quoting.

De Blowitz: "The patriotism of Her Majesty would seem more meritorious if her national costume did not suit her so well."

Queen: "You're a sceptic. Don't you think I am capable of sacrificing coquetry for love of my country?"

De Blowitz: "God save me, Madame, I only said that the gown suits you at one and the same time, as both Queen and woman."

Queen: "Well, it's a good thing when there is no contradiction between the duties of one and the rights of the other."

These gallantries concluded, the journalist was taken aside to have his private talk with the Hohenzollern Prince on whose political judgment so much seemed to depend. Charles obviously appreciated the fact that the *Times* man had not only met the Rumanian delegates at the Berlin Congress, but that he also held the Order of the Star which the King was wearing. This interview, though not directly connected with the story of the Orient Express, is an interesting historical sidelight of the age, as well as a journalistic scoop. Not often did a correspondent, dripping wet and improperly dressed, coolly collect a monarch's thoughts while stretching his legs during a break in a railway journey.

Charles—or Carol, as the Rumanians called him—spoke perfect French with rapidity and precision. At first, he talked mainly of the new palace, and the difficulty of building it, when all materials had to be brought up the hills by horse and mule. But he added, with a sweep of the hand towards the lofty ceiling, "I think it was worth it."

The *Times* man steered the conversation round, as soon as possible, to the Congress of Berlin. Was His Majesty disappointed at having to give up the province of Bessarabia in exchange for Dobrucza? His country had at least gained two ports, open to the world's trade. "I don't hold with this theory of territorial exchanges," said the King. "When you exchange, you not only give up land: you give up people. As for one of these ports, the cost of building it up will be at least twenty million francs. It isn't just a present, without strings."

The conversation then turned to the internal situation in Rumania, and the important question of the Army. Here the King was confident and categorical: his troops were loyal and well organised, and he added: "The day sudden events blow up in this corner of the globe, we shall have to be reckoned with. Our credit and finances are good: our regime is liberal. We want to show ourselves worthy of our situation."

Then the King appears to have taken over the questioning, and showed himself to be very knowledgeable on many political subjects. He particularly wanted to know about Mr. Gladstone's attitude to the occupation of Egypt.

"If you will pardon me, Your Majesty," said de Blowitz, "I would assert that any British Cabinet advocating leaving Cairo would not last twenty-four hours." The King laughed and replied : "Nobody in Europe expects you to do that !" and held out his hand. The day of the *Times* man was made. He had certainly worked hard for it.

There was another touch of tragi-comedy when the party eventually left the palace. Another handsome major-domo, with a more highly charged sense of protocol, led them down the servants' stairway instead of the *grand escalier*. But the brollies and boots had been left at the main entrance, so the whole company had to retrace their steps, before emerging into what Edmond About called "rain which was like Breton rain".

After a junket such as this, the *Compagnie des Wagons-Lits* was in no hurry to speed the parting guests on their journey. Here was a time to celebrate. At ten o'clock that night, the party went to a restaurant in Bucharest at the invitation of the King's aide, Colonel Popesco, and the manager of the Royal Rumanian Railways. De Blowitz, elated by his success with King Charles, enjoyed the blow-out. Both he and the company praised the fresh caviare —"compared with it, what one eats in the west is just boot-polish" —and the young sturgeon, served without oil or paprika, or any of the fierce Hungarian condiments "which poison under the pretext of improving". There was much talk of wars and politics, and little of railways, and the meal ended with half a dozen toasts, "All of which I could quote," wrote Edmond About, "if we'd had a stenographer with us."

The memorable dinner lasted until long after midnight, and the passengers seemed to have slept it off well as the Orient Express trundled on towards the Danube, and the river port of Giurgiu. This was, in fact, to be their last experience of railway comfort, for here they were to say goodbye to coaches with bogies, and the Burgundian chef and all the creature-comforts laid on by the *Compagnie*.

Giurgiu at seven o'clock on a bleak morning did not present a pleasant sight. There was a scramble for luggage. Porters appeared from the drab wooden hangars on the station, and officials warned everyone "Don't give your baggage to a porter without a uniform, or you won't see it again !"

A ferry stood by to take them to the Bulgarian river bank, and the town of Rustchuk, where local rolling-stock awaited them. On the return journey from Constantinople, Giurgiu, with its promise of Wagons-Lits luxury, and luncheon ready on the train, was to be a tantalising prospect. Now, with Rumanian hangovers, they were to taste the discomforts of Eastern Europe. The one pleasant item on the chilly half-hour crossing by ferry was the serving of Turkish coffee and liqueurs by the head-waiter of the voiture-restaurant, who had been thoughtful enough to bring along about twenty assorted bottles from the railway cellar.

So this, de Blowitz reflected, was Bulgaria, in whose apparent interest Disraeli broke up the Berlin Congress and took sides against Russia. The nations of Europe had, in effect, condemned Bulgaria to a useless freedom. "They spend three million francs on a royal palace in Sofia," he wrote later, "and two million on a hunting lodge in Varna. But after five years they can't build a bridge, repair a road, construct a school, and in the midst of all their infantile quarrels, they can't even put up a hut to shelter travellers disembarking from the Danube in the early hours of the morning ! They've put back the civilisation we've been bringing them by travelling on the train to their country. . . ."

The company made the familiar round-town excursion in *fiacres*. It looked to de Blowitz like a place "inhabited by troglodytes". On the square in front of the new palace of the Prince Regent, Alexander of Battenberg, nephew of the Czar, several hundred slovenly soldiers were being drilled by Russian officers. No doubt Bulgaria looked on the Czar as a liberator, a Pope and a father, but his kinsman had done little to improve the wretched conditions of his country, still nominally under the rule of Turkey. Disraeli had talked about "peace with honour", but in backing the "unspeakable Turk" he had made a wager described by his successor, Lord Salisbury, as "putting our money on the wrong horse".

No one relished the thought of the remaining journey from

Rustchuk to the Black Sea. (The only claim to fame for this unhappy town is that novelist Michael Arlen was born there, and that another novelist, John Buchan, made it the setting for his book *Greenmantle*.) The train, composed of antiquated six-wheeled coaches ran on a line constructed by the Turks, which had been laid out with complete disregard for any towns which might lie at any distance from the straight route. It was a track which led through nowhere. Cattle, buffaloes and sheep wandered aimlessly, without shepherds; the only trees were those grouped round graveyards. Bandits had attacked two of the stations en route : at one they had tortured and killed the station-master, who would not surrender the keys of his cash-desk.

Lunch was served at a place called Scheytandijk. The name, in Turkish, means "Little Devil", but as one of the company remarked, not even the big Evil One himself could have eaten the partridge that was served. But afterwards there were Turkish pastries for dessert, and a compote of peaches stuck with almonds and swamped in rose-scented syrup.

They reached Varna in somewhat liverish mood, and nothing about this half-derelict Black Sea port did anything to improve matters. To begin with, Customs officials demanded a $2\frac{1}{2}$ per cent surcharge on all baggage, and Mijnheer Nagelmackers had to produce his magic talisman in settlement. Rough weather was forecast for the voyage, but the Austrian Lloyd ship *Espero* seemed an improvement on Bulgarian railway carriages, and the *Compagnie* had thoughtfully provided their own official doctor for the trip, Dr. Harz of Liège, who had distinguished himself by tending the wounded at Metz during the Franco-Prussian War.

Quarters were comfortable for the Orient Express contingent, but the *Espero* also carried a number of Turkish emigré families leaving Bulgaria. They occupied what looked like a mere hole in the deck and their condition appeared to be about as wretched as that of the cows, horses and pigs which were herded with them. Edmond About saw a mother place her two babies, under coverlets, on the open deck, and returned to the dining saloon disgusted. But he eventually slept so well that his cabin companion had to rouse him with the dramatic cry : "Get up ! We're already in the Bosphorus !"

37

3

ON TO CONSTANTINOPLE

Down the Bosphorus to the City of Suleiman the Great—Some description of nineteenth century Constantinople, by George Augustus Sala, Lady Neave, and others—The travellers arrive—De Blowitz interviews Sultan Abdul Hamid—The return journey.

The voyage from Bulgaria to the Bosphorus had taken eighteen hours, and a leisurely sail down the straits linking Europe and Asia could not have been in more pleasant contrast.

Some of the travellers went on the bridge (de Blowitz taking with him a portable telescope) and tried to identify the villas and monuments on both shores. Many of the villas were rented by foreign diplomats, which made the *Times* correspondent all the more eager to identify them. He had particular hopes that the British Ambassador, Lord Dufferin, would favour his case for the long-desired interview with Sultan Abdul Hamid, and he was not to be disappointed.

But modern history, in a setting like this, was bound to be mixed with legend, and there were many such stories linked round the Bosphorus: just as in a port like Jaffa the traveller learns that Jonah is supposed to have set sail from here, to encounter his whale; that Saint Paul left Jaffa, or Joppa, on his journey to Turkey and Cyprus and Malta and that the rocks out in the harbour are where Andromeda was chained, to be rescued by Perseus from the sea-dragon.

So, along the Bosphorus, the thoughts of de Blowitz might turn to the goddess Europa, naked upon her bull; to King Darius and the all-conquering Persians; even to Lord Byron, whose daring exploit was to swim the Hellespont. From their vantage-points the passengers could see the "kiosks" or palaces (it is strange that this Turkish word has come to mean, in the English language, a tiny

38

stall for newspapers or sweets or information.) Many were large and costly; Armenians, Greeks, French and Turks had spent vast sums on them. But many were neglected and in ruins. There had been, perhaps, too much political change in this part of the world.

Then at last, the dream-journey down the Bosphorus came to an end as the *Espero* reached the jetty at Constantinople, below the majestic cupolas of Santa Sophia and the Mosque of Suleiman the Great, with their sharply pointed minarets. It had been a four days' journey from the Gare de l'Est, and it ended in scenes of memorable confusion. *Fiacres,* of a kind, were there to meet them, but de Blowitz declared : "It was like a sort of sixth-rate sale of horses at Tattersall's." His French colleague, however, was fascinated to see the luggage being hoisted on to donkeys, or on to the backs of the *hamals,* the human donkeys who still, in this enlightened age, hump enormous packages and furniture on their backs. The horse-drawn trams of Constantinople, pushing the Turkish citizens aside, caused much amusement, and Edmond About's imaginative eye noted the bright colours in the street markets—"the episcopal amethyst" of the aubergines, the coral of the pimentoes, the reddish purple of the tomatoes. "As for the odour," he added, "it would have given Emile Zola enough for a dozen chapters !"

Before we consider what kind of a city Sultan Abdul Hamid ruled over, let us see the Orient Express contingent to their hotels, the Luxembourg and the Angleterre, led by one M. Weil, of the Austrian Railways, and General Ahmed, an aide to the Sultan, and a distinguished dragoman. Edmond About, a man not easy to please, approved of the Luxembourg. It was clean and new, with a French manager. "Alas," he reflected in his notebook later, "the good French type of hotelier is fast disappearing in favour of a species of German diplomat, with a white tie, but with dirty hands, and whose blend of insolence and rapacity is enough to turn the milk in the tea-cups or sour the wine in the bottle. A hotel guest should be less than a friend, but more than a mere number."

Stefan Opper de Blowitz was enraptured by the view from the Angleterre. "*Je demeure, ravi, transporté, en extase ...*" he sighed. During that fortnight in Constantinople—a fortnight in which he was to spend most of his time trying to fix the meeting with the Sultan—he rose at six o'clock each morning to look out from his window. After several days, he had to draw the curtains, he says, to avoid being seduced and distracted by the scene. To him it was all fairyland : the Isles of Prinkipo in the bluish haze (scene of torture and imprisonment, from the Middle Ages to Menderes), the clatter of sabots across the Galata Bridge linking the old town with the new, Scutari with its hundred minarets, Santa Sophia in the diaphanous air—even the *caïques* on the water, which were, to him, "as if sleeping in the lascivious arms of some invisible nymph. . . ."

Life for Europeans in the Constantinople of the 1880s was an unreal existence. Three cities made up the sprawling Turkish capital—the Old City, with the Seraglio and the Great Mosques, and the largest market in the world; the comparatively new city of Pera, across the great bridge; and Scutari, across the Bosphorus. Pera became the fashionable quarter. The *Compagnie Internationale* itself built the Bosphorus Hotel and later the Pera Palas, which is still a comfortable place to stay in, but without the luxury of the Hilton, or the view from the Park.

A journalist even more unconventional than de Blowitz of *The Times*, George Augustus Sala, traveller, author, man-about-town and gastronome, made some lively and sarcastic references to the capital in his despatches to the *Daily Telegraph* and the *Illustrated London News*.

"Within the last few years," he wrote in 1877, "Pera has been blessed with a municipality, who have a very handsome town hall, and the members of which are continually squabbling among themselves. The suburb has been lit with gas and partially paved, so as to be practical for wheeled carriages; but the impediments to locomotion in general, and pedestrians in particular, are still woefully great. You must wear goloshes, or preferably jack-boots, if you walk abroad and wish to avoid being fresco-painted with mud or drenched with slush."

For any journey of any length, Sala recommended that the journey be made on horseback, but added : "You may ride as splendidly as Lord Herbert of Cherbury, or as clumsily as Hudibras did, but it will come, in the long run, to pretty nearly the same thing. You have a groom on foot, behind you, a wiry young Turk or Armenian, armed with a long switch, and he very efficiently performs the part of a Hampstead-Heath donkey boy, and pilots you through the quick-sands of Pera and the tortuous alleys of Stamboul. Everything is in the hands of your *kismet*, your fate."

The Orient Express group in 1883 were greeted with the *fiacres* which de Blowitz likened to a "sixth-rate Tattersall's". Five years before, they would have had to put up with the sedan-chairs which Sala saw in such numbers, on hire from the Hotel de Byzance, the Hotel de l'Angleterre, "and the other inns frequented by European visitors to Constantinople".

Sala gives full marks to the first-named hotel.

"The landlords (Greeks) are civil and attentive : the waiters are well-drilled : the table d'hôte is, for Constantinople, an excellent one; the Costi Fenerli, who speaks seven languages, is a pearl among dragomans, and as honest as an English commissionaire. . . ."

George Sala had been despatched to Constantinople by his newspaper at six hours' notice, via St. Petersburg and Odessa. He had already conceived an idea of the horrors of the Ottoman capital, and had, in fact, written an essay about it many years before for the old magazine *Household Words* (founded by Charles Dickens.) What astonished him was to find that the place just about matched up to his preconceived ideas.

"Substitute typhus and cholera for the plague, modify the acerbity of my remarks touching the ramshackle hotels and the dogs (which last I found on intimate acquaintance to be very good fellows) and my imaginary picture might be convertible for the real draught which I am striving to make in 1877. Perhaps it had been my fate in a previous and forgotten state of existence to flounder, for my sins, in the mud of Pera, to be bitten by the fleas of Galata, to be cozened by the hack-drivers of Scutari and to encounter the smells of Stamboul."

Sala gives a lengthy and sarcastic description of the whole city, from which we can choose only a few passages. The Orient Express had not arrived during his tenuous tenure of office, but there were already trains of a sort.

"There is no word, I am informed, in Turkish for a railway tunnel; and even the modern Greeks have been compelled to

41

manufacture a term defining so eminently a modern contrivance. They call a tunnel *upogeios diodos*—literally, an underground passage. The Turkish term is much more poetical and much more expressive. They have named the Pera and Galata tunnel 'The Mouse's Hole'. Up trains and down trains run from early in the morning until late at night through this subterranean passage which debouches, at its western extremity, hard by the Galata Branch of the Maritime and Commercial Club, a handsomely appointed and admirably conducted establishment, where strangers from Europe, properly introduced, are treated with great courtesy and hospitality."

Sala had been a correspondent in Russia during the Crimean War, so it is not surprising that in his report on the city, he also visits the Asian side, with its comparatively recent memories.

"Leander's Tower stands, like a sentinel, in front of Scutari, which has been poetically called the 'Peristyle' of Asia, for from here the Government Tartars or couriers journeying into Asia are accustomed to start, and here the Sultans of old used to hold a final review of their troops ere they commenced their expeditions to the Euphrates or the Taurus. . . . Scutari possesses, moreover, a melancholy interest to all Britons as being the site of the English burial-ground, a beautifully planted and admirably kept ceme-tery, close by that hospital made famous for all time by the labours of Florence Nightingale. . . . The bodies of some eight thousand Englishmen moulder peacefully in this graveyard. I fancy that the remembrance of their deaths might moderate the frenzy of the politicians who seem bent on hounding England on to a fresh war with Russia. . . ."

George Sala was also much possessed by death, of another kind, when he came to consider the Topkapi Palace and the Seraglio. He is merely echoing what so many have written when he says "Don't think I am launching into fine writing. Nor our Smithfield nor our Tower Hill, nor the *Champ de Mars* nor the *Place de la Concorde* in Paris, can match the old Seraglio as a human *abattoir*. . . .

"It has been the grandest, the most historical, and the most horrible slaughter-house in Europe. The modern Turk is, no doubt, the nicest of nice gentlemen. He roars as mildly as a sucking-dove : he has abolished decapitation and the bastinado : and it was from a balcony of one of the bureaux of the Sublime Porte . . . that I heard the Grand Vizier, Midhat Pasha, proclaim a brand-new and essentially liberal Constitution for the Ottoman Empire. It was the old Turk who was a barbarian and a butcher. The new or Constitutional Turk is a very sweet youth—so sweet, indeed, as to make me fear that he will melt, some of these fine mornings, in somebody's mouth. . . ."

When the Orient Express travellers were taken to the Topkapi Palace, which had been a museum for many years, after housing the Sultans and their harems since the fifteenth century, the splendours of the treasury and the jewels almost overwhelmed them, and Stefan de Blowitz, echoing what many must have thought when confronted with such a display, said to his colleagues "There are thirty of us here, and only four guards. Why don't we overpower them, and steal everything?"

Many years later, this was to be the theme of a thriller and a film about an attempted robbery of the jewels of Topkapi—and could be likened to Colonel Blood's attempted seizure of the Crown Jewels in the Tower of London.

The position of women in the Muslim world led to any number of misunderstandings in the European community. In Court Circles, a Sultana could wield immense power, even in retirement or as a widow, but for all others, the veil and their inferior position banned them from all kinds of public life. The only time the Sultan's women ever made any kind of appearance was on the traditional Friday morning "Selemlik", the traditional royal ride to the Mosque, a ceremony which not even the terrified Abdul Hamid could avoid.

Some Turks were offended at the sight of unveiled "giaour" (infidel) women in the streets : others, particularly soldiers, regarded them as fair game, and protecting their women-folk became one of the most arduous tasks the European diplomats and officers had to cope with. A woman like Lady Hester Stanhope, who lived in Turkey in the eighteenth Century, wearing man's clothes and smoking the pipe of tranquillity with Turkish aristocrats, was tolerated as an eccentric. Lady Mary Wortley Montagu enjoyed the privileged position of being an Ambassador's wife, and was one of the pioneers of Pera society. But as late as the 1890's, Lady Neave, another leading figure in diplomatic circles, reported continual embarrassment.

"We had become accustomed to having our arms pinched, and being kissed by the soldiers, but their insults in broad daylight steadily became more frequent and more daring. My sister was seized by the throat and shaken for not getting out of the way of a *mullah* who was passing in his long robes and turban, and Baroness de Braun of the Austrian Embassy who was out walking with me had a string of prayer beads flung across her face. . . . It was an opportunity which the soldiers did not fail to seize when we were caught in the crowd, to push and pinch and generally annoy the European women, who appeared to them as bold, brazen hussies, walking unveiled through the streets, in striking contrast to their own modestly veiled *hanums. . . ."* (*Romance of the Bosphorus*. Dorina Lady Neave. Hutchinson, London, 1949.)

In the higher strata of Turkish society, things were different Ladies from Europe enjoyed a great deal of adulation, offered by Turks with a slightly cynical smile. Gifts were showered on the spoiled darlings by men to whom assassination was a familiar way of life. It reached its apotheosis in the State visit of Kaiser Wilhelm in 1898, when Abdul Hamid presented the blushing Kaiserin with a daily, exotic arrangement of jewels, each one more magnificent than the last.

The European communities made a great event of Christmas, returning from their villas along the Bosphorus to Pera, to start the Season which George Sala so obviously despised. "The festive season was an exasperating time," remarks Lady Neave, "as the bearer of every gift sent to us expected *baksheesh*—boatmen, coachmen, postmen and porters—in fact anyone calling with some small offering of fruit, pot of jam, or sweets or flowers, had to be paid in tips."

The high-born Turks were not unaware that their handsome and dashing appearance, their magnificent horses, and that certain something which hinted at sexual prowess, with more than a hint of cruelty, appealed to the European ladies. A magazine of the time, *Scribner's Monthly,* printed the impressions of an English lady married to an Italian, Signora Fagnani, who, with her friends, was unexpectedly invited by the Minister of Foreign Affairs to a State Ball to be given at his summer residence on the Bosphorus. It was the very first day of her arrival.

"As the distance was considerable, we were to leave Pera at eight o'clock, so that we had scarcely time to unpack our trunks and rest, before we were obliged to prepare for our expedition. We drove in an open carriage preceded by a mussulman on horseback, arrayed in the most gorgeous style, with richly inlaid pistols in his holster, and a yataghan (Madame Fagnani seems to have picked up the Turkish word for "sabre" very quickly) by his side. He was a splendid-looking Turk named Mustapha, and he started off ahead, knocking down ruthlessly the tables and chairs standing in front of the cafés, and causing dire confusion among the women and children who thronged the streets, to say nothing of the lean, wolf-like dogs which swarm beneath one's feet in every quarter of the city.

"This was the first manifestation that we were in a land of despotic power : but our stately English coachman seemed to take it as a matter of course, and the indolent mussulmans seemed undisturbed.

"On arriving at our destination we felt as if we were living in the days of Haroun Al-raschid. The whole building was one blaze of light; no less than thirty-five thousand lamps of every hue were distributed among the grounds, and the rooms were illuminated with superb crystal chandeliers. We were received at the entrance of the garden by an officer brilliant in gold embroidery who led us upstairs, ushered us into a superb ballroom, and introduced us to the Princess of Samos, who, being the first Greek lady in the place, did the honours in lieu of the Minister's wife, who could not, of course, step out of the precincts of the harem.

"The Princess deputed her niece to conduct us to the harem, in order that we might pay our respects to Madame Ali, the Minister's wife. How our hearts throbbed as we approached the door where stood on guard two gigantic Nubians nearly seven feet high, holding enormous canes in their hands ! They bowed to our conductors, and lifting a curtain, we entered that abode of romance, which we had never expected to see. . . ."

What a first night for Madame ! Gold-braided uniforms, chan-

45

deliers, the trappings of despotism, and the vicarious thrill of the harem and the odalisque. But the first impressions of the captive ladies were scarcely up to expectations.

"We were exceedingly disappointed in the toilets of these ladies : with the exception of their undervests of Broussa gauze, they were nearly all dressed in European fabrics of various kinds, full trousers, slippers, and an over-dress more like the soutane of a Romish priest than any other garment. Instead of the long-braided tresses we had expected to see falling to their feet, their hair was cut short, and surmounted by an embroidered gauze handkerchief put on like a turban; but to compensate for lack of Oriental splendour in the rest of the dress, their jewels far outstripped our imagination.

"One young married lady, about fifteen, was dressed in a French muslin of a brilliant corn-colour, and next under it she had donned a crinoline, so that the effect of the steels, clearly defined beneath the scant folds of the transparent muslin, was ludicrous in the extreme; but the others looked at her with admiration, as she paraded her French organdie and hoop-skirt before them—her girlish face surmounted with a regal coronet of magnificent gems."

There followed a *divan* with refreshments.

"Slaves came kneeling down before us, bearing golden salvers, on which were gracefully, and even artistically, piled, candied fruits of every description; others handed iced sherbet in large gold and enamelled cups; and after the return of a few more compliments, we rose to return to the ballroom.

"The Europeans amused themselves with dancing, the others looked on, probably thinking, as a Turkish diplomat once told a friend in London, 'that the English ladies were very foolish to tire themselves with a performance which was much better executed by their paid dancing-girls !'

"At midnight we went down into the beautiful garden. Resting upon Saracenic columns of green and gold was seen a magnificent tent, literally of cloth-of-gold, embroidered with birds of plumage, made for the Sultan, at the cost of millions. Beneath it were spread tables, and a superb supper *à la Francaise* was served to us on gold and silver dishes belonging to the Sultan."

A la Francaise. . . . The analogy with the French Revolution is irresistible, and yet this Turkish regime, hedged round with the starving, the tortured and the deprived masses, did not end in revolution yet; merely with the eventual deposition of the Sultan, the hanging of his eunuchs, the dispersal of his harem, and the substitution of a similar state of affairs under another Sultan.

Madame Fagnani (she was so surrounded by exotic flowers, she might have been called Madame Frangipani) concluded: "We returned to Pera about two in the morning, and were soon lost in dreams of Fatimas and Sultanas, odalisques and bayadères. . . ."

There were, it seems, no such junketings for the visitors from the Orient Express. For de Blowitz, at least, duty came first, and the campaign to get his interview with the Sultan was under way, with all the double-talk and intrigue and false promises which accompany such requests in the Middle East. "Constantinople was about as suitable for the exercise of the journalist's skills," remarks Frank Giles, "as the Court of Genghis Khan would have been"—and Abdul Hamid had never granted such an interview before.

Why, therefore, did the *Times* correspondent, helped by men like the Ambassador, Lord Dufferin, consider the meeting so important? Partly, no doubt, it was the double lure of a scoop and a "first". Partly because Abdul Hamid, though mocked by caricatures in *Punch* and reviled by British Members of Parliament and by the French—Anatole France, with memories of bloodshed in the Armenian atrocities, called him *"Le Grand Saigneur"*—was a shy, retiring man, yet still, officially, "The Emperor of powerful Emperors, the Sole Arbiter of the World's Destiny, Refuge of Sovereigns, Distributor of Crowns to the Kings of the Earth, Master of Europe, Asia and Africa, High King of the Two Seas, the Shadow of God upon Earth."

Politically, too, his kingdom was at a cross-roads, pitied and feared by turns, wooed first by the British, then by the Germans, shunned only by the Russians. The arrival of the international Orient Express from Paris was a significant indication that Constantinople was not to be left out of the picture, and some inkling of this may have been conveyed, however vaguely, to Abdul Hamid, as he cowered behind the walls of his Yilditz Palace, with the two thousand pistols he kept in many different rooms and courtyards—ostensibly for shooting pigeons.

If the background of the interview with the King of Rumania was tragi-comical, the events leading up to the meeting between the "Prince of Journalists" and the "Shadow of God upon Earth" became almost farcical. For a time it seemed that nothing could be arranged : then one of the more helpful major-domos, Philippe Effendi, found the solution—the *Selemlik*, the traditional ride on Fridays to the Mosque.

De Blowitz was told to be at the Medidjeh Mosque between 11.30 a.m. and 12 noon. He was preparing to leave when another aide galloped up on horseback, breathless, and told him that the route had suddenly been changed, and the Mosque was at Bechik-tache. (Last-minute changes like this were not unusual, for security reasons, and since an attempt to assassinate Abdul Hamid was, in fact, to be made at a *Selemlik* some years later, the Sultan had perhaps cause for caution.)

Bewildered, de Blowitz hurried to the rendezvous, thinking that this was hardly propitious for a personal interview. Then Philippe Effendi took the journalist up to the first floor of a building overlooking the Mosque. One window was open. He was given coffee and cigarettes, and the apparently absurd plan was explained to him. If he sat on the window-sill, showing himself prominently, the Sultan might spot him, and that might make all the difference.

No one really knows, least of all Stefan de Blowitz, if this device did the trick, but he dutifully straddled the window-sill, dangling his diminutive legs. "I hope," he told his companions, "No one takes a photograph of me !"

The Sultan rode by, with his elaborate cavalcade. Maybe de Blowitz waved, or huffed and puffed. Maybe permission had already been given, and the odd demonstration was merely to show that the Englishman had turned up. After a dramatic wait, the news came through. De Blowitz was to proceed to Yilditz Kiosk, the palace itself.

There followed more cloak-and-dagger activity. He was led through a small private door, and across the gardens. "Who," he at last managed to ask, "actually gave the order for this?" "The Sultan himself," he was assured. "But he's been at prayer," said de Blowitz. It was Philippe Effendi who replied, patiently, "This is one of your European illusions. One can pray anywhere, because Allah is everywhere. One doesn't have to use a mosque for prayer. It can also be a meeting-place."

Fanfares sounded as Abdul Hamid emerged, and stepped into a victoria. De Blowitz was ushered into a following vehicle. After a short ride, they were at their destined place. De Blowitz waited till the Chamberlain, Osman Raghib Bey, appeared; then he was led through into the Salle des Maréchaux, and stood face to face with Abdul Hamid II. The Sultan extended a gloved hand to the journalist, and graciously invited him to sit with him on a rich damask sofa. Cigarettes and matches were provided on a gilded table decorated with malachite and onyx. Raghib Bey was invited to act as interpreter.

"For the interviewer," de Blowitz wrote afterwards, "there are obvious advantages in having an interpreter. You can get an opportunity to observe your subject." No doubt the interview took place at a much more leisurely and hesitant tempo than a modern television interview, with its neck-microphones and a studio manager giving a one-minute wind-up signal.

During the preliminary polite exchanges de Blowitz noted a thin, average-sized man in a marshal's uniform—blue baggy trousers, red jacket, damascened sword. He observed the Sultan's dark, dry skin, his short beard, sad mouth, bony Turkish nose, slightly twisted, and large, dark, unfriendly eyes. His voice was more highly pitched than that of most Turks, but distinct and without hesitation. He was forty-one but appeared older because he had a front tooth missing. This "evil nightmare brooding over Europe" was no ranting tyrant outwardly; rather a sad and shifty specimen in his appearance and behaviour.

De Blowitz began with some generally complimentary remarks about the hopes of Europe resting with the Sultan, as the one man who could relieve the sufferings of his people. Abdul Hamid said he was flattered, but he added that Europe persistently underestimated and even derided Turkey, believing the country could never recover. He had done his best to improve the financial position and prepare the country for liberty. This thundering lie was qualified by his contention that to give liberty without question was like giving a rifle to someone who didn't know how to use it.

49

The result might be that the man would kill his father, his mother, his family, and then himself.

Then the Sultan took the initiative. He had obviously been aware that de Blowitz had attended the Berlin Congress. What were his views? This pleased the *Times* man greatly, and he immediately asked the Sultan, "Why did you send Turks of such low calibre to the Congress, men who trembled before Bismarck?" There were regrets from Abdul Hamid. It was a sad moment, and the Turks hadn't many friends. He didn't blame England or France, but he knew there had been "clouds" between them and Turkey, and hoped they would soon disappear.

Into this dewy-eyed diversion, de Blowitz dropped the specific question "Does your Majesty refer to the occupation of Egypt?" He added that, according to public opinion in England, Turkey should have allied with her and France in the occupation.

"*Chagrin pour moi*," came the smooth reply through the interpreter. Chagrin was perhaps a mild word to describe the petty fury shown by the Sultan when Britain and France called his bluff, and took over Egypt without him.

Then Abdul Hamid wisely changed the subject. What did his visitor think of the situation in Turkey? This was the moment de Blowitz had been waiting for. He asked if he coud speak freely, and one can imagine the languid gloved hand waving in assent.

"Create an administration which will admit reforms, and you will revive your country," he declared. "You have all the liberties in your hand. Your people have all the goodwill to offer. Why not open your hand a little towards gradual liberty?"

"I am glad you asked me this," replied Abdul Hamid, in the manner of one who says "that's a very good question". He continued : "I am happy to think that you are not one of those who consider that this country cannot survive. I am indeed willing to 'open my hand'. But how far should I open it?"

De Blowitz realised that this was a *cul-de-sac* in the conversation—perhaps rather like one of those real sacks in which the Turkish Sultans sewed up their victims alive, before dropping them into the Bosphorus. But when Abdul Hamid mentioned Egypt again, the *Times* man rammed home his most controversial question. Why, he asked, hadn't Turkey supported

Britain and France? How far was His Majesty responsible for holding back—or did he bow to the wishes of his advisers?

These were bold words, for they implied a direct and well-founded criticism of the King of Kings. For saying this, other men might have been garotted, flayed alive or poisoned in that very room, and without delay. But Abdul Hamid, after a pause, made no reply to the question, and proceeded to a polite peroration which, though dutifully reported by de Blowitz, contradicted all the despotic intention history has accorded him. He had no wish to suppress existing liberties (whatever they were?) but to add new ones. He was desirous of establishing a new code of justice, and added, piously, "This country may have its weaknesses, but it also has elements of great strength. I want to heal the former, and make use of the latter."

The celebrated palaver was nearly finished. The little man dressed like a Calabrian bandit had bearded the "Shadow of God" in his den, and was hearing him say "If ever you come to Constantinople again, you must come and visit me the day you arrive. You can say it is my wish—indeed, my command."

Abdul Hamid then asked Raghib Bey to produce a box containing the Order of Medjidie (Second Class) one of the highest decorations, and personally pinned it on the grateful correspondent before the final gracious farewell. When the party left the Yilditz Kiosk, the Turks, obviously relieved that all had gone well, waved and saluted. The royal guard presented arms. As they went out into the road, de Blowitz said, "I hope we don't meet any European cartoonists on our way back!"

It is perhaps interesting to compare his brief encounter with the longer experience of a resident British correspondent, Edwin Pears of the London *Daily News,* the doyen of foreign journalists in the Turkish capital. (Later, as Sir Edwin, he wrote his memoirs, *Forty Years in Constantinople,* and a biography of the Sultan.) Pears, though apparently in the city at this time, makes no mention of the inaugural trip of the Orient Express in 1883, or of de Blowitz, and dates the beginning of the Paris-Constantinople run from the year 1888. But he pays tribute to the Wagons-Lits for maintaining a good service for twenty-five out of his forty years' residence.

51

Pears had attended in the antechamber of Yilditz Kiosk in his time, but had politely refused the very decoration de Blowitz accepted, and described the Sultan as a man devoid of any principles or aspirations, a mean, petty, dyspeptic recluse, with few hobbies other than pistol-shooting (his minions would throw oranges into the air, for him to hit in flight) and reading reports of his spies and secret police. But the *Daily News,* being a Liberal paper, maintained an attitude to the Turkish question very different from that of the Conservative *Times.*

Stefan Opper de Blowitz, with brief-case crammed with notes (his method, thanks to a prodigious memory, was to write down little at the time of interview, but everything later) prepared to return to England, a happy man. He must have scribbled furiously on his way home by the Orient Express, since the concluding chapters of his long book on the whole journey are a summing-up on Turkey, and the seven devils which seemed able to destroy her—chief among them the bribery, or "baksheesh"—breaking faith with Europe, the harem, the national debt, the absence of roads.

He re-lived his interview with the Sultan, and described what he would have said if he had been able to tell him what he should do. He reiterated his belief that the "Sick Man" was not incurable, but would need England and France to stand by him. Constantinople, he predicted, would continue to be, for the politician with hindsight, the central point of Europe's struggle between nations. It is all quite a lecture, in the grand manner. Let there be a three-power agreement between England, France and Turkey: this would at least keep the Russians at arms' length, "willing to wound and yet afraid to strike". Prophetically, he concludes: "There is in Europe only one possible cause of conflict and eventual warfare—the hatred between France and Germany."

When it came to saying goodbye to the Bosphorus, the literary style of the *Times* man ran as purple as the shadows of the evening, and he can only be quoted in his original French.

"La sirène du Bosphore avait revêtu son costume le plus doré. Plus que jamais, elle avait parfumé son haleine et constellé de milles perles rayonnantes sa robe d'azur et d'éméraudes. . . ."

This was the man who had found equal delight in the colours of the wagon-restaurant, with its shaded lights and wine-bottles, more than two weeks ago in the Gare de l'Est. After a journey as successful as this, he had a right to relax, and luxuriate in his surroundings. On the *Espero,* he got up to look at the Black Sea by moonlight, and out came all the adjectives again. He saw the lighthouse at Varna in the dawn. With de Blowitz was a Queen's Messenger, one of the type destined to become faithful commuters on the Orient Express, Sir John Pender.

It was a great joy to de Blowitz to see the big Wagon-Lit cars on the station at Rustchuk, and to hear the chatter and watch the to-and-fro of the passengers. The *Compagnie* kept its promise by having a French luncheon all ready for new arrivals, and later, de Blowitz was once again lulled by "the *berceuse* of the wheels" in the bogie-carriage.

He had a fleeting view of Szegedin in Rumania, a brand-new town in which three thousand houses had been built in four years, and a triple dyke against floods, all at a cost of sixty million francs. Yes, the new Rumania seemed the country of the future in this part of Europe. Hungary he saw, too, by day, and after the plain was past, he found the countryside charming, particularly the neighbourhood of Esztergam, with its immense Byzantine cathedral.

At Vienna, the train filled up, and things livened up. These Viennese were smart and amusing—especially the ladies. Once again de Blowitz savoured the occasion. Walking down the corridors of the Orient Express, he declared, was like a stroll along the Rue de la Paix. The gentlemen glanced appreciatively; the ladies glanced back roguishly. And in addition to this *coqueterie* on wheels, there was the scenery which God, immortal landscape-gardener, had spread out before the eyes. "The landscape flies at your feet . . . the streams seem to flow under the wheels . . . villages and houses shine like morning stars . . . and from your Rue de la Paix you can see the minuscule population of a little world under your observation. . . ."

In this mood of momentary exaltation, the "Prince of Journalists" and the most spectacular and successful of all those on M. Nagelmackers' guest-list, is wafted back to Paris.

His two interviews appeared in London on November 6th and 8th, 1883. It was a time of opening horizons. Henry Irving and

Ellen Terry had just begun a theatrical season in New York (and to cross the Atlantic at that time by Cunard Line cost from 12 to 15 guineas cabin class, and 4 guineas in the lowest class.) Gilbert and Sullivan's *Iolanthe* had just passed its 350th triumphant performance at Mr. D'Oyly Carte's Savoy Theatre, "The Only Theatre in London Fully Equipped with Electric Light". Vladimir Pachmann, the pianist, was on a concert tour, and Messrs. Maskelyne and Cooke presented themselves as "The celebrated interweavers of refined mirth and profound mystery, at the Egyptian Hall, Piccadilly". More relevant to Egypt, Mr. Gladstone had some comments to make about the British withdrawal from Cairo.

But pride of place, on both days, went to a long report from "Our Correspondent on the Orient Express", and the interview with Sultan Abdul Hamid ran through five closely printed columns. *The Times* had even given him a leader which, though somewhat lofty and patronising, praised the "energy and persistence" of their man on the spot.

Others of the Orient Express party had left Constantinople some days earlier, after a final champagne party at one of the hotels, which coincided with the christening of the manager's daughter. He named her Leopoldine, after the King of the Belgians, and in recognition of the fact that the *Compagnie Internationale* was primarily Belgian, and under royal patronage.

We leave Edmond About equally as grateful as de Blowitz for the resumption of Wagons-Lits comfort in Rumania, but with thoughts about Turkey which were less political than social. Thinking of the dark-eyed Oriental beauties, he was scandalised that Abdul Hamid had issued an edict, replacing the traditional filmy *yashmak* by an opaque covering. This, he affirmed, would bring about a chorus of protest, not only from the makers of *yashmaks* in Turkey—there were reputed to be more than 60,000 of them—but from the people themselves. "Abdul Hamid," he wrote, "cannot be deaf to the cries of his subjects." But he, as well as de Blowitz, had formed a somewhat indulgent opinion of the "Shadow of God upon Earth".

So ended one of the most talked-of, successful and memorable journeys since railways began.

4

"EN VOITURE, S'IL VOUS PLAIT!"

The story of the Wagons-Lits Company continued—Relations with Thomas
Cook & Sons—Silver Jubilee banquet for Nagelmackers—The First World
War—The Simplon-Orient Express—The history of Car No. 2419 in two
world wars.

The success of that first exhausting, exhilarating trip on the
Orient Express by Wagons-Lits had proved one thing : that
Turkey, and other places in the Middle East, were destined to
become popular with tourists. Constantinople was already
fashionable, partly, no doubt, because Disraeli had backed the
Turks and the British Government were expressing the pious hope
that the "Sick Man of Europe" was not so sick after all. Partly
because the international train had opened up the mysterious East
in a painless way.

The second reason recommended itself to the eventual rival of
the Wagons-Lits—the British travel agency of Thomas Cook &
Son, already veterans in the job of sending distinguished clients
out to foreign parts. Cook's is still the most famous travel agency in
the world, but its later activities are routine compared with the
early experiments started by Cook himself, a Bible-punching, tee-
total idealist from Leicester, whose English pleasure-trips date
back as far as 1845, and whose first continental tour (to Belgium)
was in 1856.

The British firm was the first to enjoy success with the Grand
Tours in Egypt (for the Pyramids and the Nile) and Palestine (for
the Holy Land), and the Cook family saw no reason why the same
success should not take place upon the Bosphorus, and among the
ruins of Troy and Ephesus.

Every month they issued their magazine *The Excursionist and
Tourist Advertiser*. The edition for April 19, 1884, makes it quite

clear that they were making a bid for the travellers to Turkey.

"For some years we have been strongly urged by influential ladies and gentlemen interested in Eastern Europe to open out a system of travelling arrangements on a similar basis to those which we have established for Palestine, etc., to enable one or more travellers or small private parties to visit districts of great interest, especially to classical and historical students.

"We have given considerable attention to these requests, and we have been watching for favourable opportunities, but through political and military troubles, and brigandage formerly existing in certain districts, we have not thought it advisable to induce travellers to visit the above districts until we have had the opportunity of thoroughly satisfying ourselves as to the perfect safety, and that the journey can be accomplished with some degree of comfort.

"Mr. John M. Cook, our managing partner, visited Turkey and Greece twice during 1883, thoroughly investigating the question, especially of facilities and safety, and we have decided that the time has now arrived when we may without doubt do everything we possibly can to induce travellers to visit these interesting districts."

So John M. Cook, of Thomas Cook's, had got off the mark early, realising the potential value of the market. But why should British tourists take such time and trouble to visit such a distant area? Cook's had the answer.

"With Constantinople for a centre may be visited the principal battlefields of the Russo-Turkish war, the Dardanelles, and the reputed site of Troy.... At our Constantinople office will be found competent dragomans and guides, who could be engaged for tours of any description, at 170 Grande Rue de Pera."

Egypt had been a notable triumph, and was to continue as such for many years, but the first visit of Mr. Cook to Greece and Turkey had been as early as 1868, with a small number of travellers. When the 50th Anniversary of Thomas Cook and Sons was celebrated, the chronicler of that event noted the possibilities.

"Since the direct line to Constantinople by way of Vienna, Budapest, Belgrade, Sofia and Philippopolis was opened, the mode of travelling between Europe and the East has been revolutionised. Most of the notable travellers in the East, the Ambassa-

56

dors and Government officials, have availed themselves of the advantages held out. At times of political excitement and disturbance, travelling in that part of the world is attended with special inconvenience. Happily, Messrs. Cook have been able, through the medium of trustworthy representatives, to give efficient aid to the distinguished persons who have put themselves under their care." (*The Business of Travel*. W. Fraser Rae. Cook & Son, London, 1891.)

In other words, Cook's were only too willing to book passengers on the new Orient Express, but they must have realised that the Wagons-Lits Company were not unaware of the tourist possibilities, and had the advantage of providing the only travel facilities to the new area of competition. Wagons-Lits, indeed, built hotels in Constantinople to house the travellers—the Bosphorus Summer Palace Hotel, and the Pera Palas. At that time they were complete with typical Victorian plush settees and potted palms—everything as a contrast to the Turkish reality outside.

Troubles in Bulgaria held up the idea of a direct Paris-Istanbul train, but in 1885, an agreement was made by Wagons-Lits with the Serbian Government, for a route via Belgrade to Nish, in addition to the journey to the Black Sea. Between Nish and Plovdiv (the old Philippopolis) passengers would have to travel by horse-coach for two days, and it was not until 1889 that there was any direct rail connection with Turkey without change of carriage. This seems to have been the main break-through.

The difficulties with Bulgaria were overcome, but not without hold-ups over protocol. George Behrend describes one of these :

"Nagelmackers sent one of his lieutenants to Sofia, a Viscount de Richemont. The Viscount had to see Prince Ferdinand personally to obtain his signature, but he was not allowed to do so without a court uniform. This he did not have with him, but he obtained an audience with Ferdinand by appearing attired as a Captain of the Prince's own police; whereupon Frederick is said to have exclaimed 'What a ridiculous country!' " (*The History of Wagons-Lits, 1875-1955*. Modern Transport Publishing Co., London, 1959.)

As far as rolling-stock was concerned, the Wagons-Lits carriages were ahead of their time. Nothing impressed foreign associates

57

more than the result of a railway accident in Rumania in 1889, between Bucharest and Jassy. In a collision, the entire train seemed to fall to pieces—with the exception of one coach belonging to Wagons-Lits. It was made of teak, and this hard wood was used right up to the time of steel coaches. The Jassy incident is still talked about at headquarters in Paris and London.

The Compagnie Internationale celebrated its Silver Jubilee at Liège in 1898, with a banquet, in the Royal Music Conservatory, honouring the Director-General, Georges Nagelmackers.

The reporter of the local *Journal la Meuse* gave a full and affectionate coverage of the event, describing the Belgian town as the "cradle" of the company in 1873. (Nothing much else has happened in Liège—apart from two wars—except for the birth of M. Georges Simenon, writer of thrillers, who has not to my knowledge ever involved Inspector Maigret in an Orient Express case.)

"If little Belgium," the reporter commented, "has no say in the European consortium; if she is too small to create fear in other countries, she is well-loved through the world, and the reason is the extraordinary success of the great enterprises which are born on her soil."

The great enterprise in this case was the *Compagnie* itself, and in proud flowery language, the Director-General was praised by M. Neef-Orban, President of the Wagons-Lits Council, and by M. Lechat, Paris Director of the Company, before an audience of distinguished persons brought there by special trains, and including the Vicomte de Ségur, the Marquis de Beauvoir, Comte Chastel from Paris, and Sir Francis Evans from London, as well as an assortment of Belgians and Dutch. Before drinking the loyal toast to King Leopold I, and praising "Mr. Nail-maker", the company sat down to the following menu :

Huîtres de Beernham

Turtle soup : Potage Reine

Truite Saumonée à la Chambord

Selle de Chevreuil à la Duchesse

Poulardes Valois

Chaudfroix de Langouste à la Parisienne

Truffes au Champagne
Bécasses à la Monaco
Parfait de foies gras
Plombière Impératrice
Fruits-Desserts

The ice-creams, contained in model Wagons-Lits fashioned out of nougat by a local confectioner, were the success of the evening. The speeches, conventional rather than inspiring, reflected variations on this theme of adventure rewarded by success.

A Vice-President of the Company, Lord Dalziel of Britain, an astute financier, was equally ambitious in his ideas. He began as a major ally of Pullman, and developed all-Pullman car trains on the London, Brighton and South Coast Railway. One of them, making a daily run to Brighton at an average speed of 50 m.p.h., he christened "The Southern Belle".

Having a foot in both camps, Dalziel was able to supervise connections between Pullman services from London to Dover and Wagons-Lits trains from Calais to Paris. He must have bitterly regretted the shelving of plans to build a Channel Tunnel in the years before the first world war. His other plan was to extend the Orient Express route through the Middle East, reaching Baghdad, Aleppo, Basra and Damascus, and linking up with the Wagons-Lits service operating from Cairo up through Palestine. The progress of this service is referred to in a later chapter.

Georges Nagelmackers died in 1905, but by that time there was no doubt about the thriving future of the *Compagnie Internationale*. The ambitious plan of a run to Istanbul in 1883 had been followed by the "Nord-Sud" Express concept, linking seven capitals; St. Petersburg (Leningrad), Berlin, Paris, Madrid, Lisbon, Brussels and London, with allowances made for the three different gauges of railways in Russia, Central Europe, and the Spanish Peninsula. A strange survival of this concept is to be found today on the façade of Blackfriars Station, London. Among the many place-names carved in the grimy stone is the destination ST. PETERSBURG. The Spanish-Portuguese portion still survives as one of Europe's crack expresses. Even more ambitious horizons were envisaged when the Czar of Russia, in 1898, called on the *Compagnie* to equip the first Trans-Siberian Express from Moscow to Peking. It was to become the most luxuriously appointed train of its kind in the world.

The full-length portrait of Nagelmackers, with his arrogant, challenging face, described by de Blowitz as being of "a slightly Arab type", dominates the board-room of the Wagons-Lits headquarters in Paris, and stands almost as high as the ceiling.

A year after the death of Nagelmackers, the longest railway tunnel in the world, the Simplon, was opened to traffic. It linked Switzerland and Italy, between Brig and Domodossola, and an international train between Paris and Milan was immediately inaugurated, and eventually prolonged as far as Trieste.

The Treaty of Versailles (1919) saw a spectacular revival and extension of this Simplon line. In previous years it had been a case of the *Compagnie Internationale* importuning and inviting governments to approve new routes. This time the Allied governments gave orders for a route to be re-opened. Articles 321 to 386 of the Treaty mainly concerned international waterways, and the future of Switzerland and the new Republic of Czechoslovakia, but they also touched on international rail transport. Since the primary object, urged by the French, was to maintain speedy and regular communication between the West and the new countries in the Balkans, any Grand Express of international repute would have to avoid the defeated lands of Germany and Austria.

The obvious choice was not the original Orient route, but the one through the Simplon tunnel, which brought in Italy. Students of history might well find in this decision an echo of earlier centuries, when Europe was first divided into nations, and when the Hapsburg Empire, which included Austria and Spain, found communications between these countries threatened by wars in France and the German States. Milan therefore became the vital junction for the Emperor Charles V. European wars, up to the reign of France's Louis XIV, were largely fought to obtain or safeguard routes between east and west, and between north and south. Now, in 1919, this pattern was repeated, not with armies, but with railways.

The first train left Paris for Istanbul on April 15, 1919. The route : Dijon, Lausanne, the Simplon, Milan, Venice, Trieste, Zagreb, Belgrade, Nish and Sofia. Italy was pleased : work on her mammoth railway station at Milan had begun again (the foundation stone was laid in 1906, the year the Simplon Tunnel opened, but the station was not completed until 1932, when Mussolini was already being credited abroad with the one virtue of making Italian trains run to time). Milan, with its concourse in marble and granite, 700 feet long, its handling of well over six million passengers a year, is still one of the wonders of the railway world, and is as imposing as the Colosseum in Rome.

Beyond Italy lay the newly-created Kingdom of Jugoslavia. French anxiety to establish friendly relations was reciprocated by the leaders of the new state, which had sent delegates to Paris, eager to discuss the train and its implications. Never before had a Grand Express enjoyed a greater political significance. The Swiss and the Dutch gave support to the project, and in 1920, the "S.O.E." (as the Simplon-Orient Express is known in railway circles) could offer through Wagons-Lits to Athens via Thessalonika.

The human driving force which turned a compulsory political move into a highly successful commercial proposition was the Director-General of the French P.L.M. (Paris-Lyon-Mediterranée) railway, M. Noblemaire, aided by a M. Loiseau, former President of the Paris Chamber of Advocates, and a man with considerable knowledge of Balkan conditions. P.L.M., representing France, became the "Administration Gerante"—the Top Member of the group—an honour awarded at the International Timetable Conferences in the case of all Grand European Expresses. The original Orient Express of 1883, sponsored by the Chemin de Fer de l'Est, did not resume its run until 1932.

Owing to shortage of rolling stock, damaged track and so on, the S.O.E. could not become a daily service until 1921. Its main advantage was its saving in time. According to Wagons-Lits handbooks, the Paris-Istanbul journey, which had in the past taken $96\frac{1}{2}$ hours, was reduced to 56 hours, and the trip to Athens 59 hours. It is ironical to think that these runs are *quicker* than the Direct-Orient times of 1966, but in those days the Simplon-Orient was an

61

all-sleeper luxury affair and, more important still, it was an express!

Other variants from the S.O.E. were to emerge as Europe settled down after the disruptions of war. The Fetesti bridge over the Danube made Rumania accessible, and opened up another route to the Black Sea port of Constanza, as an alternative to Varna (then a miserable place but today the headquarters of Bulgaria's tourist drive, inviting capitalist West Europeans to "come unto these yellow sands"). It was a longer boat journey from Constanza to the Bosphorus, but as late as 1929, according to a contemporary timetable, this was still the route.

Summer Train Services from May 15th, 1929

ORIENT EXPRESS: on Tuesdays, Thursdays and Saturdays from London:

London (Victoria)	11.20 (first day)
Calais	15.10
Paris (Est)	19.50
Munich	11.10 (second day)
Vienna	18.45
Budapest	0.25 (third day)
Bucharest	17.55
Constanza	22.45

The Simplon-Orient became the most celebrated of all the expresses, and the one which captured the imagination of several writers, but the inability or unwillingness of post-war Germany to co-operate in the matter of servicing trains (the Germans were, in fact, busily reviving their own highly successful wartime system *Mitropa*) led to yet another route with the inspiring initials S.A.V.E. (Swiss-Arlberg-Vienna-Express).

This made its way through Switzerland at night, using the Arlberg Tunnel, and continued a picturesque course to Innsbruck, that mellow and superbly placed town, Linz and Vienna. Later extensions brought S.A.V.E. to Budapest and, in 1932, to Bucharest, and the word "Orient" was attached to it.

But though the Swiss part of the journey may have been enjoyable, experiences in post-war Austria were not so happy. That country had suffered severely from dismemberment of her Empire, and the new republic was largely situated in mountainous districts without coalfields. The Austrians were, however, able to electrify the line between Salzburg and Vienna. The Arlberg-Orient was the first express to be revived after World War II, but the railway writer Peter Allen sums up on the later stages :

"This train is but a sad reminder of its former glory, as only an odd coach or two struggles east of Vienna and through the Iron Curtain to Budapest and finally on to Bucharest. In July 1953 it still had some of the best coaches in Europe in its make-up, but it also contained some very local Austrian stock, with an open-vestibule four-wheeler bringing up its rear."

This final comment suggests as undignified a picture as the present-day attachment of odd goods trucks to the Direct-Orient Express. It is certainly in contrast to the prestige enjoyed by the *Compagnie's* trains during the halcyon years of peace and at certain times of international crisis. The car itself became a symbol. In one spectacular case, it became not so much a carriage, but more a conference room.

The first world war meant the sudden shut-down of nearly all *Compagnie Internationale* services. When Belgium was over-run, the headquarters were transferred to Paris, where they still remain, the Belgians retaining only the original registered office. Wagons-Lits vehicles in Allied hands were obviously useful for emergency purposes, such as field headquarters for Generals and as mobile ambulances. Marshal Foch employed no less than three such coaches for his desk-work and conferences and map-reading. As the war drew to a climax, the Marshal ordered yet another dining-car to be specially equipped, for a special event.

This car, No. 2419, was destined to become the most famous in the history of the *Compagnie*.

It was Weygand (Foch's Chief of Staff), ironically enough, who was to take charge of it just before the Allied victory, in October, 1918. General Weygand, who died as recently as 1965, at the age of 96, was to escape the German reprisal at the surrender in 1940. A cloak of secrecy covered the movements of No. 2419, until it suddenly arrived at the Forest of Compiègne, outside Paris, attached to Marshal Foch's train. What followed is a matter of history. But what befell No. 2419 after 1918 was a classic case of *de haut en bas*. After triumphal appearances at various victory centres, and an unsuccessful attempt to install it in the Invalides, the precious relic ended up at Réthondes, not far from the scene of its original triumph, nine years later.

The strange setting for defeat obviously impressed a former corporal in the German Army of the first world war, one Adolf Hitler, who had the (dining) tables turned in June 1940 by hauling out No. 2419 into the exact spot at Compiègne for the second act of surrender. But this time it was the French who were surrendering.

No. 2419 then rumbled into captivity in Berlin, a mute symbol of human folly and vanity. But history was to ring the changes once again. The Allied bombing of the Anhalter station in 1944 at first seemed to have included the destruction of this much-tried veteran. Later researches made by railway historian George Behrend, suggest that the Nazis hung on to it to the end, keeping it in the town of Ohrdruf, in Thuringia, until the day the American tanks were on the outskirts. Then, a special S.S. detachment was detailed to blow up the old car, which had once more become a bitter symbol of defeat.

5

WIDER STILL AND WIDER

Anglo-German rivalry—Influence of the Germans on the Turks—The *Drang
Nach Osten* and the Baghdad Railway—The Taurus Express—Ambitions of
Lord Dalziel—Luxury travel between the wars.

Air travel obviously enlarges the horizons of the tourist trade.
Families who would earlier have spent their annual vacation at a
near-by seaside resort now travel thousands of miles on a comparatively cheap "package" holiday anywhere from Bermuda to the
Balearics, from Morocco to Israel. But it must not be forgotten
that certain parts of the Middle East—notably Egypt—were already favourite holiday centres for a select few more than a
century ago, with Thomas Cook as the pioneer. Both Cook's and
the Wagons-Lits company had invested a lot of money in the area
of the Nile. The Grand Tour became fashionable, and Cook's were
particularly enterprising at arranging any kind of journey, from
the matron in muslin who wanted to see Luxor and the Abu
Simbel statues, to a Royal State Visit, such as the one Kaiser
Wilhelm II made to the Holy Land in 1898. Mr. Frank Cook was
in charge of all the arrangements, and did his best to encourage the
somewhat naïve view that the Imperial tour had a sacred rather
than a political significance, and that the Kaiser's stay in Constantinople as the guest of the Sultan, and the elaborate arrangements
made by Abdul Hamid for his comfort in Palestine, were merely
an exchange of courtesies. But the Sultan had long experience of
German business men and technicians, and favoured them. Subsequent history shows that there were to be further, far-reaching
results to the visit, and that Germany's celebrated *Drang Nach
Osten*—the Drive to the East—was closely tied up with railway
concessions.

A year after the Imperial visit to the Sublime Porte in Constantinople, a convention was signed between the two countries, granting the German Anatolian Railway an extension of their system to Kuwait, on the Persian Gulf. This was the initiation of the Baghdad Railway, a Teutonic dream which only a world war could dispel. Political observers and writers in Britain and Russia watched its progress with increasing frustration. Professor Charles Sarolea of Edinburgh University declared: "By this convention, Germany has secured, with one stroke of the diplomatic pen, what England and Russia have striven for generations to obtain. . . . She has added to her sway not only the Turkish dominions, but the ancient Empires of Semiramis and Nebuchadnezzar, of Cyrus and Haroun al Raschid. . . . Finally, the German company has obtained the concession of the proposed line between Aleppo and Mecca, the line which will be taken by all the pilgrims to the City of the Prophet. . . . The Holy Land will become a German province. . . ." (*The Baghdad Railway: German expansion as a Factor in European Politics.* Oliver & Boyd, London, 1907.)

Professor Sarolea pointed out that Britain had neglected the chance of building the Suez Canal, and had ignored the opportunity of helping to run the Trans-Siberian railway. Britain and France, he wrote, should take the lead in internationalizing the main railways in the Middle East.

But opinion in Britain itself was divided. Since the inauguration of the railway from the Asian side of the Bosphorus to Angora (Ankara) in 1893, there had been considerable support for the German project, largely out of dislike for the alternative French or Russian influence in the area. Prime Minister Lord Salisbury indeed welcomed the concession of the Anatolian Railway as a move which came in line with British interests in the Persian Gulf. Imperialist supporters such as Cecil Rhodes and Joseph Chamberlain also supported the concession. The railway had become a considerable pawn in the political game. In the words of a Turkish Liberal Minister of Finance, quoted by a British historian "When you entered the board-room of the Baghdad Railway Co., you breathed the atmosphere of the Minister's office in the Wilhelmstrasse". (*A Short History of the Middle East.* George E. Kirk. Praeger, New York, 1948.) The British had to be content with two directors on the board.

The Germans went ahead with their plans, the most ambitious being to build a tunnel under the Bosphorus, linking Europe with Asia. This task might well have proved impossible, and the Great War of 1914 made it entirely academic, but at the time the project had all the dramatic quality of the Channel Tunnel between Britain and France, which was being canvassed and debated throughout this period.

The Anatolian Company proposed two alternative routes as a result of the agreement. One, the old imperial route of the Romans, lay through the north, through Angora and Shivas, avoiding the mountainous ranges of the Taurus. The second, the southern line, followed the valley of the Meander river, ascended and descended the Taurus mountains, and continued along the plains of Mesopotamia. (This is the present route of the Taurus Express.)

The inaugural trip of the Orient Express in 1883 was not directly connected with these later activities, although the two anonymous German journalists in the official party may have already had some inkling about their country's attitude towards the East. Perhaps that is why they were ignored by the Belgian and French contingents on the journey.

By the beginning of the twentieth century, German surveyors were a familiar sight in Turkey. They had been given forestry rights, mining rights and a monetary guarantee per kilometre of track which the Sultan was entirely unable to pay, unless he were to sell his jewels in Topkapi Palace ! The terminus of the Baghdad Railway at this stage in the proceedings was to have been Basra, but the Germans put pressure on Sultan Abdul Hamid to persuade the Sheikh of Kuwait to cede twenty-five square miles of his territory, providing the Germans with a terminus, and access to his spacious harbour for German liners.

Britain may have been slow in her acquisition of inland routes, but as a maritime nation she had little to fear, at that time, from competition. The Sheikh coolly replied to the Sultan : "It was pleasant to receive a communication from my nominal overlord. We have not heard from you for a hundred years. You have always left us to the tender care and solicitude of the British Navy. With regard to your special request, I have to inform you that you are a little too late, for the British Consul from Basra recently visited me, and, in consideration for all that the British have done for us, I gladly strengthened our agreements, and now I am not permitted to give any of my territory to your German friends without the sanction of the British authorities."

The Turks mobilised an army on the borders of Kuwait, but later the Sultan lost heart, and the Germans had to be content with the railway station at Basra. Those were the grand days when a British gunboat in the Gulf made all the difference to political alliances. Aleppo became an important junction on the line, and already in the Balkans railway trucks could be seen bearing the proud if somewhat exaggerated sign BERLIN-BAGHDAD. Thanks to the ingenuity of German surveyors and engineers, nearly twenty tunnels were constructed through the Taurus Mountains. When war came, and the armies of Allenby and the brilliance of Lawrence of Arabia swept triumphantly through the area, they captured immense amounts of German rolling-stock and equipment.

After 1918 the vanished German dream became the British dream. Resisting pressure from the French Government, and even from an American financial group, the Chester concession, Mustapha Kemal (Ataturk) allowed a group of British bankers to buy the whole bankrupt stock of the Anatolian railway. Behind the operation could be seen the influence of Lord Dalziel, who had become Director-General of the *Compagnie Internationale*.

His railway concept was even more ambitious than the German one : not only a drive to the East to Baghdad, but a link with the South, through Beirut, Haifa and Gaza, right down to Cairo, where Wagons-Lits business flourished. The Taurus Express, connecting with the Orient by specially timed ferries across the Bosphorus, had made the Paris-Baghdad route a reality by1930.The service became popular, and at one time the company possessed sixty Wagons-Lits and twenty dining-cars, all on the Asian side. The special sidings and repair shop still show a good muster of these "Yatakli Wagons", as they are labelled in Turkish.

In the years immediately before the second world war, the time-table and handbook for the Simplon-Orient and Taurus Expresses, printed in French, English and Arabic (but not in modern

Turkish), shows an impressive system on an almost Napoleonic scale, involving the whole Eastern European and Middle-Eastern complex, with the Dalziel extension through Palestine to Egypt, and a shipping connection between Basra and Bombay. Pretty ladies and handsome gentlemen are seen reclining in railway luxury, and there is even provision for small dogs to accompany passengers, so that Madame's poodle or Pekinese could travel with her on the Grand Tour, on payment of 20 per cent of the Wagons-Lits supplement.

This was the heyday of the "Sleepings". On the Simplon-Orient Express, hot and cold showers were available during the summer months. Meal-tickets insured adequate nourishment throughout the journey. Hopefully, the time-table promised new Wagons-Lits routes in Iraq and Jugoslavia, already dated 1940 and 1941. There were also fare and supplement reductions of up to 40 per cent for those on the staff of "certain important accredited Companies" who were making long-distance bookings to places like Aleppo and Baghdad. Parties of six or more "effecting the journey from Orient to Europe or vice-versa" were also given a 40 per cent reduction.

According to Wagons-Lits documents in 1939, the journey from Haydarpasa to Aleppo took only thirty-five hours, and Cairo could be reached in three and a half days. Paris to Beirut was reckoned as a four-day journey, and to Baghdad, six days. These were great achievements of the 1930s, but air travel has obviously superseded them in the post-war years.

6

THE TIME-TABLES TURNED

George Bradshaw's first time-table—Cook's Tours begin—Mark Twain on Thomas Cook—How international expresses are organised—Mysteries and misunderstandings at International Time-Table Conferences—End of the Simplon-Orient Express—Hopes for new routes.

International trains do not only raise problems such as politics and Customs regulations. In each case, a time-table has to be agreed, and the proceedings of Europe's International Time-Table Conferences, begun as long ago as 1872, can be as acrimonious as a full session of the United Nations, and contain as much tough bargaining as a meeting of Europe's Common Market.

The idea of a time-table with an official status started, it seems, in Britain. George Bradshaw, a map-printer, engraver and publisher, issued his first local time-table in 1839. Before that, picturesque but fallible stage coaches had given approximate times of setting-down and picking-up, often lettered in gold leaf on notice boards outside the hotels or staging-posts. But "Bradshaw" became the trade-name for the whole of Britain as soon as the railway system established itself. The name passed into the dictionary and the language, a Bradshaw time-table became, like the time-signal at Greenwich, the ultimate authority.

Thomas Cook, a contemporary of Bradshaw, was also anxious to establish some reliable list of arrivals and departures, but in the first phase of his activities, he confined himself to his famous Excursions, and later his Grand Tours, all in Special Trains, a fact which did not endear him to the railway companies. On Tuesday, June 18, 1850, he announced a "Charming Excursion to Cheltenham, Gloucester, Bristol, Exeter and Plymouth" leaving his native Leicester and allowing his passengers up to five days in the West of

70

England. A time-table was given, and a "Brief Guide to the beauties of the Tour", with the current local attractions.

Six years later, having tried his hand out at the Paris Exhibition, Cook offered a "Grand Circular Tour of the Continent", heading for Antwerp by way of Harwich, and personally conducted by himself. Starting, obviously, with the battlefields of Waterloo, the route lay along the Rhine to Cologne, Mainz, Heidelberg and Baden-Baden, returning via Strasbourg and Paris. From then on this remarkable man built up the far-flung organisation which, as we have seen earlier, could conduct the German Kaiser and his large retinue to the Holy Land via Constantinople, and which built up, in association with the Wagons-Lits company, an unassailable position among international travel agencies. Cook even competed with the well-established and rapidly expanding American Express Company, not in Europe but on their own territory, a tourist invasion which is only just beginning to be canvassed once again, more than a century later. American Express was already running nine hundred offices in the United States, but had not yet considered Europe to any great degree as a tourist playground. Cook's were advertising American tours with a choice of five shipping lines, and an average return fare from Liverpool to New York of 25 guineas first class, and 16 guineas second class. As far as conducting American "innocents" abroad on the continent is concerned, Mark Twain, who had little opinion of European standards of travel, paid the company this tribute : "Cook has made travel easy and a pleasure. He will sell you a ticket to any place on the globe, or all the places. . . . He provides hotels for you everywhere, if you so desire; and you cannot be overcharged, for the coupons show just how much you must pay. . . . Cook is your banker everywhere, and his establishment your shelter when you get caught out in the rain. . . ." (Quoted in *The Thomas Cook Story*. John Pudney. Michael Joseph, 1953.)

There is still, today, in Cook's head office, the Eastern Princes' Department, as well as the Pilgrims' Department—and Cook's Continental Time-table is to Europe what Bradshaw was until recently to Britain. The companion-company of Wagons-Lits issue their own French-language time-table and guide, with a cover in their livery of dark blue and gold, but this only gives their own

Table 28
DIRECT-ORIENT EXPRESS

Day	arr.	dep.		arr.	dep.	
A	..	z1430	**London** (Victoria) 50 ... ⋀	1450z	..	
32	1855	1919	Calais (Maritime) 🚉	1130	1205	
⋁	2233	2253	**Paris** (Nord) 50	7 25	8 10	9
A 529	2316	d2350	**Paris** (Lyon) 151	6 29	6 57	
B 168	6 00	6 20	Vallorbe 🚉 158	2334	0 08	520
	7 00	7 07	Lausanne 251	2248	2257x	
	7 32	7 34	Montreux	2221	2223x	
	9 19	9 27	Brigue 🚉 251	2014	2037x	191
	1005	1025	Domodossola 🚉	1913	1933	
PO	1223	1320	**Milan** (Cent.) 352	1610	1715	
	1705	1730	Venice (S. Lucia) 390	1144	1240	
	1954	2014	Trieste 390	8 30	9 32	OP
⋁	2044	2110	Poggioreale Campagna 🚉	7 23	8 00	
B PO	2119	2225	Sežana 🚉	6 09	7 14	
C	0 21	.. ⋁	Ljubljana 791	..	4 05	OP
B D41	..	1556	**Munich** (Hbf.) 684 ...... ⋀	1348	..	D46
E	1753	1815	Salzburg 🚉	1130	1205	E
⋁ 735	2152	2208	Villach (Hbf.) 🚉 759	7 23	7 50	734
B 907	2300	2330	Jesenice 🚉	5 07	5 55	
C	0 25	.. ⋁	Ljubljana 793	..	3 45	908
C PO	..	1 07	Ljubljana 791 .... ⋀	3 23	..	
	3 10	3 30	Zagreb	0 58	1 13	
	9 00	9 56	**Belgrade** 791	1843	1935	OP
	1334	.. ⋁	Crveni Krst 792	..	1458	
PO	..	1343	Crveni Krst 792 .... ⋀	1440	..	
	1734	1800	Skopje	1050	1110	
⋁ 402	2130	2210	Gevgeli (Yug. T.) 🚉	6 30	7 10	OP
C	2315	0 00	Idomeni (Grk. T.) 🚉	6 43	7 25	
D 2	1 15	1 55	Thessaloniki 897	4 40	5 25	401
D	·1142	.. ⋁	**Athens** 897	..	1901	I
C	..	1356	Crveni Krst 802 .... ⋀	1428	..	
⋁ 4	1555	1634	Dimitrovgrad (Yug.T.) 🚉.	1208	1248	
C	1856	1935	Sofia (Bulg.T.) 🚉	1115	1150	3
D 546	a0 45	a1 20	Svilengrad 🚉	3 20b	4 35	
5	a4 06	a4 45	Pithion (Grk.T.) 🚉	0 19b	0 40b	
⋁	a5 05	a5 45	Uzunköpru (Turk.T.) 🚉 .	2325c	0 01b	
D	a1230	.. ⋁	**Istanbul** 901	..	1630c	6

Paris branch

A page from a recent Cooks International Timetable shows the route to Istanbul to be a procession of frontier stations.

services, and for a comprehensive guide to European trains, Cook's Continental Guide is essential. Since 1952, it has been under the editorship of Mr. J. H. Price.

There are two ways of looking at a time-table. One is purely practical, and solely connected with your route—including those important little beds and crossed knives and forks at the foot, telling you at what stages you can sleep and eat en route. The other is surely the blissfully imaginative, in which you indulge in a vicarious day-dream, just as G. K. Chesterton asserted he could enjoy all the thrill of going on holiday by packing up his luggage, hiring a horse-cab to call at his house, bowling down to the Continental platform of the station—and going home again.

This super-Bradshaw from Cooks can tell you not only how to get from Paris to Istanbul, but what time the ferry-boats leave from Italy to Sardinia, and about the hard and soft class route from, say, Krasnovodsk to Samarkand, which is no longer a poetic golden road, but a railroad to a town in the Soviet Union. Mr. Price has all the answers at his finger-tips. Some of the distances are enormous—not only the 1800 miles from London to Istanbul, but the 1662 miles involved in the journey from Moscow to Sofia on the Danubian Express. This makes it about the second longest train journey in Europe, and Communist throughout, whether the class is hard or soft.

There are other surprising discoveries chosen at random:— that, for instance, three times a week you can go from Copenhagen (and Denmark is surely considered politically congenial, whatever the trains are like) to Moscow on the Ostsee Express, via Berlin and Warsaw: or from Stockholm to Bucharest through Prague and Budapest on the Balt-Orient Express. The two frontier stations between Hungary and Rumania are called, respectively, Biharkeresztes and Episcopia Bihor, and the trains arrive in the middle of the night—as always. Add to this the Egyptian trains (the Hydrofoil service up the Nile to the statues at Abu Simbel), the local from Aleppo to Beirut, and the diesel service from Haifa to Tel Aviv, and you will see that Mr. Price casts his net wide, and without any political bias.

After the earliest experiments in international travel in the 1880s, further difficulties arose in addition to political ones. Fox-

73

well and Farrer, who compiled a book of the major trains in Europe as early as 1889, complete with time-tables and comparative speeds, commented on the troubles of the young Wagons-Lits organisation.

"The Company gets more obloquy than it deserves from English travellers," they assert, "since the very large supplements which are charged on its cars" (in 1889 they were between 20 per cent and 35 per cent of the normal fare) "are not the fault of the Car Company, but of the monopoly system which prevails on the Continent. . . . It is obvious that an alien growth such as theirs cannot maintain as proper a control over details as the railways themselves could, and since Prussia will not have the international services at all, a serious break in European communication is threatened for the Car Company." (*Express Trains English & Foreign*. Smith Elder, London, 1889. Reprinted by Ian Allan, London, 1965.)

Foxwell and Farrer, however, give two alternative Orient Express time-tables of the year 1880, the first running through Munich, Vienna, Budapest and Bucharest to Constanza on the Black Sea, the second branching south from Budapest to Belgrade and the frontier town of Zaribrod. They give times, mileage, and speeds. The average, twenty-seven to twenty-nine miles an hour, they find disappointing in so distinguished a train.

The annual International Time-Table Conferences were, however, already in being, and have continued ever since. They are held in a different country each year. It need not be in a capital town—the last Conference in Britain was held in 1949 in the picturesque and appropriately Oriental setting of the Royal Pavilion at Brighton. Three of the recent settings have been in Sofia, Vienna and Stockholm. Since the Second World War the proportion works out roughly at two Conferences in Western Europe to one in Eastern Europe. The Swiss, with that genius for centralised and simon-pure neutrality, represent the headquarters of the International Union of Railways, and the Time-Table Secretariat is located at Berne.

Each representative at the annual Conference has one vote as a member, plus one vote for every thousand kilometres of track used by trains passing through his country. Long before the Conference meets, with the usual polite speeches of welcome and goodwill, a lot of work has gone on by correspondence to prepare the ground, particularly if the train is a truly international one, such as the Direct-Orient Express, including six countries in its whole journey. Alterations and suggestions have been exchanged, and presumably most of the delegates know what problems may arise.

After the first half-day of polite talk the Conference divides into sub-committees, to consider the particular international expresses under review. Some concern very few countries. The Sud Express —as old in years as the Orient Express—can be left to the French, Spanish and Portuguese representatives. With other more complex organisations one administrator is appointed as the *Administrateur-Gérant* for that train, the Chairman. It might be that French Railways have chief responsibility for the Simplon-Orient, West German Railways for the Tauern Express, the Swiss for the Direct-Orient Express, and so on. The main expresses are, however, dealt with first, and the Istanbul line is usually first priority.

It calls for the attention of no less than twenty-two members of the Conference. Does this mean, then, that as well as being a present-day failure as a train, it is also an international headache? Not necessarily. It's obvious that with airline competition, the "carriage-trade" of the Grand Dukes and the opera stars and the King's and Queen's Messengers has disappeared, and that, from the economic point of view of the six countries concerned in the journey from Paris to Istanbul, the train has to be considered as a local proposition. This is why it stops at every station in Switzerland, and most of the Italian stations. This can only be agreeable to the long-distance passenger provided he accepts the fact that his train is, for the moment, a local train, and not a Grand European Express.

One reason for the slowness of the run through Italy from Paris is readily explained by Mr. Price. There are two departures for Istanbul, one from Paris, the other through Munich. The Paris section, which is the old "Simplon-Orient" route, takes three hours longer than the German run. It leaves at midnight, and therefore the Time-Table Conference agrees that it shall dawdle through Switzerland and Italy until it connects with the other train, in

Jugoslavia. Otherwise one could have left Paris at 3 a.m. instead of midnight, but who wants to do that?

Arrivals and departures of trains are very important to members of the Conference. It is said that the Jugoslavs finally killed the "Simplon-Orient" because, as scheduled, it landed Jugoslavs in Belgrade in the middle of the night, and was not profitable for Jugoslavs wanting to work in Germany. There wasn't even much chance of selling ice-cream or slivovitz en route, let alone booking any local traffic.

So it was decided to close the famous Simplon-Orient, to the regret of many, on May 26, 1962. Obviously, the Wagons-Lits Company was ready to organise another schedule, which came up, the next day, as the Direct-Orient. The Turks and Bulgarians wanted to keep the original proud name "Simplon-Orient", but were outvoted by a committee headed by the implacable Swiss. The twenty-two members kept the train in being under the new name. No wonder—the time was more acceptable to the Jugoslavs, since it reaches Belgrade at about nine in the morning, with passengers who have not been fed the night before, and are obviously glad to have arrived.

The new Istanbul Express, started in May, 1965, runs from Munich, and there are signs that it will not be just two coaches attached to local trains and taking pot-luck in the Balkans. The West Germans are a very potent force as travellers—either as businessmen or tourists—and theirs is a voice which calls more loudly in matters of transport than any other European country today. Moreover, their country employs thousands of Jugoslavs, Greeks and Turks, who travel home two or three times a year for their holidays.

One of the major disadvantages of these Time-Table Conferences, from the point of view of such organisations as Wagons-Lits, is that Sleeping and Restaurant Car Companies can attend only as observers, with no power to vote. Thus the *Compagnie Internationale,* while it owns its cars and blazons its name upon them, is at the mercy of the railway administration in every country. Restaurant car facilities can only be provided if the car can be cleaned, watered and refitted for the return journey in the country where it is operating. In recent years, this has been the major drawback for travellers on trains such as the Orient, the Jugoslavia and Balkan Expresses. If the Wagons-Lits Company is forbidden to provide the food and drink, there's no point in providing their own voiture-restaurant. Their only privilege lies in the bed-linen which, with Paris as the great laundry centre, can be provided from the conductor's own locker. This is small consolation for the hungry traveller who reflects that the company owns the large Paris food store, *La Maison Raoul Dautry*, and the magnificent hotel and restaurant at Orly Airport.

It is a curious international anomaly that the only item of equipment common to *all* countries is a key. The three-sided, flat-ended Berne key (Switzerland again) will lock or unlock any railway carriage in Europe.

These are some of the reasons why a time-table, involving so many different interests and national attitudes, is not as simple as it looks when laid out neatly on Mr. Price's printed page.

7

APPROACHES TO THE ORIENT

Britain overcomes her isolation—Channel Tunnel prospects—The Golden
Arrow's "millionaire" service—The Dunkirk Night Ferry, favourite with the
Duke of Windsor—A Purser's reminiscences of famous passengers.

In a London newspaper of the 1930s appeared the headline :

GREAT STORM IN ENGLISH CHANNEL:

CONTINENT ISOLATED

The implications behind it caused lasting amusement among
European observers. Equally telling is the story of the foreign visitor who, on arriving in London at Victoria Station, saw an evening
paper poster which read

ENGLAND FACING DISASTER

A little further on another poster proclaimed

LITTLE HOPE FOR ENGLAND

Wondering what terrible political or financial catastrophe had
struck Albion, he stopped to buy a paper with the headline
ENGLAND COLLAPSE. The verb in the plural might have
given him the clue. England were losing a cricket-match against
Australia.

But the large notice-board above Victoria Station pronounces it
to be THE GATEWAY TO THE CONTINENT, as if to
confirm that Britain regards herself as part of Europe, has made
efforts to join the Common Market, and is now actively support-
ing that hundred-year-old project, the Channel Tunnel between
Dover and France. Londoners may yet see a board on a Wagons-
Lits coach saying LONDON-ISTANBUL, a sign which would
have rejoiced the heart of Lord Dalziel.

The Tunnel idea, first seriously suggested in Paris in the reign of
Napoleon III, resulted in the formation of The Channel Tunnel
Company in 1872—just a year before the *Compagnie des*

Wagons-Lits. But while the international railway company flourished from the start, the Tunnel company floundered. The most steadfast opponents of the scheme were the military commanders on both sides of the Channel; it was said that Sir Garnet Wolseley, the General who had won the Ashanti campaign, had scored a decisive victory in scotching the Channel Tunnel campaign. But he had not killed the idea. More voices were raised in its support, among them that of the young Winston Churchill. In 1930 the project was defeated in the House of Commons. Through two world wars men have asked themselves what difference a Channel Tunnel would have made (particularly after the British retreat at Dunkirk).

One thing is almost certain. If the Channel Tunnel is ever built, it will be a railway tunnel, even if the rolling stock is mainly devoted to carrying cars; and since it would not be possible to bore direct through the twenty-odd miles between the two coasts the overall length of the Tunnel is likely to be about thirty miles. Until this is done, those who do not wish to fly to Paris head for Platform 8 at Victoria Station, the needle's eye through which the continental camels must pass.

It is a depressing, even degrading, exit from the metropolis, with none of the excitement of foreign carriages and names. A facia board in blue-and-yellow proclaims the famous all-Pullman service of the Golden Arrow, but the design has not been changed since it was first put up in 1929, and the surroundings, the ancient notice-boards, the forbidding iron railings, the lack of seating for those who wait, perhaps for hours in the holiday season, make this a drab bolt-hole for those thinking of sun and sea and adventure. The domes and minarets of Istanbul would seem very far away indeed.

But once inside the Golden Arrow, things are very different. The immaculate train leaves at ten o'clock precisely every morning of the year except Christmas Day. A blue-and-white jacketed attendant stands at the entrance of each Pullman car. The first-class cars have names—Rosemary, Minerva, Pegasus (which contains the original travelling bar, the Trianon) and the second-class have numbers. But the service is the same, and British Rail are as proud of their Golden Arrow part of the journey as the French are of

79

their *Flèche d'Or*, which continues from Calais to the Gare du Nord. It was Dalziel's ambition to provide a "millionaire" atmosphere on the London-Dover Pullman, and to maintain it throughout the remainder of the 280-mile journey. In British railway annals, it has equal fame with the Royal Scot, the Flying Scotsman, and Cornish Riviera Limited, but it was designed as a link with just such a train as the Orient Express.

The important aim was to maintain a continual standard of comfort and service. Dalziel had to overcome initial French opposition, since he insisted that British rolling-stock should be used throughout (the cross-Channel boats were British anyhow). It is odd to find national pride so sensitive in the prosaic matter of train equipment. Not until after the second world war were the French allowed to provide carriages at Calais.

When the war-interrupted service was restored (April 15, 1946) the Gare Maritime at Calais still looked like a battlefield, and the famous cross-channel ship *Canterbury*—veteran of Dunkirk and later off the D-Day beaches at Arromanches—was still painted in battleship grey. Her master, Captain Tony Walker, who had served in both these naval epics, was still in command, and remained so for years to come. A new class of locomotive, the "Merchant Navy" Pacific, hauled the train from London, bearing a large Golden Arrow above the boiler plates, and somehow, despite all their difficulties, the French had mustered the essential Pullman coaches, to preserve the exclusive character of the train. Only four years later did French Railways succeed in their plan to add ordinary coaches, in the interests of economy.

During the high season there are many different ways of reaching Paris from London, but only two British Rail services have lived up to the pre-war standard of the Grand European Expresses. Second to the Golden Arrow is the unsung, unspectacular but ever-reliable Night Ferry via Dunkirk. It has been favourite for travellers like the Duke and Duchess of Windsor, who rarely use any other route. In this service, started in 1936, there is complete continuity apart from different restaurant cars, for the Wagons-Lits are shipped aboard the ferry, and the *de luxe* passengers need not stir from their beds until the call for breakfast. With cars for both Paris and Brussels the Night Ferry looks more continental

than any other boat train, though the surroundings of its departure from Platform 2 at Victoria are even more dreary than that of
the Golden Arrow.

But there is something of the frontier post (so alien to England)
on that platform. If you are travelling by sleeping-car throughout,
you are the nearest thing to a foreign element in all British railway
practice. Once you have passed the barrier, no one can follow with
a platform ticket to say goodbye. Holders of night-sleeper tickets
(the most expensive way of getting to Paris, by land, sea, or air) are
segregated from those hardy souls who intend to travel by ordinary
carriage to Dover, and then doss down on a couch aboard the
ferry. These have an entirely separate entrance from that of the
train, and have to be there at least half an hour before departure.
The effect of the division is almost dramatic in its completeness;
especially as the ferry also carries cars and coaches, which come
aboard at Dover.

It is a safe, leisurely way out, and perhaps that is why it recom-
mends itself to royalty and diplomats. The Queen herself went on
the Dunkirk Ferry for her state visit to Paris, and she has received
many royal visitors and heads of state on the red carpet at Victoria
Station's Platform 2.

My own view of this route from London to Paris is that it is
much better on the return journey. Going out, the arrival at Dunkirk at four in the morning is apt to be accompanied by a certain
amount of cavalier treatment—or at least noise—as the coaches
are off-loaded from the ferry, and there are few hours of sleep left
to recover before breakfast is called. On the journey to England,
the evening meal on the train in France is certainly better, if more
expensive, and the departure at midnight is preferable, and
painless.

The outward run at one time passed through Canterbury, until
the Folkestone line was electrified in 1961. On this line the train
passes near Chartwell, home of the late Sir Winston Churchill, and
on one occasion during his Premiership the train was stopped
specially to pick him up at Sevenoaks. The entire station had to be
closed for this to be done.

Procedure for securing the Wagons-Lits cars when on board,
and for disembarking them on the ramp, is highly complicated,

81

and has undergone several changes. The vital performer on this operation is a powerful diesel shunting engine which moves with cat-like tread, easing each carriage gently on to French soil. As a sleeping passenger, you may of course be awakened by the sudden hiss of the Westinghouse brakes, or the staccato heart-beat of the Westinghouse pump, to say nothing of the sound of the wheel-tapper.

Then you are in Dunkirk, and are soon speeding through the battlefields of World War I, past Arras, past Hazebrouck, to the nine o'clock rendezvous at the Gare du Nord. There is something solid and permanent and imperturbable about the Night Ferry. It has scarcely ever been cancelled, and it is said that Hitler planned to use it for his triumphant entry into England.

A man who has many tales to tell of cross-Channel passengers is the celebrated ex-purser of the Golden Arrow ship *Invicta*, Sydney Mason-Springgay, who has served out so many landing-tickets to the famous as well as the unknown. Now retired, Mr. Mason-Springgay lives in Folkestone, and he readily recalls some of the passengers he has looked after between Dover and Calais.

One of the men he knew well was Lord Dalziel himself. "When he died, he had a million in the bank," says the purser, "and yet, on his trips over, he couldn't bear having to pay the port-dues, which, as I recall, were one and five pence in those days." Port-dues are sums which are levied even for those who have a free travel pass, and today the amount from Dover to Calais is about a pound, or three dollars.

Dalziel always travelled alone, and always paid the purser himself. "On one occasion," said Mr. Mason-Springgay, "he hadn't got the right amount, so he gives me one shilling and six-pence, saying 'You can pay me back next time.' Sure enough, on his return journey he called me over and said 'Sydney, you owe me a penny, remember?' "

Mason-Springgay's memories include occasions of high politics and diplomacy. He remembers the funeral of King George V in 1936, when for the first time he had a delegation from Russia to look after. The chief representative was the massive figure of Tukachevsky, Marshal of the Red Army. They had travelled on the Simplon-Orient Express in order to avoid going through Nazi Germany.

The following year, for the Coronation of King George VI, the Russians sent another delegation to London. Mr. Mason-Springgay expected to see some familiar faces, but this time the party was headed by Mr. Litvinov, the Foreign Secretary, a man whom the purser described as being "such a contrast—all smiling, like Mr. Pickwick". He asked why Marshal Tukachevsky had not paid a return visit to Britain. Mr. Litvinov smiled and said, "He has been unavoidably delayed." In fact, the great Stalin purge had taken place, and the Marshal had been deprived, not only of freedom to travel, but of life itself.

King Carol of Rumania also travelled on the same route for the royal funeral, a disastrous journey for him since, after a riotous night before the event in London, he had to be accompanied in the procession by a masseur, who in turn had to be put in the uniform of a Rumanian colonel, to conceal his identity among all the nobility.

Ambassadors, ex-Premiers, Dukes and Duchesses, stars of stage and screen : the purser has seen them all and talked with them all. Among the diplomats, he remembers that when Sir Robert Vansittart travelled with his lady, she always had the same maid with her; that Sir Maurice Hankey (later Lord Hankey) Secretary to the British Cabinet for many years, on his way to Egypt, prided himself, even at the age of eighty, on having a cold bath every morning, and used to greet Mr. Mason-Springgay with the remark "I hope you didn't miss your bath this morning". He also recalls that the King's Messengers, the couriers who were once regulars on the Grand European Express, were often handcuffed to their diplomatic cases; and the occasion when Mr. Nubar Gulbenkian, with customary orchid in buttonhole, brought three passports with him—Armenian, Persian, and British. Prince Yousoupoff, the man credited with having killed Rasputin, was another famous passenger who passed through.

Then there were the un-political, non-diplomatic personalities. Mr. Mason-Springgay remembers Serge Diaghilev en route for a London triumph : the Osbert Sitwells, who travelled under the unlikely name of Parkinson and always brought an enormous amount of luggage : Chapliapin, Pavlova, both Sacha and Lucien Guitry on the same day : the list is endless. And as far as visitors' books are concerned, both Mason-Springgay, the purser, and Alfred Terry, *Invicta's* chief steward, have enviable collections. Where else but in Mr. Mason-Springgay's diminutive office on that crossing, could one find one page which contains the signatures of Arnold Bennett, Rudyard Kipling and Albert Einstein.

Other railway authorities could describe their own approaches to the Orient—particularly M. Nagelmackers' own countrymen, who send off the Jugoslavia and Balkan Expresses to Istanbul from Ostend and Brussels, and the Dutch, with their terminus at the Hook of Holland. But there is a special, almost endearing, quality about the connections with London, partly because of the traditional character of the original luxury services, in which even the rose-colour of the lamp-shades in the Pullman car has not changed for generations, and partly because the British are a law unto themselves, and when a storm rages in the English Channel, and the boats cannot dock, it is hard luck to be isolated on the Continent.

8

THEY WENT BY COACH

Travellers' Tales: The Pre-Railway Age. Marco Polo—Alexander Kinglake, *Eothen,* and the Pasha of Belgrade—King's Messengers' tales—The Courier who collected a Zoo.

"It should be known to the reader that, at the time when Baldwin the Second was Emperor of Constantinople, where a magistrate representing the Doge of Venice then resided, and in the Year of Our Lord 1250, Nicolo Polo, father of Marco, and Maffeo, the brother of Nicolo, respectable and well-informed men, embarked on a ship of their own, with a rich and varied cargo of merchandise, and reached Constantinople in safety. . . ."

The Travels of Marco Polo

Seven hundred years ago, when Venice held "the gorgeous East in fee", the Polo family made the Bosphorus their start for a visit to the Court of Kubla Khan and other strange and exotic places, returning to Constantinople after their first journey. Through the centuries, this city has held a lure for travellers. It is not, like Mecca or Jerusalem, a place of pilgrimage. It has never been a peaceful or comfortable place. But long before the cry of "Go West, young man!" was heard, men and women preferred to go East, with Constantinople as the threshold of a new world. Since 1453, when Mohammed II conquered and sacked the Byzantine stronghold, there has been less cause for Europeans to go there, particularly after the "infamous" Turks, at the height of their power, reached the gates of Vienna. When the Turks retreated and withdrew towards Asia, the travellers returned, until the railway age brought the Sultan's mysterious domains within reach of the ordinary tourist.

The first railways operated in England in 1830, and four years later, there was a remarkable prophecy about this method of travel, when Alexander Kinglake, a young man of Scottish stock, though born in Devon, decided to leave his legal studies at Lincoln's Inn and make a Grand Tour of his own choosing, accompanied by his friend Lord Collington.

His account of his journey begins in Belgrade, and passes through Turkey, the Lebanon, Palestine, Egypt and Cyprus. It is contained in *Eothen*, a book which was to become a classic. The name is Greek, and means "from the early dawn" or "from the East".

Kinglake and Collington found Belgrade still garrisoned by Turkish troops under the command of a Pasha. . . . "They wore the old Turkish costume; vests and jackets of many and brilliant colours divided from the loose petticoat trousers by heavy volumes of shawl, so thickly folded round their waists as to give the meagre wearers something of the dignity of true corpulence. No man bore less than one brace of immensely long pistols and a yataghan, or cutlass, with a dagger or two of various sizes. This carefulness of his arms is a point of honour with the Osmanlee (Ottoman); he never allows his bright yataghan to suffer from his own adversity. . . . Again and again you meet turbans, and faces of men, but they have nothing for you—no welcome—no wonder—no wrath—no scorn. . . ."

But there was a welcome from the Pasha: Turkish coffee and hubble-bubble pipes for the travellers at his castle. Soon the party was ready, with its "Tartar" or courier-guide, and all the baggage horses, ready for the fifteen-day ride to Constantinople. Their first stopping place was a simple Servian village, and Kinglake reflected: "The first night of your first campaign is a glorious time in your life. It is so sweet to find oneself free from the stale civilisation of Europe !"

While in this early stage of the journey, Kinglake devises a remarkable imaginary conversation held between himself, the Pasha, and the interpreter or dragoman: remarkable, because it has to do with railways—and this was in 1834. Kinglake gathered that the Pasha was deeply interested in the vast progress which had been made in the uses of steam, and appeared to understand the structure of our machinery, which he demonstrated in a manner worthy of Laurence Sterne or Lewis Carroll. Kinglake as the Traveller in the dialogue, had convinced him that both Houses of Parliament had met, and assured the integrity of the Sultan's dominions from the Speaker's chair.

"*Pasha*: Wonderful chair! Wonderful houses! Whirr! Whirr! All by wheels!—Whiz! Whiz! All by steam! Wonderful people—Whirr! Whirr! All by wheels! Whiz! Whiz! All by steam!

Traveller: (to the dragoman) What does the Pasha mean by that whizzing? He does not mean to say, does he, that our Government will ever abandon their pledges to the Sultan?

Dragoman: No, your Excellency; but he says that the English talk by wheels, and by steam.

Pasha: I know it—I know all—the particulars have been faithfully related to me, and my mind comprehends locomotives. The armies of the English ride upon the vapours of boiling cauldrons, and their horses are flaming coals! Whirr! Whirr! All by wheels! Whizz! Whizz! All by steam!"

It was to be another fifty-one years before a whiz-whiz train bound for Constantinople was to reach Belgrade, and one wishes that this remarkable Uncle Toby of a Pasha could have lived to see it. He ended up with this tribute:

"The English are foremost and best; for the Russians are drilled swine, and the Germans are sleeping babes, and the Italians are the servants of songs, and the French are the sons of newspapers, and the Greeks they are weavers of lies, but the English and the Osmanlees are brothers together in righteousness. . . ."

The Pasha had provided relays of horses at distances of perhaps twenty miles, though on two occasions the party covered sixty miles with the same beasts. Nothing remarkable occurred through Servia. Indeed, Kinglake notes that, because it was night, they missed "the only public building of any interest that lies on the road. It is said to be a good specimen of Oriental architecture; it is of a pyramidical shape, and is made up of thirty thousand skulls, contributed by the rebellious Servians in the early part of this century. . . ."

At one stage on the long trek to Constantinople his companion,

Lord Collington, was taken ill and for part of the journey was conveyed in an araba, "a vehicle drawn by oxen, in which the wives of a rich man are sometimes dragged four or five miles over the grass by way of recreation. The carriage is rudely framed, but you recognise in the simple grandeur of its design a likeness to things majestic. . . . He suffered greatly, for there were no springs for the carriage, and no road for the wheels. . . . Poor fellow, poked into an araba, like a Georgian girl!"

On their last day before the Bosphorus, they were assailed by a cold wind that came "straight from the steppes of Tartary, keen, fierce, and steady as a northern conqueror". But at last, the imperial capital came in sight.

"We crossed the Golden Horn in a caique. As soon as we had landed, some woe-begone fellows were got together and laden with our baggage. Then on we went, dripping, and sloshing, and very like men that had been turned back by the Royal Humane Society as being incurably drowned.

"Such was the condition of our party, which fifteen days before had filed away so gaily from the gates of Belgrade. A couple of fevers and a north-easterly storm had thoroughly spoiled our looks.

"Even if we don't take a part in the chant about 'mosques and minarets', we can still yield praise to Stamboul. We can chant about the harbour; we can say, and sing, that nowhere else does the sea come so home to a city; there are no pebbly shores—no sand-bars—no slimy river-beds—no black canals—no locks or docks to divide the very heart of the place from the deep waters.

"All the while that I stayed in Constantinople the plague was prevailing, but not with any degree of violence. Its presence, however, lent a mysterious and exciting, though not very pleasant, interest to my first knowledge of a great Oriental city; it gave tone and colour to all I saw, and all I felt—a tone and a colour sombre enough, but true, and well befitting the dreary monuments of past power and splendour.

"The coats and the hats of Pera are held to be nearly as innocent of infection as they are ugly in shape and fashion; but the rich furs and the costly shawls, the broidered slippers and the gold-laden saddle-cloths, the fragrance of burning aloes and the rich aroma of patchouli—these are the signs that mark the familiar home of plague. . . .

"Perhaps as you make your difficult way through a steep and narrow alley, shut in between blank walls, and little frequented by passers, you meet one of those coffin-shaped bundles of white linen that implies an Ottoman lady. Painfully struggling against the obstacles to progression interposed by the many folds of her clumsy drapery, by her big mud-boots, and especially by her two pairs of slippers, she works her way on full awkwardly enough, but yet there is something of womanly consciousness in the very labour and effort with which she tugs and lifts the burthen of her charms. She is closely followed by her women slaves. . . .

"She turns, and turns again, and carefully glances around her on all sides, to see that she is safe from the eyes of Mussulmans, and then suddenly withdrawing the yashmak, she shines upon your heart and soul with all the pomp and might of her beauty."

Those who travel but (in these days, at least) tell no tales are the Diplomatic Couriers, carrying mail which may be routine or revolutionary. They have been about the most consistent users of the Grand European Expresses over the years, and on all occasions are inseparable from their diplomatic bags. The Foreign Office and State Departments are also at pains to keep them separated from other passengers.

In England, the office of a Royal Courier, with his Silver Greyhound badge, is a very ancient one, and jealously guarded. It was established in 1454 by King Henry VI. The first title of King's Messenger dates from 1485. One John Norman was to be "among His Majesty's Messengers, and arrears of fourpence halfpenny to be paid to him"! The company of King's Messengers, forty strong at the end of the Civil War, would have been disbanded by Cromwell, but sixteen of them escaped to the Continent, to await the restoration of Charles II.

Though they retained their royal title, the Messengers gradually came under the Government's wing. They wore a uniform (which all detested) and carried with them an essential Way Bill or *Lettre de Part*. Today they are indistinguishable from all ordinary passengers, except for their diplomatic immunity from Customs examination and a certain amount of privacy and segregation. This was enforced rigidly in the nineteenth century by Lord Palmerston, who forbade members of the Diplomatic Corps to take anyone else in their horse-carriages. To this Lord Granville, in a further injunction added : "A Messenger, while travelling on service, must never be accompanied in his carriage by his wife, or by any other female."

One Messenger, Captain Wheeler-Holohan, has told the whole story of the Corps, with its badge of a Silver Greyhound, in entertaining detail. Much of it concerns the earlier years, and the rigours of travel for the Messengers, before the Wagons-Lits Company smoothed their path to foreign parts.

"Each Messenger possessed his own carriage. In normal times, these vehicles were kept permanently at Dover, and were big, strong vehicles, built in England for the Messengers themselves to their own orders and specifications. They were as light as could be compatible with great strength and cost anything between two and three hundred pounds. The coaches were so fashioned that the seats could be turned into beds; they had commodious receptacles for the despatches and personal baggage of the King's Messengers, lockers for wine and food, and specially contrived racks for arms. A pair of pistols and sword were always within easy reach. . . ." (*The History of the King's Messengers.* Grayson and Grayson, London, 1935.)

So the Messenger had to be a marksman as well, presumably, with licence to kill, precursor of James Bond.

The carriage or "diligence" was not always the agreed mode of travel. When despatches were urgent, the Messenger took to horse, particularly in the Balkans, and the regions east of Vienna, where roads were virtually non-existent. The Messengers of old had an itinerary as varied as any airline today, but not so predictable. Here is the journey of one William Ross in 1804. "He was sent from Whitehall to Vienna. From there he was sent to Trieste, and then back to Venice. Back again he went to Trieste, and from that port to Corfu. After a period of quarantine, he left Corfu for Constantinople, journeying via Vienna back to London. He was nearly nine months away."

In 1849 Colonel Charles Townley undertook the journey from

Belgrade to the Bosphorus, with very urgent messages for the British Ambassador, Sir Stratford Canning. Guides (Tatars) were laid on for him at Nish and Philippopolis (Plovdiv) because of the importance of his mission. He had to abandon half his luggage before even leaving Belgrade (where, no doubt, Kinglake's Pasha was still celebrating the spirit of England with his "Whirr! Whirr! All on wheels! Whizz! Whizz! All by steam"). Colonel Townley kept having to order fresh horses on his way to Sofia, and continued riding through the nights. At Sofia he had a steam bath, and was able to carry on, like a John Gilpin or a Paul Revere, in pouring rain and feeling "sick as a dog".

"Ah, the misery of that night of mud!" he wrote in his report, as quoted by Captain Wheeler-Holohan. "That night of mud, and darkness, and watchfulness! Twenty times I turned in my saddle, feeling sure that the day must be breaking. But the day breaks not the earlier for men's wishes. . . ."

A bit of a philosopher, Colonel Townley. The exhilarating turning point of the journey was the sight of the Sea of Marmora. "Although the heaviness of sleep came over me, and my eyes had become so weary and bloodshot that I could scarce see out of them, I got into the saddle with a light heart, well knowing that I should witness the morning's sun shining on the mosques and minarets of Constantinople."

He reached the British Embassy in Pera five days and eleven hours after setting out. The distance was 820 miles, and Colonel Townley was told, by a grateful Ambassador, that this was the fastest time ever recorded in winter.

"I can claim credit for obstinacy," wrote the Colonel, "if for no other quality. . . . Breakfast was prepared for me, and I should imagine I looked like a hungry wolf, as they placed food on the table; in fact, I could hardly summon sufficient good breeding to keep my fingers out of the dishes. . . . It was astonishing how little tired I felt at the time : and after having had a Turkish bath, and being well stewed, I felt fit to go back again to Belgrade."

Most people would feel that Captain Townley had done the Corps of Messengers proud.

Most Messengers merely had to contend with getting official

91

despatches through, but there were other surprising side-lines to the job, and two of Wheeler-Holohan's colleagues had very odd experiences. One, Martin Haworth-Leslie, a former Master of Foxhounds, was asked to provide a private zoo for Sultan Abdul Hamid, to be built in Pera. His Irish friend was Head Dragoman to the Sultan, an important and influential post. Haworth-Leslie secured an elephant and a tiger, and on his way through to Vienna on duty was able to get a couple of giraffes from King Victor Emmanuel and the Royal Zoo in Turin, as well as a number of birds. A lioness which he bought in Antwerp brought him much trouble, since it broke loose and killed a woman in a nearby street. He was allowed to house the animals in the London Zoo pending delivery to the Sultan, and eventually put them all on board ship bound for Turkey—and the Sultan paid up. But it was a strange task even for a Queen's Messenger to undertake.

Abdul Hamid was clearly fond of giving such assignments to his English aides. At another time a Messenger, with his bags packed ready for the journey to Constantinople, was told he had to take out a special present for the Sultan, consisting of "eight canary birds valued at twenty-five pounds". The Messenger was further entrusted with a paper bag of bird-seed, a bottle of tonic, and a brush to clean out the cage.

"He rashly consented to the task," reports Wheeler-Holohan, "but had infinite trouble with the enormous cage which contained his charge, and which constituted a difficulty to every railway guard and conductor who caught sight of it. Possibly the scruples of those worthies were overcome by a liberal distribution of *baksheesh,* and the seed and the tonic evidently suited the canaries' constitutions, as the interested travellers reached the Yilditz Kiosk quite safely. . . ."

As far as the normal journey of a Messenger in the railway age is concerned, Wheeler-Holohan has described a typical journey, starting from the arrival at the French channel port.

"When the ship docks, his special porters take his baggage ashore. They know the work, and he passes through the passport control and Customs with very little fuss—just a fleeting sight of the red passport and the murmur "Courier du Roi" is enough.

"At the platform the famous Express is drawn up, and for a

moment the Messenger has an unpleasant fear that he will never get all that stuff into the *coupé* compartment. However, the conductor knows him, and so does the *baggagiste,* and the load is pushed in, the ginger-coloured sacks inevitably sticking in the window as the eagle-eyed station-master approaches. . . . The train eventually moves off, and the worst part of the journey is over. The Messenger gradually shakes down in his home-to-be for several days and nights, and so trundles across Europe. . . ."

The Messenger has various people to contact on the journey, and the ginger-coloured bags are officially handed over. "A well-known novelist," writes Wheeler-Holohan, "has described him, rather unkindly, as 'the morose, dyspeptic, Vichy-drinking denizen of the Wagon-Lit'. Where is the beautiful lady who will decoy him into her compartment, and drug him with a scented cigarette or jab him with that dagger concealed in her garter, the while her Hercules of an accomplice breaks into his *coupé* and pinches the ginger sacks? She doesn't appear, and she won't. It is a pity to spoil the illusion, but she doesn't exist. For years the members of the Corps have been waiting for her, blonde or brunette as they would like her to be, looking forward to the test and to the excitement she most inevitably would provide—but we have given her up. At last the terminus is reached, right on the other side of Europe. The Messenger is met by the Chancery servant or *kavass.* The journey is over; the Messenger signs the Ambassador's book or leaves his card. He is automatically under the latter's orders. . . ."

The *Couriers du Roi* continued to use the Grand European Expresses exclusively until a few years ago, but with the advantage of direct flights the airlines have now claimed them, and another colourful chapter in Orient Express history draws to a close.

9

THEY WENT BY TRAIN

Travellers' Tales: The Railway Age. The Orient Express from many Angles—The Case of the Upturned Duchess—A Musical Spy—The "Pimpernel" travellers—Beverley Nichols's journeys—Strolling players—Driver King Boris—Trials of a *Life* correspondent—Peter Allen and the Simplon-Orient—Disillusions and delays—Marghanita Laski relaxes—The hard way for students—A Johnny Morris journey—George Behrend recalls a memorable ride—Joseph Wechsberg's tribute to Wagons-Lits conductors.

Apart from the Travellers' Tales which signify the changed conditions of a once luxurious service, there are a number of embarrassing and even farcical incidents to add to the story of the Orient Express. On one occasion, at an unidentified station in the Balkans, the train was searched, and passports were confiscated. One passenger, to his great distress, was hauled off the train by military police, and taken to the station-master's office. But the incident turned out to be as hilarious as the story of Michel and the music-score. It was the station-master's birthday, and he had been looking for a man who had been born on the same day. After scanning all passports, he found his counterpart, and the Orient Express was held up for half an hour, while champagne was ordered, and birthday toasts drunk.

Another story of embarrassment comes from one Colonel Crompton, a distinguished master-electrician, whose London firm provided not only illumination for large installations such as the Ring Theatre in Vienna, after it had been burned down in 1885, but for the Crystal Palace Exhibition, the Dalai Lama's immense Palace in Tibet, and private houses of such public figures as Lord Randolph Churchill, Sir Winston's father.

Colonel Crompton also had time to write his own life-story, and the following incident occurred soon after he had joined the Orient Express to arrange the lighting for Belgrade. He arrived at

94

Whitsuntide in 1890, at a time of near-revolution. King Milan had abdicated in favour of his son Alexander, but his Queen refused to leave the capital. On Whit Monday an angry crowd assembled in front of the palace. Troops were called out, and opened fire. Crompton continues : "I was in the crowd, and near to us was a high official from the German Embassy. We all had a narrow escape, for of the forty or fifty persons killed by the firing some fell close to us, one woman actually at my feet, her brains being scattered over my clothes. I ran to take shelter in the doorway of a house out of the line of fire, and there saw a copper disc about four feet in diameter and curiously engraved. This I used as a shield, and afterwards bought from the proprietor as a souvenir of this tragedy. The owner told me that it was one of the ancient dinner trays around which the Serbian families used to squat down to eat their meals." (*Reminiscences*. R. E. Crompton. Constable, London, 1928.)

Colonel Crompton was no ordinary business tycoon. When Queen Natalie was finally driven out of Belgrade, he gallantly offered her his rooms at his hotel in Semlin, on the north bank of the Danube. Later in the same year he went on to Sofia, to investigate the possibility of lighting the Bulgarian capital by harnessing a torrent some ten miles out of the city. There he found equal unrest, with Prince Ferdinand, a stranger from Coburg, at odds with his Prime Minister Stambulov. When Crompton met Stambulov to discuss his water-power scheme, the Bulgarian Prime Minister was in such fear for his life that throughout the interview he had a loaded pistol on the desk pointing towards the Englishman.

"In spite of all precautions," the Colonel adds, "the poor fellow was murdered a few months later."

Crompton has one amusing railway experience to relate, in the course of one of his numerous journeys to Vienna.

"I was sitting with my face to the engine in the outer seat of a table of four in the Pullman dining-car of the Orient Express. Another man was seated on my left, and the two-seat table to my right on the other side of the gangway was occupied by an Austrian lady and gentleman. On a curve just outside Munich, owing to a rail being out of place, our carriage suddenly leaned over hard to the left, and I was forced violently against my companion. When the carriage righted itself I found that the Austrian couple had both fallen over, making a complete somersault. The lady's head had got underneath our table, and her legs were upright in the air. While the other ladies screamed with laughter and the men endeavoured to keep grave faces, I grappled with the difficult task of holding the inverted lady's petticoats together, and at the same time freeing her head from the table legs.

"After I had succeeded in disentangling the lady, her husband thanked me and handed me his card. He was an Archduke. I handed him mine, and thought the matter was at an end. But three days later I received a pressing invitation from the Archduchess, asking me to call at her house at the hour of afternoon coffee, as she wished to thank me personally for the service I had done her. When I went into the room, the Archduchess got up from her chair and came forward to meet me, telling her guests, chiefly ladies, 'This is my English friend, who saved my life, and has seen more of me than my husband himself.' We afterwards became great friends. This adventure was for several days a matter of court gossip, and the old Emperor himself told me he had heard all about it, and that I was a man to be envied. . . ."

Though the period between the end of the nineteenth century and the first world war was perhaps the period of the train's greatest glory, no great changes took place. The story told by the railway historians Foxwell and Farrer in 1889 merely hinted at the various difficulties an International Company might encounter among so many rival nations.

The outbreak of war brought an end to the great experiment. With Belgium over-run, and Turkey an ally of the Central Powers against the Allies, the Wagons-Lits Company ceased to operate on anything but a very limited scale, though their captured rolling-stock must have been useful to the Austrian railways. Trains of a sort ran from East to West, particularly since Switzerland had become the neutral clearing-house and point of contact between the warring nations. One highly entertaining story about railway espionage is told by the British archaeologist Sir Leonard Woolley, whose excavations at Ur of the Chaldees brought him world fame.

14. Thomas Cook, founder of the world-famous travel agency which bears his name and pioneer of holidays abroad as we know them today.

15. Our man in Constantinople! An unknown Cook's interpreter who must have reassured many a bewildered Orient Express passenger of the 1880's on arrival in the then Turkish capital.

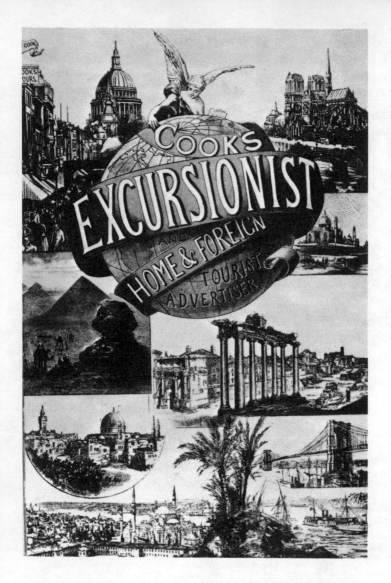

Cook's house magazine, *The Excursionist and Home and Foreign Tourist Advertiser.*

16. The cover of the issue of April 8, 1899, with an evocative view of Constantinople in the bottom left-hand corner.

17. A page from the issue of June 11, 1883; announcing, between notices of a Wagner Festival at Bayreuth and P. & O. steamers from Gravesend to India, China and Japan, the commencement of a Through Service by rail to Constantinople, in 80 hours.

the calamities inflicted by the floods last autumn on a great part of the country, and particularly on the Purserthal, the Etschthal, and adjacent districts, seem to have excited a general opinion that the visiting of that country would be interrupted. Such, however, is not the case, as the governor of those provinces, the Imperial Stadtholder in Innsbruck, has explained in an official communication. The railways mostly frequented by travellers, it is stated, have only partially suffered by the floods, which destroyed chiefly the less accessible and unfavourably situated parts of the Alpine regions, so that the regular railway communication has been perfectly re-established in every direction.

WAGNER FESTIVAL AT BAYREUTH.

The late celebrated Composer, HERR WAGNER, during the latter days of his life, completed all the arrangements in detail for the performance of "Parsifal" during the coming Summer, and no more fitting demonstration of respect to the memory of so great a man could be shown than in carrying out his own plans for a representation this year of his last work.

A council of management has been formed at Bayreuth, under the patronage of His Majesty KING LUDWIG II. of Bavaria, the *dramatis personæ* has been arranged, and it has been decided that twelve representations of "Parsifal" shall be given, to begin on the 8th of July, and to be continued on alternate days throughout the month.

We have prepared a programme, showing the various routes to Bayreuth, with other particulars, which can be obtained at any of our offices. We shall also be pleased to give quotations for other and more extended tours, combining France, Italy, Switzerland, The Tyrol, &c.

THROUGH SERVICE TO CONSTANTINOPLE.

A new service, called the "Oriental Express," consisting exclusively of wagon-lits and a restaurant saloon, has been established between Paris and Constantinople, leaving Paris every Tuesday and Friday, and from Constantinople every Thursday and Sunday, accomplishing the journey between Paris and Constantinople in eighty hours.

P. & O. STEAMERS FROM GRAVESEND.

The Peninsular and Oriental Steamship Company's steamers for Bombay, Calcutta, China, and Japan, now leave Gravesend on Tuesdays at noon, instead of Wednesdays. The direct steamers for Australia leave Gravesend every second Wednesday, from June 6th, instead of alternate Thursdays, as formerly.

NEW ARRANGEMENTS IN AMERICA.

We have lately entered into an arrangement with the New York West Shore and Buffalo Railway Company for the issue of tourist tickets over that Company's lines, so far as completed. The construction of this line is being pushed on with great rapidity, and it is expected that it will be open as far as Albany by the middle of June, and through to Buffalo in August.

This line extends along the West Shore of the Hudson River, and through the valley of the Mohawk, connecting the important cities of New York, Newburgh, Kingston, Albany, Utica, Syracuse, Rochester, and Buffalo, besides furnishing another independent highway between the Great Lakes and the principal Atlantic seaports. As regards the character of the car equipment, it is only necessary to state that it is to be furnished by the Pullman Car Company, and will embrace many new features designed to promote safety and pleasure in travelling.

18. The impressive Haydaparsa Station, in Istanbul. Situated at Scutari, on the Asian shore, it is the terminus for the Taurus Express which runs to Aleppo and Damascus.

19. The Orient Express in Turkey : a rare photograph taken in 1910.

20. The Simplon-Orient Express, initiated after the First World War, passing the Château de Chillon near Montreux in Switzerland.

21. *"En voiture s'il vous plaît!"*: the Simplon-Orient Express at Milan.

22. The Arlberg-Orient Express, with *fourgon* and five coaches, in Austria, 1930.

23 and 24. Two period pieces: the cover of an Orient Express timetable, 1929; and a double berth wagon-lit, from the Wagons-Lits Handbook to the Taurus and Simplon-Orient Expresses, 1938.

25 and 26. Orient
Expresses in the
1920's.

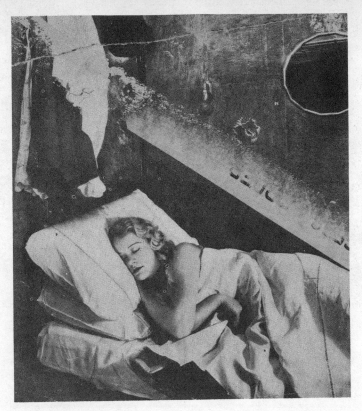

27 and 28. Wagons-Lits comforts by night and day in the 1930's, from the Wagons-Lits Handbook to the Taurus and Simplon-Orient Expresses, 1938.

29 and 30. Approaches to the Orient. Above, the Night Ferry, Victoria-Dunkirk-Paris: started in 1936 it is still the favourite route of many royal personages, including the Duke of Windsor. Below, the Golden Arrow, Victoria-Calais-Paris: the "Millionaire's Route" initiated in 1929. Both are shown leaving Victoria Station.

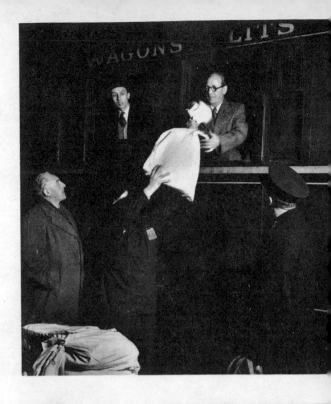

31. The British King's and Queen's Messengers have been among the most consistent users of the Grand European Expresses. Here a Queen's Messenger receives a sealed diplomatic bag on the Orient Express.

32. Royal Engine Driver: King Boris III of Bulgaria had his own elaborately equipped and decorated wagon-lit, but liked nothing better than to take charge of the footplate himself.

In 1916 Woolley was a prisoner-of-war in Constantinople, and in a volume of memoirs (*As I Seem to Remember*. George Allen & Unwin, London, 1962) he tells one tale of a Syrian, French-speaking Levantine called Michel, working as an allied agent. While not directly connected with the suspended Orient Express, the story shows that it was possible to go right along the old route, through Bulgaria, and for the agent to get his report through to Switzerland—but not without difficulties for Michel.

"I realised," he told Woolley, "that musical notes could perfectly well stand for alphabetical letters or even syllables, and I bought a lot of properly lined musical paper and I wrote out all my reports in musical notes; and it was very good. But it nearly got me into trouble. . . . I had got permission from the Turks to go into Switzerland, as a neutral country, to buy agricultural implements which the Government of Southern Syria needed very much indeed, and they gave me permission to do that, so I travelled quite easily up to the Turkish frontier . . . At the frontier of Bulgaria I was sitting in the train and soldiers and officials came round looking for contraband, and they came into my compartment.

"I said 'I have nothing to declare,' and they opened my bag and there was nothing; then suddenly they saw on the rack over my head another dispatch case, and they said 'What is that?' and I said, 'Oh, that is music.' They said 'Music? Let us look.' So I took down the bag and opened it and showed the man all this music. And he looked at it and said, 'This isn't music!' I said, 'Of course it is.' He said, 'No, music is printed and this is written by hand! This sort of thing isn't allowed : all manuscripts are confiscated!' I protested, 'But you *can't* confiscate it! Of course it's written by hand : it's my own composition. I am a great musician and I'm going now to Sofia by invitation of the Government to give a concert of my own music.' 'Well,' he said, 'That may be, but this is manuscript, and it is against the rules, so I must call my superior officer,' and in a minute or two up came an officer with two or three more soldiers and they looked at it and said 'Nonsense, this is spy work! Come along with us,' and they dragged me out of the compartment."

Michel now thought the game was up, but one of the porters on

ORIENT-EXPRESS

FOXTROT

Composed and Arranged by
Gerhard Mohr

Banjo

UNITED MUSIC PUBLISHERS LTD.

Had he taken the Orient Express, the "Musical Spy" (see opposite) could have found a better theme tune in this foxtrot of the thirties.

the platform remembered that the stationmaster (Woolley doesn't name the station, but it may have been Svilengrad) was a musician, and had a piano on the premises. So the little procession made its way to his office. "We've got to have these tunes played," he was told, "to prove whether they're music or not."

By this time Michel felt really desperate.

"The stationmaster sat at the piano and he opened the first piece of music that I'd got and looked at it, and he looked very puzzled, and then he lifted his hands and he brought them down on the keys—and it was terrible! You never heard such dreadful noises as came from that piano; and they all looked at each other and began to smile. Then the stationmaster went on to the second thing. The first thing had been the name of the town and the second thing was the number of guns there ... and I heard a perfectly good chord came up, a very pleasant little chord, and I sat up and I said to myself, 'Michel, you are a musician after all,' and the stationmaster looked pleased. The next thing was the number of troops, and that came. It was difficult to play, but it sounded well, and then there was another place name, and it was terrible, and the stationmaster tried and tried and at last he turned round and he said, 'This is too difficult for me.' I said, 'Of course, this is *modern* music,' and the stationmaster said, 'I don't know much about modern music.' I asked him, 'Do you know the works of the younger Strauss?' 'Strauss,' he said, 'I've heard of him. He is a very modern master.' 'Modern master! He is old-fashioned: he is out of date,' I said. 'This is the new music, the stuff that *I* write. I am a great musician.' "

Michel concluded "And they all took off their hats and they bowed to me and said, 'Certainly you shall go to Sofia and you shall play before the Government Circles of Sofia, and we shall be congratulated for letting you through the Customs.' So, I have got safely through, and here is all my music. I have got a complete list of nearly all the garrisons of Turkey."

Say It with Music is the title of a once-popular tune, and this seems to have been carried out literally.

A family which must often have travelled by the Orient Express between Hungary and England were the relatives of Baroness

99

Orczy, remembered as the authoress of *The Scarlet Pimpernel* and many other richly-embroidered period novels.

The Orczy estates were in Transylvania, and the Baroness's son, John Orczy-Barstow, recently told a story on the radio in England about his uncle, the local squire and overlord (*B.B.C. Home Service,* February 3, 1965).

"We were leaving to come back to England, mainly because the term had started at Harrow for me, and my uncle's property was some twenty-five miles from the nearest railway station and you had to get up at about four in the morning and drive in the coach and five to the station. Uncle and aunt came to see us off, and we discovered we were two hours early for the train. Uncle complained bitterly to the stationmaster, for not having a train there at the right time, and he said, 'Besides, we're all very hungry.' So the stationmaster said, 'Oh, but I've got breakfast awaiting you upstairs if you'll only join us, your honour.' We all trooped up to a magnificent breakfast, with popcorn, which is the staple meal as a rule, bread and butter, honey, coffee, cream, everything you wanted, cigars, liqueurs, Tokay; and suddenly my uncle looked at his watch and said, 'Good heavens, but the train's been gone two hours!' 'Oh no, your honour, it is waiting for you.' They'd held up the train for two hours until we were ready to take it. That was typical."

The train service wasn't always up to the standard required by the Baroness's brother. The following occurred later in his life when he was recalled for military service. Orczy's nephew relates:

"He had to travel to a town called Novagarod, which was half way between Transylvania and Budapest, and there was only one train. He got his sleeper and he tipped the sleeping car attendant to wake him up and throw him out of the carriage at Novagarod, which was at about three in the morning. However, uncle woke up and realised he was in Budapest and not in Novagarod at all. He hadn't been woken up. Furious, he summoned the guard; he also summoned the stationmaster at Budapest and cursed: I think he would have put to shame an English sailor. By the time he'd got them all trembling with anguish and apprehension, the sleeping car attendant blurted out: 'Your Lordship's language is nothing to the man whom I *did* throw out at Novagarod. . . .' "

What of travellers who tried their luck on the Orient Express after the 1914-18 war? Certainly everything, diplomatically, was done for them. This was the only train in history which was "written in" to a peace treaty. The Treaty of Versailles included a special proviso and instruction by the Allied Powers that the Orient Express should be started "without delay". Defeated Germany pleaded, not without cause, that she was unable to raise the rolling-stock or guarantee the safety of the lines, so the first revival was the fashionable Simplon-Orient through Italy.

By 1921, with the end of the local war in Macedonia, it was also possible to open up the additional route to Athens, via Salonika. These arrangements were no doubt more political than practical. For a consortium of victorious countries to re-establish railway connections with Turkey, the defeated enemy, with a line to Greece through a hinterland not often out of trouble, was asking a lot of the various railway authorities—and of the long-suffering passengers. But a few years later, everything was going along in fine style, with no serious setbacks.

The best account of the contrast between these grim early days in the 1920s and the subsequent pleasures of the journey in the 1930s has been chronicled by Beverley Nichols, who started out for Athens in 1921, as a bright young author recently down from Oxford.

As President of the Oxford Union, Mr. Nichols had had the formidable task of entertaining Winston Churchill before and after his visit as one of the speakers in a debate. In London, he wandered round rather disconsolately, looking for a job, but his first book, *Prelude,* was an immediate success. Churchill read it and liked it, but lectured young Mr. Nichols on the necessity of discipline in writing. "It is like any other job," he said. "Like marching an army, for instance. If you sit down and wait till the weather is fine, you won't get very far with your troops. It's the same with writing. Discipline yourself. Kick yourself. Irritate yourself. But write. It's the only way."

Nichols's London publishers thought up a solution. They suggested he should go to Greece, to contact King Constantine and his family, and find documents which might relieve the King's un-

101

popularity with the Allied powers. In a later book (*Twenty-Five*. Cape, London, 1926) he recalls his immediate reaction.

"Would I go to Athens? Would I go to heaven? Just imagine if *you* had just come down from Oxford, were still at heart an undergraduate, and were suddenly given the opportunity of embarking on an adventure which gave every promise of situations as fantastic as ever occurred to the peppery imagination of William le Queux!"

His hopes high and his credentials assured, Beverley Nichols left for the Balkans by train—but soon experienced disillusion.

"Let us get straight on to Greece, for it is easier to do that in a book than in the so-called *train-de-luxe* which totters across Europe, falling over bridges, blundering through ravines, and waiting for a whole day at deadly looking hamlets in strange countries. It is all right until you reach Fiume. Till then you have a comfortable dining-car with regular meals, and a sleeping compartment in which it is possible to sleep and not to freeze. But after that, God help you. They take off the dining-car, and you have to depend for sustenance on what you have got with you. And if you have got nothing, it means you have to clamber out of bed in the middle of the night and go into some filthy little railway café, to bargain for black olives and dusty chocolate and sour bread. At least, that was how things were in the winter of 1921."

This was certainly not a good year for that part of Europe, particularly Jugoslavia. In a prophetic moment, Nichols writes "Make no doubt about it, Jugoslavia is a coming country." He adds, "But if you could see its capital, the town which, by the august dispensation of the Peace-Makers, has been set in authority over many fair and cultured cities of the Austria that was, you would say it was a back slum of London, set on a hill, subjected to an earthquake, and then cursed by the Creator. . . ."

Belgrade seemed to him the most sinister and most melancholy of all the cities he'd ever visited. "It would appeal to Poe. We arrived at about dawn, and I woke up to look out on a dreary, broken-down station, snow-bound, and to hear the monotonous echo of some soldiers singing round a little fire they had built on the platform to keep them warm. I dressed and went outside with some Greeks, who spoke bad French. We were all terribly hungry

102

and were determined to eat some breakfast or die in the attempt."

The Belgrade breakfast didn't improve matters.

"It was quite as depressing as a Dostoievsky novel. We had it at the best hotel in the place, and it consisted of bitter coffee, white butter made with goat's milk, and bread so sour that it was almost impossible to eat. There were no eggs, no meat, no sugar. One was back in wartime England again, with a difference. . . ."

Before rejoining the train for Athens, Beverley Nichols had another quick look round Belgrade.

"They don't build houses to last in Belgrade, because they know that in ten years or so there will be another war, and the whole thing will be blown to pieces again. This is the sort of spirit one met the whole time. Nothing permanent. No trust. No faith. No hope. I looked into a photographer's shop and saw a photograph of the Parliament in session. So pompous, so threadbare, so utterly, damnably sad. All this may have been the effect of a bad breakfast and a cold morning. . . ."

The next time Beverley Nichols writes about the train, he is a mature, well-known writer on his way to Istanbul in the more leisurely and luxurious days of the mid-1930s (*No Place Like Home*. Cape, London, 1936).

"A bell tinkles in the corridor of the Orient Express. Lunch! We get up, with hunger gnawing at our inside, filled with delight at the prospect of eating crisp rolls, and potato mayonnaise, and veal and *petits pois* and slabs of *fromage du pays*, washed down by white wine, drunk *from a tumbler* (which is the only way to drink white wine). And not only does the prospect of the food allure us, but the fact that we shall be devouring it in a fantastic chariot of steel and glass, hurtling through a foreign country. There must be something seriously wrong with the man who does not enjoy lunching in the train.

"As we gulp a glass of our white wine we look out through the window and see a black river rushing below, spitting and fuming against the rocks. What river is it? What rocks? Who knows? Who cares? All that matters is that we are alone and free, *free*. Nobody can telephone to us. Nobody can ask us to lecture on the Victorian novelists. It is beyond the realms of possibility that anybody, for at least twenty-four hours, will ask us to open a chrysanthemum exhibition. This is life! More wine! And a little more of that delicious cheese, if it would not incommode you. . . ."

Heading for Hungary in this state of exultation, Mr. Nichols is a very different person from the disgruntled young man longing for Greece. He is trying to fathom the mysteries of a Hungarian menu card, in which potato mayonnaise looks like *Eroleves finom Meteltel*, and the final mysterious item is called simply *Gsumses*. This traveller even likes crossing frontiers in Central Europe (in later stories it will be seen that not everyone shares his enjoyment) even though the customs officials begin to look more and more sinister as the train heads for the Black Sea, and the port of Constanza.

Life on the Express could, in Beverley Nichols's opinion, be a very pleasant experience.

"Although quantities of people have sung the romance of travelling in stage coaches, or on foot, or in small wet ships, it never seems to have occurred to anybody to sing the romance of travelling by Wagon-Lit. Because, I suppose, it is rather expensive, and can be very comfortable (though it can also be agony). And anything that is expensive and comfortable must also be, in the eyes of the average man, entirely devoid of adventure.

"Yet, what could be more improbable, more uplifting, more . . . well romantic is really the only word, than the moment when one wakes up at night from dreams of England, and suddenly sees, through the thick plate glass, a golden moon scudding along the top of some strange Rumanian forest? For a moment you stay lying there, luxuriating in the warmth of your comfortable bed. Then you slip out, put on a dressing-gown, press your nose against the icy pane, and stare out.

"It is three o'clock in the morning. You are somewhere in Rumania, charging at sixty miles an hour through the winter night. Yet you are clad in a thin silk dressing-gown, and the smoke from your cigarette curls, without a quiver, to the ceiling. Only gods, surely, should be entitled to travel in this manner! Only gods should be allowed this astonishing command over the elements."

Nichols, with an eye for contrasts, compares the scene outside with the arrangements made for his comfort by the Wagons-Lits company.

"The train pants. We are climbing. Sparks fly past the window. We enter a tunnel. . . . We switch on the lights. We look round our room, this strange little oasis of peace and comfort, almost of domesticity, in the surrounding chaos. There are our clothes, swaying on the coat-hanger. There, on the table, is our money, our passport, and an empty glass which contained the Vichy we drank after dinner. . . .

"Half waking, half dreaming, we stare around us. Underneath the window is a brass plate in three languages.

IL EST DANGEREUX DE SE PENCHER EN DEHORS

(This should surely read "Ne Pas se Pencher", but let it pass)

NICHT HINAUSLEHNEN

KIHAJOLNI VESZELYES

"We have no intention of pencher-ing ourselves *en dehors*; it would be far too cold. Besides, it is so agreeable inside. We *like* our little Wagon-Lit."

Ah, those happy far-off days in the 1930s, when the international train was king. True, Beverley Nichols was on an interesting assignment, for on this trip he achieved as much journalistic success as de Blowitz, the *Times* man of fifty years before, having interviews with Queen Marie of Rumania and King George of Greece. But this time the Athens visit came after the trip to Istanbul. His Wagons-Lits experiences will find an echo with many travellers in those days.

"Far, far away are the lights of a town. Shall we stay up for it? Shall we glare out, arrogantly, at sleepy porters on ice-bound platforms and watch, in pyjama'd ease, the activities of barbaric officials? No, too sleepy, too . . . sleepy." He has no difficulty in getting off to sleep. "This, I repeat, is how the gods would travel, were they so inclined."

Praise of the highest order for a peak period in the train's success. Nichols even enjoyed the transfer, at Constanza, to the nondescript vessel which took him down to the Golden Horn.

A royal traveller closely associated with the Orient and Tauern Expresses was King Boris III of Bulgaria. But this monarch was no mere V.I.P. traveller. On a number of occasions he preferred to become the engine driver. George Behrend recalls that when, in 1934, the regular driver was injured by a blow-back from the boiler, and his clothes set alight, Boris extinguished the flames himself, and took control, driving the train on to Varna.

It has been recently reported by a frequent and distinguished traveller on the Orient, living in Italy, that King Boris's elaborately equipped and decorated Wagon-Lit was still in use along the route.

The period between the wars saw a very wide variety of transcontinental travellers. The inevitable King's Messengers and couriers, naturally; crowned heads and princelings with their retinues, and gentlemen on important diplomatic missions. There were even people who almost commuted on the train. The theatrical touring company known as the English Players provided one remarkable example of group travel.

For nearly twenty years, from 1922 until the fall of France in 1940, Edward Stirling led his company to more than thirty countries and over two hundred towns. It is a record probably without parallel. Their repertoire was necessarily limited, because of language difficulties. The favourite authors were Shakespeare, Shaw, and—Edgar Wallace! But other plays like St. John Ervine's *The First Mrs. Fraser* and the First World War drama, R. C. Sherriff's *Journey's End* were performed the length and breadth of Europe.

The Orient Express route became a familiar one to the English Players. Their favourite spots were Rumania, where they played five times in Bucharest, before the redoubtable Queen Marie, and in Jugoslavia, where they played eight times in all. They reached Constantinople in 1931, the first British company to play in the Turkish capital, and Edward Stirling, like so many others, fell for the unpredictable atmosphere of the city, and the contrast between the serenity of the setting and the cruelty of the old Sultan's regime.

Then they were off by the Simplon-Orient to Bulgaria, again the first British group to perform there. Shaw's *Candida* was produced first in Plovdiv, then in Sofia. "Sofia," enthuses Mr.

106

Stirling, "with the scintillating uniforms of its officers and the flamboyant costumes of its peasants, is one of the most charming towns in Europe. The market place is a fascinating sight not only because of the brightly-dressed, fine-featured people; but on account of the Gauguin-ish still life which the blazing fruit, wine, corn and flowers create. The country abounds in roses, and it gives one an odd feeling to hear that the decisive battle of Shipka, in 1877, was fought in the midst of the rose-gardens on the sunny slopes of the valley of the Maritsa river. . . ." (*Something to Declare*. Muller, London. 1942.)

Arms and the Man, also in the repertoire, was an obvious choice; the setting for the play is in a small Bulgarian town near the Dragoman Pass. Bernard Shaw, when asked by a lady from Sofia why he had chosen her country for such a disparagingly anti-military farce, is said to have replied, "I had to find a country constantly at war, and as I didn't want to make it Ireland, Bulgaria was the only one which fitted my requirements".

There had been demonstrations in Vienna when Stirling's company had put on *Arms and the Man*. In Sofia there were none: only congratulations from the Bulgarian Minister who attended the first night.

Belgrade, Zagreb and Ljubljana, all on the Orient route, were visited several times through the years, and the English Players remained highly popular. Reading a list of Edward Stirling's East European assignments is like reading a Wagons-Lits timetable:

Rustchuk, the ferry-station on the Danube, which had caused such misery to the voyagers of 1883, and was still, in the 1930s, without a bridge: Budapest, Bucharest, Novi-sad, Prague (a performance attended by President Masaryk), Constanza on the Black Sea, terminus of the Orient Express in the 1920s, and even the frontier station of Subotica, where Graham Greene' Dr. Czinner met his death.

In 1949, a *Life* magazine two-man team—reporter Roy Rowan and cameraman Jack Birns—set off on an assignment on the Paris to Istanbul run, at a time when the Cold War was blowing and the Iron Curtain had a very hard, metallic ring about it.

Rowan looked up his pre-war time-table and reckoned the 1939 journey at fifty-six hours. Their own Odyssey on the Arlberg-Orient took eighty hours and he had heard of others lasting up to over a hundred hours. The delays could be summed up in one typical phrase: "The Bulgarians flag the train at every mud-hole." He also noticed that, on the Wagons-Lits cars, notices were in two alphabets, Roman for the Croats, Cyrillic for the Serbs.

Like most other Orient travellers, Rowan and Birns were lulled into a false sense of comfort and well-being in Switzerland and Italy, with photographs of the Château de Chillon as the train flashed by, and an amusing Italian conductor, Alfredo Piccinini. Much depended on the conductor, even in those days. But after Switzerland, there were only seven first-class passengers left, among them a U.S. courier called Croasdale. They discussed the only likely case of a genuine murder on any Orient Express in all that long history of the train.

In February of that year the body of Eugene Karp, a U.S. Naval Attaché in Bucharest, and a friend of Robert Vogeler, was found by the line a few miles from Salzburg. Subsequent enquiries have never given a satisfactory solution to the tragedy. But it is surely remarkable that in over eighty years, no other similar incident has been reported, although the fiction writers have amply made up for the deficiency.

There is one authenticated case of a raid on the train, quoted by Dr. Fritz Stockl of Austria. During the Thracian troubles of 1891, in the neighbourhood of Tscherkeskeni, the partisans of one Athanasos derailed the train, and made off with four representatives of the Berlin Travel Bureau. These gentlemen were released only on payment of a ransom of 100,000 francs. The direct rail connection with Turkey was then only two years old. From then on, throughout the Macedonian troubles, the Orient Express seems to have borne a charmed life, though not a comfortable one. The Jugoslavs and Bulgarians insisted on providing their own restaurant cars, "with disastrous digestive results". (They were lucky to have any attention at all from the Bulgarians.) Eventually two coaches got through: the same number as on the run today.

Messrs. Rowan and Birns were very glad to arrive, because they hadn't travelled hopefully, but at least Jack Birns obtained (and retained) some interesting film.

Fifteen years later a television team from N.B.C. made a somewhat similar trip, starting full of nostalgia and ending with the inevitable disappointment. A critic of the *San Francisco Chronicle,* Terence O'Flaherty, took them to task for not dwelling more on the nostalgia.

"The Orient Express," he wrote, "was a train of intrigue and romance, crossing ten national borders and tied with enough diplomatic tape to wrap a mummy. It is still a real thrill to see the handsome cars—deep blue with gold trim—like a string of Brooks Brothers gift boxes. . . ."

In the immediate post-war years frontier difficulties were obviously mounting up. The U.S. journalists from *Life* didn't expect to enjoy the trip: to them it was a job to be got through, and something of a scoop to bring back pictures taken behind the Iron Curtain. But there is another description of a journey in the same year, 1949, undertaken on the Simplon-Orient by another type of traveller—a business man who is also a railway-lover, a man who can describe the steam locomotive as "surely the most human and most appealing of all the machines made by man". This love of railways is ardent in Britain, where clubs are formed to preserve, in their exact original working order, country branch lines which have officially been closed down.

Peter Allen, ex-Harrow and Trinity College, Oxford, who eventually became a Deputy Chairman of Imperial Chemical Industries, is also a member of the Stephenson Locomotive Society, and the Railroad Photographic Club of Boston, Mass. Put these together, and you will see why Mr. Allen, on this as on all his many journeys, looked forward to the experience. He wanted to see the steam engines!

Allen's railway reminiscences (*On the Old Lines.* Cleaver-Hume Press, London, 1957) cover a very wide area, including the continent of Europe, the Near East, Australasia, and the Far East, and both the North and South Americas. He admitted certain omissions, such as a ride in the "Chief" across the United States (since rectified)—most of Africa, also now corrected; "the longest straight stretch in the world across the Nullarbor Plain (Australia)

109

with the world's only railway grand piano" : and the Trans-Siberian Express.

Peter Allen has, however, made up for it by describing railway rides in such odd places as Hawaii and Ceylon, Peru, Chile, and Ireland. For him, the locomotive is what matters. For him, they are still "human and appealing" be they a Southern Pacific in San Francisco, a British built engine at Buenos Aires, or a wood-burner on the Meklong Railway in Thailand.

Yet he gives pride of place, in all these journeys over the globe, in the Rockies, in the jungle, in the desert, to this post-war run on the Simplon-Orient Express. It is worth quoting at length :

"That year we left Paris at a quarter past eleven on a Saturday evening and arrived at Istanbul dead on time at 6.45 the following Thursday morning. Altogether our two through carriages covered 1880 miles in 101 hours, passed through eight countries, changed direction five times and employed the service of no less than twenty locomotives.

"Merely to pass through the Iron Curtain and emerge on the other side seemed justification enough for making the journey : but the journey itself was simple enough. Three days a week there were through coaches from Paris, though on the day I went I was the only passenger, indeed the only person on board, who went the whole way.

"Provided you had a transit visa for Turkey, it was quite easy to get visas to travel through Jugoslavia and Bulgaria, and with these there were no difficulties in walking about quite freely in Zagreb, Belgrade or Sofia.

"Nowadays, with Jugoslavia turned friendly to the West, the difficulties are less . . . the journey has been cut to less than seventy hours. Much of the time has been saved by cutting out the long stops, and it has taken away much of the charm of wandering around in Balkan towns, and time for photographing the engines.

"The Simplon-Orient in those days was quite a study, as it changed character several times during the trip. From Paris through to Trieste, it was a pretty respectable fast train by any standards. Next morning, however, as we got near Ljubljana, the first Yugoslav town of any size, we were clattering along through farming country in pretty disreputable company, some very elder-

110

ly coaches attached to the back of us and some cattle trucks next the engine.

"On the stretch from Belgrade through Serbia we had sleepers for Skopje as well as Nish and Sofia attached to our through carriages and a fine Yugoslav "Pacific" built in Germany at our head. Coming up through the Dragoman Pass between Yugoslavia and Bulgaria, which showed us some grand mountain scenery, we were a very light train and so continued all the way to Sofia. . . . Later we ran through to the Bulgarian border as a local, stopping at all stations. . . .

"In 1949 food was a problem. There were officially no dining cars from the Sunday night, when we left Italy, until Wednesday afternoon, when a Turkish diner converted from an old baggage car was added to the train at Adrianople, or Edirne. However, the Jugoslavs did add a diner, which kept the wolf from the door on the Monday of the journey, and then a number of meals "ashore", supplemented by an iron ration from home of half-a-dozen hard-boiled eggs and a bottle of brandy, proved to be quite enough to live on."

Bulgaria did not, of course, receive United Nations aid at the end of World War II, but she had been well supplied by Nazi Germany. Peter Allen describes some of the locomotives as being built as late as 1943, "clean, well-kept and smartly painted, black with red wheels and frames, and often with lights for inspection after dark. The passenger service was hauled by Pacifics and big 2-8-2's built just before the war."

In contrast to Rowan and Birns, he found the Bulgaria of 1949 a "pleasant surprise". "We were over twenty-four hours in the country, with twelve hours to wander about the capital. I had always pictured Bulgaria as the essence of remote primitiveness, but I found an attractive countryside with pleasant small towns and clean and well-kept farms, a smiling, attractive land."

The remainder of the journey was very different. Most passengers on the Orient Express today would not experience the food problem of seventeen years ago, but in 1949 the civil war in Greece had meant considerable delay and disruption after Svilengrad, on the Bulgarian border. A Turkish railways locomotive (actually, the author notes, a French-built 2-8-0 of pre-1914 vintage) took

111

over, but pushing five empty wagons ahead of it, to explode any mines on the track, and with trucks carrying soldiers and an armoured car bringing up the rear. The two through coaches of the Orient Express were sandwiched in between, and the train set off down the Maritsa Valley at twenty miles an hour "apparently ready for anything".

"There was still much evidence of Communist activities along the line, in burnt-out stations and fortified police posts guarded with sandbags and barbed wire, although the troops and people looked cheerful enough, and there were many children about.

"In many ways I think this railway journey across Europe was the most memorable I have ever made," writes a man who had at the time of writing covered 250,000 miles in fifty-eight countries. "It was with a great feeling of relief that we crossed the frontier into Greek Thrace, passing the 'last enemy' in the shape of a Bulgarian tommy-gunner standing with his weapon slung as we crossed the line. I remember, too, our arrival at the Turkish frontier, where the Greek guard turned out with impulsive courtesy to present arms to the train, while a few yards further on the stolid Turkish sentry stood impassively staring straight ahead. I remember, too, stopping early that evening at some wayside station in Turkey while a great moon rose out of the downlands of Thrace. In the distance were the lights of a village where a dog was frantically barking and some near-by gas engine was thud-thudding away in the dark, while an ancient engine with a vast, tall funnel crept past us on the other track. . . ."

Allen, being a true enthusiast, soon found his way across the Bosphorus to Asia, and the station of Haydarpasa, starting point for the Taurus Express to Baghdad, favourite line of Agatha Christie. In the marshalling yards he noted a number of powerful German locomotives of pre-war years, and a vast Czech-built 2-10-0 mixed-traffic monster. "Anatolia," he explains "is a tangled mass of mountains, and climbing power and adhesion come before speed, so that these huge engines do much of the passenger work."

We leave him busily taking photographs on the spot, but there he was challenged by an official, and hauled away towards the main office for using his camera thus. When, however, he established that he was a member of the Railroad Photographic Club of America, and produced his passport, the official stopped and smiled.

"He held out a hand like a leg of mutton," writes Allen, "and said 'Ah, Inglees!' And that was that."

The tip of Eastern Thrace, where Allen's train had to look out for mines, has always been the most troublesome spot on the whole run. The area became an intermittent fighting ground involving Greeks, Turks, Jugoslavs and Bulgarians for most of the past century. The Dutch author Den Doolard wrote a powerful novel about the guerilla *comitadjis* along this part of the route. Today the Direct Orient Express makes a most undirect sortie into Greek territory at the frontier station of Pythion. Nothing much happens now, but Turkish immigration officials turn up here, and there's usually an argument on the desolate platform as to who shall be allowed on the train.

A British author, J. A. Cuddon, at one time a resident in Istanbul, has left a moving description of local passengers' plight, a situation which must have taken place only a few years ago (*The Owl's Watchsong: A Study of Istanbul*. Horizon Press, New York, 1962). The Wagons-Lits supplement-paying passengers would have been screened from meeting such refugees, who would have been nearby on the third coach attached to the other two at this point.

"As I waited at dawn for the train to Istanbul to leave from Pythion, a troop of Turkish people who had been expelled from Jugoslavia boarded the coaches. They had nothing but what they carried.

"One family was in my compartment: the father, a wiry, resilient man and very much the master of his flock; his wife, a shell, emaciated, sunken-eyed, dark brown eyes deep in the sockets of her worn, wasted face. In black, she crouched in the corner, a beaten, dying woman, the bones of her skeleton pressing through her papery skin. And her terrible eyes would turn and see nothing: defeated, lack-lustre, the eyes of the dying and the hopeless and the helpless. She was death—and yet she had given birth to so many.

113

"There were about seven or eight children; the eldest a boy, the apple of his father's eye, but half-imbecile; then a daughter, already a withered old woman of sixteen in a rag of a dress. Her nose ran and she coughed and coughed. And then there were all the little ones from about ten to four, like a Giles cartoon incarnate. They had all been dressed somehow, fed somehow, kept alive.

"All their possessions were in sacks and old suitcases and cardboard boxes. Soon the smells of earth and poverty began to fill the compartment. They were going home. They had been driven out, their land requisitioned. They had nothing really : some hope, a good deal of courage, self-respect, resource, the best of the human qualities surviving in the endless salvaging of human dignity.

"The head of the family kept his brood in order. He talked in a courteous and dignified manner. He smiled occasionally. He offered me a cigarette, wanting to know if he could help me in a foreign land. He already regarded the foreigner as a guest of his country, though he had only just returned to it himself for the first time in forty years. And therefore, as a guest, I was to be treated with respect and courtesy and what generosity was available. His cigarette and his goodwill were eloquent.

"From time to time his wife would turn her dying eyes, turn her death-mask beneath black head-dress, towards him and me and see nothing. The journey of two hundred miles took twelve hours, and in that time she never spoke."

Disillusion, delay. Mishap, misapprehension. Most of the travellers' tales about the Orient Express during the last few years seem to reflect this pessimistic outlook. In 1957 the explorer Barbara Mons and her husband set on a marathon journey, to penetrate the remote land of Hunza, one of those unheard-of countries bordering Tibet. They knew they were heading for very primitive (but, as it turned out, very friendly) conditions, and thought they were starting in a most civilised way (*High Road to Hunza*. Faber & Faber, London, 1958).

"The Simplon-Orient Express began as a very dashing train, with superb French food. When it came out of the Simplon Tunnel the food became Italian and rather less tender. Next day we were in Jugoslavia, going slower and the food indifferent; and when we passed Nis and started off in the direction of Bulgaria, we had quite ceased to be an Express and there was no food at all.

"Nowadays everybody except us goes to Istanbul by air. Only one carriage went all the way, and the only other English passenger after Venice was a nice Queen's Messenger bound for Sofia. At every junction we got hitched on to a new train, so that it proved impossible to apply the maxim—'never lose sight of your luggage'—or the van that you put it in.

"It appeared that it was unusual to travel through Bulgaria without a diplomatic passport. But everyone was nice; in fact, in Sofia there was quite a charming little incident. It was the evening of the third day and we had nothing left to eat, having been given totally wrong information in London about restaurant cars. We alighted at the station and made our way to a food stall with the Bulgarian money we had been given in exchange for a pound note. We chose two rolls of milk-bread, two bars of chocolate, and two cakes, and put down our money. The man indicated that it was not enough. As we were trying to make clear that in that case he must take back the cakes, a poorly-dressed spectator stepped forward, paid for them, shook hands with us warmly and made off.

"The snow which covered Western Europe changed to floods, dramatic in extent: large areas of northern Greece were under water. It transpired that ours was the first train to run through for three weeks. For several hours before Istanbul the line passes through country of appalling monotony: hundreds of miles of absolutely featureless plains. The train stopped at every station and a crowd of locals crushed into all the carriages except ours, to alight at the next station where a handful of houses were dimly visible. This went on for hour after hour. The heating on the train ceased to function. We had almost given up hope when at midnight, eighty-six hours after leaving London, we saw the lights of Istanbul. . . ."

The same sad story of a train in decline is told by the much-travelled author Bernard Newman :

"The words Simplon-Orient Express conjure up a vision of one of the world's most famous trains hurtling across Europe from Paris to Istanbul. It may begin by hurtling : but by the time it reaches the Balkans it has long lost its enthusiasm : even on the return journey it is so dispirited that it takes a couple of days to recover its original energy.

"A lengthy halt in Sofia affords an ample rest before the train begins the slow climb through bleak mountains to the Dragoman Pass.

"From Sofia to Nis is only 125 miles, but it takes six hours of the precious time of the Simplon-Orient Express. Small wonder that I found only about a dozen people on the train, for most people prefer to fly.

"Yet they miss one experience. The railway follows the course of a mountain stream, the Nisava. Then it has to force a way between rocky mountains. . . . The rocks, rising sheer for a thousand feet or more, have been carved by wind and water into fantastic shapes, with a new and more extravagant vista at every turn." (*Unknown Yugoslavia*. Bernard Newman. Herbert Jenkins, London, 1960.)

But Bernard Newman, one of the first writers to recognise the value of visiting resurgent countries like Jugoslavia and Bulgaria, wrote about the train more in sorrow than in anger. So much for serious comments on the journey.

One feature in recent years has been the increasing number of adventurous students who take advantage of the cheap, second-class, non-sleeper accommodation, to get to Turkey, or more often Greece. Given an enthusiastic party of fellow-students, occupying a complete compartment for three days and nights, a good if exhausting time can be had by all. Here are some notes by an Oxford student, Sara Stuart, who made the journey by Orient Express to Athens two years running, and who describes how it is possible to distribute the personnel for the night journey :

"Eight people in the carriage. Two on floor, head to toe. Two on each seat. One in each luggage rack. My favourite was the luggage-rack, although there was always the fear that you might fall off on to the mass of humanity below. Added to all that, there were eight people's rations for three days, which went steadily 'off' as we progressed south and it got hotter. . . . At the Jugoslav border grey-clad men with dirty great guns in their belts leapt on to the train and started issuing declaration papers to everyone and removing all the passports. The door of our compartment had inadvertently got jammed, and unfortunately the red-faced official thought we had locked it from the inside. He looked very comical standing gesticulating outside and heaving away at the door, and we were soon all grinning broadly, which was like a red rag to a bull. Eventually one of them squeezed through the window, making a very undignified entrance. . . ."

Well, it's a great life, when you're young, and the second-class return fare is still only about a third of the airline ticket. . . .

The Istanbul Express of 1965, leaving from Munich, offered modern rolling-stock, but the second-class, non-sleeper journey continued to be something of an ordeal, even for hardy youngsters. Some typical experiences come from two student nurses of the Middlesex Hospital in London, Harriet Studholme and Elizabeth Schollick.

Sensibly, they stocked up with food bought at a Munich super-market—salami, bread, tomatoes, fruit, and lemonade. They were not with a party, and therefore might have been considered fair game by some of the other passengers. To their surprise, a young man whom they disliked at first—a persuasive Syrian from Damascus—turned out to be their helper and guardian angel, buying them food at wayside stations, commandeering a transistor radio from a Turkish traveller, ordering people to help "these poor starving English girls". The arrival at Sirkeci station is always bedlam, and the two nurses had no idea where to go to find the Student Hostel where they were due to stay. "We were just surrounded by screaming Turks," said Miss Studholme, "and frightened to death." But Hassan, their Syrian friend, got them a taxi, and took them to the Student Information Centre, and didn't even try to date them afterwards.

Perhaps this is why Nurse Schollick summed up her advice to Young Girls heading for Istanbul by the day-coach : "Get yourself male protection. Then you'll be all right." She also quickly learned the art of changing dollars and travellers cheques on the Black Market, and remembered to keep back enough money for the return journey for them both. In Istanbul, you can only buy a railway ticket (apart from the purely local ones) with a travellers'

117

cheque or with money changed at an accredited bank, and at the current rate.

Many students can be seen getting off the Orient and Istanbul Expresses, carrying rucksacks with their national flag, and again, you feel that it's the lure of being on the edge of Asia which has brought them there, despite the discomfort. "It's about as far as you can go on a short holiday," said Elizabeth Schollick. "And part of the fun is the great unknown—the element of danger, if you like. We were told not to go there, because it wasn't safe. We thought we knew better, so we went. And it was."

A recent tribute to the sleeping-car itself comes from an authoress, internationally known as a lively satirist, Marghanita Laski. In writing about trains she hasn't quite got the lyrical touch of Beverley Nichols, but she is obviously a devotee of this sort of travel, according to an article in *The Guardian* (April 19, 1965).

"All trains are to be cherished, but my subject isn't more or less amiable daytime trains where you get in, sit down, get up, get out. I am speaking of the train as home, oasis, retreat, the train as a machine for living in for at least one and preferably many more nights."

These thoughts were inspired by a return journey on the Simplon-Orient which (at least until recently) was not renowned for the modernity of its rolling-stock.

"Most of us who respond to the appeal of a sleeper started with a Wagon-Lit, and to Wagons-Lits glamour inalienably clings, in spite of their refusal to keep up with the best in train architecture. They aren't air-conditioned, their ash-trays are in the wrong places, their upholstery is fusty, their toilet arrangements grubby, their daytime seating uncomfortable (best to keep your mattress and pillows all day); but still one can't but look on them with love, the vestigial nouveau-art decor, the little hook for the gentleman's watch, and, never to be omitted from the count of pleasure, the outside *look* of the blue coaches with their supremely evocative destination boards. . . ."

Ah, those destination boards! So Miss Laski, as well as James Bond, fell for their lure.

She made the all-too-familiar discovery that, somewhere in

Jugoslavia, the Orient Express becomes "entirely a local train, with a few through coaches thrown in". But even this does not deter her from the away-from-it-all feeling of the Wagon-Lit passenger.

"Once in your sleeper after due preparation and with at least eighteen hours ahead to anticipate, total relaxation is achieved. You are safe, isolated, unburdened, in a gently rocking cradle. No one can get at you, write to you, ring you up, and around you are strangers. Usually at a moderate speed, strange, changing country slips by. Apart from the dutiful trot on the occasional platform, no effort whatsoever is called for. . . . And you don't necessarily take a sleeper in order to arrive somewhere. I've been to Istanbul and back, just for the journey. The peace that can be achieved in a sleeper on a train is elsewhere unobtainable this side of the tomb. . . ."

Finally, three completely contrasting accounts of *la vie du rail* across Europe. The first is a highly fanciful and possibly implausible tale about "Arrest in Budapest": the second, a very detailed description of a return journey on the Simplon-Orient by a railway historian with a gusto for the good things of life, as well as a keen eye for coupling-rods and the exact classification of carriages: then a tribute, by the well-known *New Yorker* writer Joseph Wechsberg to that one-time guide, philosopher and friend, the Wagons-Lits conductor.

Johnny Morris is a pint-sized, perceptive but perpetually worried reporter for the British Broadcasting Corporation—a sort of Walter Mitty of the microphone, on whom all sorts of minor disasters fall; a traveller with tribulations, but with a lively sense of humour.

In 1959 Morris, with a small BBC team, made what he calls a "jaunt" by rail from London to Istanbul. It is perhaps an axiom that every train which finally reaches the Bosphorus is some sort of express called Orient. He started out on what is now called the Jugoslavia Express, but all he called it was "the train for Istanbul". It began with the north sea crossing to Ostend, and took the route followed by Graham Greene's *Stamboul Train*— Brussels, Liége, Cologne, Salzburg. But from this point onwards,

"Mitty" Morris and his colleagues turn east to Vienna and Budapest.

Somewhere in Germany, his imagination conjures up the atmosphere so essential to the thriller writers.

"We lean out of the carriage window, and there on the platform is a *spy*. Must be a spy, he's got his best spying outfit on. It's unbelievable—a black slouch hat, smoked dark glasses with gold rims, a big hook nose that looks as though it's made of plastic, a loose dark cloak, a black ebony swordstick, and believe it or not, he walks with a limp."

"He stops to spy on a large man in leather short trousers eating an enormous frankfurter off a cardboard plate; then he spies for a long time on a big blonde girl with a prominent chest; then he comes over to our carriage and spies quite openly on the four of us. ..."

Typical official trouble begins in Hungary :

"Our visas say quite clearly in Hungarian and English that we are allowed transit only through Hungary. We mustn't stop. We must pass right through the country without getting off the train. Now this is an extremely difficult thing to do because all trains stop at Budapest and there's very often half a day's wait before the next train leaves for Jugoslavia."

In Vienna the tourist people had assured them that they could stay overnight in Budapest if there was no train for Belgrade until the morning. They settled in at a restaurant, under the surveillance of a strange official.

"The waiter goes away and comes back with a bottle of Tokay and a small Union Jack. He places the Union Jack carefully in the middle of our table, pats it gently and smiles. The stranger comes back. The police have telephoned. They say you must leave on the eight o'clock train tomorrow morning. But we can stay here? Yes, you can stay for the night—what's left of the night. It's all very unfortunate. He pivots easily on a heel and glides out into the night.

"Six o'clock in the morning in Budapest is equivalent to about a quarter to ten in London as far as activity is concerned. The streets are active and busy, the trains are crammed with standing silent Hungarians, the paper sellers look as though they've been there all night.

120

"The eight o'clock train for Belgrade leaves promptly at eight. What time do we get to Belgrade? About eight tonight. Twelve hours—we might be able to get a bit of a snooze in. We half doze, and with tired eyes watch the great Hungarian plain slowly turn round as we lumber on. And we arrive at the frontier post Kelebia between Hungary and Yugoslavia at about 11.30

"The passport official is pale and ill and he has got chocks of wadding bunged in his ears. It isn't even white wadding, it's yellow wadding. He looks like a tallow candle. He looks at our passports, closes his eyes, then opens the window and gives a shout which we later discover means: 'Turn out the guard and call Madam Kloplosh. We've got a right lot here.'

"Within half a minute a clumping platoon of soldiers with automatic rifles had got us surrounded and Madam Kloplosh comes creaking down the corridor. She is probably about sixty but looks over eighty. Her face is like a large dead autumn rhubarb leaf.

"Our visas aren't in order. We should go out on another line, not this one. Makes no difference, but we have broken quite a lot of law and we must get off the train for examination and interrogation. We drag our suitcases from the racks, and are marched about a hundred yards down the track to the Customs house and herded into a room. Two soldiers are posted at the door. Well, here we are in a sort of prison.

"It's quite comfortable, really, with four easy chairs, a table, a radio and an uninterrupted view of the railway line and the flat, sodden Hungarian plain. . . .

"Then the door opens and in stump about eight sullen, uniformed officials. There are chocolate uniforms, buff uniforms, pale green uniforms and some very sinister-looking gents in assorted freelance mufti. The head chocolate major knows four words of English. He salutes and says, 'Which is the leader?' We say we haven't got one. This annoys the chocolate major. We say we're going to Istanbul on holiday. The major wants to inspect our suitcases. This takes three to four hours, and when they find the cine-camera, they're really on to something.

"It is impossible to make any contact with them. Their intelligence seems to have been drilled away and wadding stuffed in.

121

Perhaps that was what was coming out of that chap's ears. Can we telephone? No. Eat? No. Drink of water? No. Lavatory? No. And then they turn and stride away.

"It's wonderful what hunger will make you do. It turns the tremulous man into an adventurous fool. The last decent meal we had had was lunch in Vienna thirty-six hours ago. One of us strides to the door and opens it. We all follow him. The guards make no attempt to stop us. Well, you couldn't escape from a desert like this."

They do, eventually, but a visit to a local café yields no food and no drink except a local Kelebian concoction which Morris describes as "a mixture of vinegar and battery acid".

Help eventually reaches them from an odd quarter. In the same waiting-room there's a chess-team from, of all places, Israel, and one of the team, who speaks English, Hungarian and German, makes enquiries on their behalf. There are assurances that the BBC party will be put on the eleven o'clock train for Belgrade that evening.

"The officials are waiting there. We grab our suitcases and scramble on the train. It's unbelievable we're free: they're letting us go. Goodbye Kelebia, good riddance.

"Well, let's get a seat. Not a hope: every seat on the train is taken. People are sprawled about all over the place. We try the Wagon-Lit. We find the attendant. He's in bed in his pyjamas but still wearing his ornamental gold braid hat. He's drunk, quite drunk. 'Keine platz, keine platz. . . .' He slides back on his pillow and his smart hat turns slowly sideways. We creep down the Wagon-Lit and peep into each compartment. They are all solid with sleepers. And then we find one compartment for two. The beds have been slept in but there's no one about. We bundle up the old linen and we pack ourselves and the ten suitcases into the tiny box space. And we travel through the night to Belgrade.

"Belgrade is a vigorous, active city. It's not a particularly beautiful city but it bounds along with the times or at least it tries very hard to. It desperately wants to be a modern city, and in some respects it is. And yet walking about in all this modern-looking scenery are a lot of very unmodern-looking Serbs and Croats. They have an old-fashioned way of dressing and I must say it's

122

very attractive. Look at this gentleman coming along. On his head there's a sort of sheepskin tea-cosy. Perhaps that's what makes the Serbs so hot-headed. Then a military type jacket and a pair of very low, underslung breeches. It's a very sensible general-purpose outfit. You can climb mountains in it, ride horses in it, shoot wolves in it, jump off moving buses in it, do folk dances in it, go to war in it. It's a brilliant rig-out but it looks a little incongruous against a reinforced concrete background."

So on, un-molested, deeper beyond the Iron Curtain into Bulgaria :

"The journey to Sofia is slow but extremely beautiful. No one worries much about fast trains with all this wonderful scenery about. It's just a single line and it roams and winds and puffs. It meanders through miles and miles of maize and fields of giant sunflowers. We had no idea that Bulgaria was so beautiful. We had no idea that Sofia was such a lovely city.

"We leave our palatial marble hotel that night and the train leaves for Istanbul. There's no restaurant car and we dawdle along the single track all night long and most of the day. We creep across the frontier and then trundle through Turkey. We've become very hungry again. Eating is most erratic on these journeys. You never know what to expect. We haven't eaten now for fifteen hours. In any case we haven't got any Turkish money and they can't cash travellers' cheques on the train. We are limp with hunger and thirst. We wouldn't mind even a glass of Kelebian battery acid.

"Then a little man appears in the doorway. He's wearing a black jacket and there's a certain look about him that makes us think he's a waiter. He *is* a waiter : they've just hitched on a restaurant car. Would we like some lunch? Well, the dear man! A slice of bread, some potato peelings, a handful of dried peas, and what's left in the saucepans. It's funny, you know, but that's pretty well what we got, except that I was the lucky fellow that day. I got the free give-away prize with the meal—a well-matured but tough Turkish cockroach. . . ."

They were obviously being accommodated in a converted *fourgon*. These still exist today, but their standard is somewhat higher than this vehicle in 1959.

"The restaurant car is filthy, crusted with dust, and tiny. It only

123

seats about a dozen. At one end there's a bunk made up with blankets. That's where our waiter has a doss-down after lunch, I suppose. At the other end is the kitchen. The cooking or warming up is done on a formidable cast-iron range. It's an elaborate 1902 model decorated with assorted cast-iron fruits and fully fluted. It's chock-a-block with boiling saucepans. Every time the train lurches, the saucepans spew out boiling water and fat. It surges and cascades over the cast-iron fruit, flows down the fluting and slithers in the scuppers. The cook skids about in the grease. He doesn't seem to mind. He smiles and winks at us. 'Marvellous what you can do, isn't it?' he seems to say."

The party then remembers that they have no Turkish money, and when the Orient Express finally pulls into Sirkeci station, the waiter leads them, suspiciously, to the money-exchange, with the bill in hand. Morris is alternately intrigued and baffled by his first look at the Turkish capital:

"Two million people live in Istanbul, and they all come out into the streets every day to trade and barter and haggle and squabble and squat and eat melons and spit pips and go to sleep. Look, there's a couple of tired Turks flat out on the pavement fast asleep. Look, there are thirty bootblacks all in a row. Look, over there, twenty letter writers and several people having letters written for them. It's useful if you can't read or write or think of anything to say. Er—'Dear Fatima. Dear Fatima . . . many moons have waxed and waned since we dined and wined together last. Say you will join me in a little Turkish delight or something. Sorry to hear that Mustapha was run over by a tram last week. Yours till the Bosphorus dries up. . . .' "

Johnny Morris also likens the minarets to guided missiles or space rockets. The muezzin appears, chanting uselessly above the din of the traffic:

"We wait just a minute to be sure he isn't launched into space by mistake."

After this astonishing journey with his colleagues, and a few days wandering around Istanbul, they decide they can't, after all, face the journey back by train, and so don't qualify for the author's projected medal, struck for those who have travelled both ways.

"You know, it's all very beautiful, but I shan't be sorry to get away. The plane leaves tomorrow afternoon at 2.40. Plane—yes, we've been shunted and buffeted in trains for a fortnight, and we so look forward to being treated like precious punnets of out-of-season strawberries by the air company. . . ."

Chicken!

George Behrend is a railway historian and travel writer: an affable, ebullient Englishman who lives in the Channel Islands. From Marlborough College, he went up to Oxford, and soon became known for his interest in transport. His life has some parallels with that of Peter Allen, in that he interrupts his ordinary job (in his case, farming) with railway travel, particularly on the Continent and preferably with the Wagons-Lits Company, of whose history he is the official chronicler (*The History of Wagons-Lits, 1875-1955*. Modern Transport Publishing Co., London, 1959). Mr. Behrend has the railway expert's sentimental attitude towards steam locomotives, as well as a full knowledge of the jargon which may be baffling to the layman, but is immediately understood by most schoolboys, or those who have model railways of their own. My own model railway of the past, which had the distinction of being Number One Gauge—today everything is miniature "00" —taught me, a layman myself, much about this expertise. The railway enthusiast can tell without looking out of the window whether he is being hauled by a French "Bo-bo" or its Swiss equivalent; knows where the rolling-stock was built, carries a set of time-tables with him, as a serious concert-goer would carry a score, and knows all about the problems of crewing and victualling and signalling. He would refer to the Orient group as the O.E., the A.O.E. and the S.O.E., rather as theological students refer to the O.T., the N.T. and the B.V.M.

George Behrend's account of the main expresses is told in detail and with great zest (*Grand European Expresses*. George Allen & Unwin, 1962). Though he has not so far arrived at Sirkeci station on the Direct Orient or Istanbul expresses, he has one very engaging description of a pre-war return journey from Athens by the S.O.E. It is a good example of a "railway" writer with a sense of fun and a feeling for humanity as well as for locomotive classifications.

125

"Shall I ever forget him, that hall porter in the Hotel Grande Bretagne? One of those men whose lives are one vast mass of complicated commissions, arrangements and pleasantries; who speak about six languages; whose excursion facilities are always better than those of the travel agents, and who can fix anything, or so the ignorant traveller is led to believe. Surrounded by a number of underlings whom they treated in an off-hand and peremptory manner, hall porters were personages of whom even the managements were shy.

"This particular porter differed from most of those found in every large hotel in all the capitals of Europe, because he made no effort to conceal his nationality behind a bluff cosmopolitanism. He was Greek and proud of it : 'No train tonight', he shouted in a curious accent, both hands raised in a manner unconsciously identical with that of a British shunter creating an emergency stop.

"The startled passengers paused uncertainly in the lobby, their bags packed, some even at that moment being carried by the porter's underlings to a waiting taxi. Something must be wrong, for such emotional behaviour was usually reserved for double-crossing dragomen; his deferential obsequity had suddenly deserted him.

" '*Pourquoi?*' he lapsed suddenly into French, shrugging his shoulders and spreading out his hands. '*Je ne sais pas, on me telephone de la gare.... Accident* ... no train tonight,' he said again finally, triumphantly, with a wicked smile, for of course the departing passengers had already tipped him and would now have to do so again.

"It was not possible to find out anything more, nor to do anything else but have dinner in *Le Petit Palais,* as the hotel also called itself. After dinner it was announced that a goods train had become derailed, blocking the line at Thermopylae. There would, assuredly, be a train tomorrow.

"By going down next morning to the Wagons-Lits office in Constitution Square, before its doors opened, it was possible to steal a march on the other passengers, who cheerfully believed their reservations to be in order. To spend yet another night in Athens, simply in order to return to England via Budapest and

Vienna, was considered impractical; the tickets had to be altered to the Simplon-Orient Express.

"In those days telegraph charges were high and always paid by the passengers; luckily only one wire to Belgrade was necessary. In view of the circumstances two single berths were sold at second-class prices, but not before the other two English, staying in the hotel, had entered the office. While waiting for the wire to arrive, it was entertaining to watch their faces. Angrily they demanded to know why they had to come to the office at all: where were their reservations? That they had booked berths on a Wednesday and had not got any for Thursday was utterly beyond them. The idea that only two through sleeping cars per day were permitted by the Jugoslav Railways was not only incomprehensible, it was intolerable, stupid, foreign—Jugoslav in fact (fortunately they did not say Greek). So, if they could not go on Wednesday because the incompetent Greeks—'it was a landslide, madam'—could not stop their trucks from falling off the line, they would go on Thursday; two double berths please. What? Full? What about these people here? They had taken the last two, had they? Well, what was going to be done about it? Berths in the Berlin car? But they did not want to go to Berlin! What did they think they were—Nazis?

"The agent respectfully suggested that they might be able to change into the Istanbul-Calais Car, avoiding a change at Paris. Should he enquire if there was room? Yes, by all means. What was he waiting for? The agent made out a chit for two telegrams, to Sofia and Trieste.

"The allocation of berths in the Grand European Expresses was one of the more closely guarded secrets of the company. In the through cars various cabins are held by different agencies along the line for intermediate passengers.

"So at the same hour on the same evening, the passengers found themselves once more in the hotel lobby, and soon afterwards were locked for safety in the station waiting-room to await the arrival of the Simplon-Orient Express from Piraeus. The cars came up from the port in charge of the Greek cleaners, who handed them over to the French and German conductors at Athens Station. There were four cars, but it was the two teak ones at the front of the train that attracted attention, for in place of the familiar brass letters screwed

127

into the cant rail they bore the Company's title in Greek; one was an R3 third-class car for Salonika, the other an R class car for Istanbul via Alexandropolis. Next to them were the blue and gold coaches, and right at the rear another teak car of Wagons-Lits, smoke pouring from its kitchen chimney.

"Dinner would be served as soon as the train started : but this the train did not do. The passengers were settled on board, their hand luggage stowed by the cleaners. The conductor, refusing to allow anyone out, himself got down on to the platform to chat with a Greek, perhaps the owner of the room in which he lodged during the day's brief respite from six nights' continuous travelling. At the head of the train, beyond the ordinary carriages, a massive 2-10-0 was outlined against the clear moonlight of the early December night. It whistled rather mournfully, crowing in quasi-American style.

"The conductor was evidently used to late starting : he continued to talk to his friend as if starting on a thousand-mile journey across Europe was the last thing he was about to do. Suddenly the train rushed out of the station; the short cut-off and the five pairs of driving wheels gave it a quick and quiet getaway. The conductor had ignominiously to run after his car and jump on to the running board; with a wry smile, he fastened the latch which effectively bolts the door from the inside.

"The best thing about travelling in the Simplon-Orient Express in this direction was that the food and the dining-cars gradually became superior. This teak dining-car came off at Amfiklia, after serving soup, risotto with shell fish, mutton pilaf, sauté potatoes and beans, cheese and fruit. The Naousa red wine went down well with the mutton, but the cheese was rather strong, as was the Turkish coffee and Ouzou. The menu was hand-written in Greek and French in the usual Wagons-Lits style.

"The journey from Athens to Salonika is one succession of climbs and descents; one could hear the hard working of the engine, the echoing whistle in the tunnels, or the sudden wheezing of the brakes Stops were frequent and long, but next morning, at about 8.0 a.m., the Simplon-Orient Express was passing between Mount Olympus and the sea, in the neighbourhood of Platamona. Here the railway is more level than the road, and as recently as

128

1960 it became necessary to stop trespassers, in particular Grecian beauties in bathing costumes, walking out with their beaux. One of these young ladies so captivated a passing driver with her good looks that he ran into the train in front !

"Thessaloniki Station is a terminus : normally there was a twenty-minute delay here but the Express was late. It arrived at 8.25 a.m., and left again at 8.30. Presumably it was frequently late in arriving at the frontier, and the unaccustomed haste was an effort to show the Greek flag. Another massive 2-10-0 of the same class came on at the rear of the train, pushing another teak dining-car, which belonged to the now defunct Yugoslav Division of the Company.

"Breakfast was continental style. Moreover, the crew did not allow the passengers to linger as it was apparently essential to clear the car before reaching Idomeni, the frontier. No doubt the fuss was partly due to the crew being Jugoslav and their French was somewhat limited. The train, which had been pursuing its leisurely way up the Axios Valley and passed through a gorge at the back of the Salonika plain, now stopped at a small Macedonian village where soldiers came aboard. Their grey field uniforms and swarthy, unshaven faces distinguished them from the soldiers in the neighbouring village, who had brown uniforms. They all looked as though the passage of the express was an unwarranted intrusion, from which they would retire to sleep until the passage of the returning express in the evening, when perhaps some incautious travellers would provide the wherewithal for the evening's drinking; the Macedonian frontier was reminiscent of the Irish border with the Six Counties. With a flourish, the 2-10-0 snorted off into a siding, and from the single track main line a diminutive Henschel 2-6-2 backed on in its place. The 2-10-0 was still on its siding when the train left, for no doubt it also had all day in which to turn and go back from Djevjelija to Idomeni, to await the evening train.

"For the whole morning the landscape was one long sea of mud; in fact only three motor-cars were passed during the entire day. At this time of year there were no nude damsels bathing in the Varda, as the Axios calls itself in Yugoslavia, where the conductors at one time had instructions to pull down the blinds !

129

"Shortly before 1 p.m. the train arrived at Skopje; here the engine was replaced by another of the same class, and the exchange provided the only chance to stretch one's legs, although the train stopped frequently for a few moments elsewhere along the line. After Skopje there was luncheon of hors d'oeuvres, pork and odd-tasting pastry, and very local cheese. Jugoslav mineral water tasted most peculiar; Dalmatian Riesling was no thirst-quencher either, but its tippling qualities were enhanced by the fatigue of the journey.

"There was something soothing in the rumbling of the train as the wheels clicked over the short rails, the background music to the flamboyant luxury of the sleeping car, which seemed the more ostentatious by contrast with the primitive countryside. The struggling peasants, who ploughed through the mud, tending their cows and goats, or who now and then struggled with their chickens and bundles in or out of the ancient wooden carriages up in front, seemed at variance with the rest of the train. Here was something set apart, unworldly almost; even the conductor, dozing on his seat at the end of the corridor, seemed some sort of extra-terrestrial being, although, descending to the track at every major stop, he seemed to know everyone along the line. The splendid isolation of first-class travel, lolling on the regal plush, one's head against the antimacassar, one's feet in carpet slippers, with nothing to do, is completed when even kings must wait for one to pass; and in a passing loop in the neighbourhood of Ristovac the south-bound Simplon-Orient Express waited, with an extra sleeper, in which King George of Greece was known to be travelling privately.

"As it grew dark the train rolled into Nis. The dining-car and the ordinary coaches were shunted off, to run on in the slow train to Belgrade. The main train was delayed in coming from Dimitrovgrad on the Bulgarian frontier; it could be heard a long time before it arrived, for the line curves right round into Nis, necessitating a reversal. For this reason the Direct Orient Express today divides at Crveni Krst, reached by a new spur built since the war.

"At Nis the Simplon-Orient Express changed its appearance. No longer was it made up of railway carriages. There were seven steel sleeping cars, a steel diner and two Wagons-Lits *fourgons*.

The dining-car was based at Trieste and worked through from Svilengrad, the Bulgarian frontier with Greece. Headed by a huge black German Pacific, the whole express roared off through the night, at twice its former speed, while an elegant dinner was served by the Italian *brigade*. The rolls were Bulgarian, the wine was Jugoslav, but the spaghetti and the meat were unmistakably Italian, as was the *gelati* that had travelled in the refrigerated compartment successfully to Svilengrad and back. The bill did not bear either the Company's title or any other heading; it was divided into squares and stated only, in Yugoslav and French, that it should be attached in case of complaint. Through the glass partition the sleeping-car conductors from Paris, Calais, Berlin and Ostend could be seen having dinner together.

"Having turned in early, with the intention of watching the shunting operations at Belgrade from the advantageous position of a single berth compartment, it was distressing to wake up at one o'clock in the morning at Vinkovci, where the Bucharest portion of the Simplon-Orient Express was attached. There was thick snow at Zagreb and Ljubljana, where water squirted from a dozen leaks in the hose pipe which was filling the dining-car tanks.

"An expansive 'meat breakfast' was served before Rakek, at that time the Yugoslav frontier. The train descended the steep hill to Postumia (Pivka), and on the way Mussolini's Alpini were much in evidence.

"After two days and two nights on the train from Trieste to Svilengrad and back the crew were relaxing in the diner before being relieved. The journey from Postumia took little more than an hour. I had an unquenchable thirst and demanded a bottle of Fiuggi as soon as the frontier was passed. The *chef de brigade* gave me a look I can remember even after twenty-five years; but the Fiuggi was produced, and so was an enormous piece of blank paper for sales in Italy, which had to be made out specially to account for it.

"At Trieste the dining-car was taken off during the forty minutes' wait that elapsed in the station. When the new dining-car appeared, with a different crew, it proved to be the same vehicle; it remained in the train all the rest of the day.

"During lunch the engine was changed at Cervignano from elec-

131

tric back to steam, but owing to the short time (about seven minutes) spent in Venice, it was not possible to see what sort was used. Lunch was delicious, particularly the Gorgonzola cheese, which was very different from those evil-smelling fabrications proffered with such a flourish in the Balkan dining-cars.

"The line from Trieste goes inland. Only at Mestre does it come down to the water's edge, to cross the causeway to Santa Lucia Station at the back of Venice, where all trains have to reverse. A single *sandolo* was all the water traffic visible. *Sandolos* today are notably lacking, their place taken by innumerable motor-boats. A large 4-6-2 of the 691 class was waiting at Venice to take over the train to Milan, across the great Lombardy plain through so many historic places—Padua, Vicenza, Verona, Brescia. There were plenty of interesting trains on this part of the journey, ranging from the 740 class 2-8-0 goods engines to the 640 Moguls on the secondary line trains. The ubiquitous 835 0-6-0 tank engines sometimes hauled branch trains of four-wheeled open-ended carriages, and were much in evidence as the Simplon-Orient Express wove its way into Milano Centrale, that monumental station, the largest in Europe, where black-shirted Fascists strutted up and down.

"The station was bursting with uniforms—Carabinieri, militiamen, railway officials and Wagons-Lits staff. The latter renewed the ice-boxes and the food supplies and removed the empties from the Simplon-Orient's diner. The authorities took great interest in the passengers, who were only in Italy for a day; but outwardly all was calm, serene, benevolent.

"At Milan, where the train reversed for the last time, two 685 class 2-6-2 engines were attached for the steep climb to Domodossola. Many more passengers had come aboard, and in the *carrozza-ristorante* dinner was almost ready. One could follow the train's progress on the map in the corridor, alongside the Customs *carnet* for the carriage.

"The dinner was very Italian. Clear soup, ravioli, steak tortellina, belpaese cheese, fruit and cassata. Finally a *cappucino* instead of the thick Turkish coffee, and Strega to go with it. The train roared through Gallerate, but later stopped at Arona and Stresa, where Lake Maggiore matched the colour of the sleepers, a

132

dark and dirty blue. The train ran ever more slowly as it climbed into the Alps. It is a difficult pull up to Domodossola, but nothing to the climb from there up to Iselle, at the mouth of the Simplon Tunnel. The Italians did not electrify the whole line until 1951, and because of the many spiral tunnels and cramped space at Iselle, the Swiss have for years operated the Italian line from Domodossola onwards.

"At Domodossola one could hear the slam of the carriage examiner's hammer, and I so far forgot Mussolini and all his works as to lean out to see if the wheel-tapper was a Swiss. On the down platform, standing in the light of a lamp standard, something moved, and looking more closely to my horror I saw an officer levelling a revolver straight at me. The first phrase that one learns in Italian—*E pericoloso sporgersi* (it is dangerous to look out)— took on a new and harsher meaning. Scarcely had I pulled down the blind and assumed a position of feigned sleep when there was a discreet but peremptory tap on the door. The conductor, troubled, entered with an Italian officer, who snapped something about passport. *'Inglese'*, I heard the conductor say, and then *'Athene-Londra'*. The officer tried to make me understand without response, and then they mercifully withdrew.

"The chromatic whirring of the Westinghouse electric pump on the Swiss engine was as balm to the nerves, and the heavy roar of the train inside the twelve-mile Simplon Tunnel restored the feeling of closeted serenity. The train stopped with a jerk at Brig, where there was more tramping up and down the corridor—no doubt the frustrated Italian was telling his Swiss colleague about the incident. Soon those comforting bells heralded the departure down the Rhône valley to Lausanne, where the dining-car came off, to await the arrival of the Simplon-Orient Express from Paris."

Joseph Wechsberg, contributor to the *New Yorker* and author of *Looking for a Bluebird*, is Czechoslovak by birth, and an American by adoption. The variety of his jobs—ship's musician, croupier, beer salesman, soldier, diplomat, journalist, *claquer* at the Vienna State Opera—is one thing. But his travels make any trip by any Orient Express seem like a local commuter's journey into town. Surprisingly, however, he has been on these trains many

133

times, although his memories cover mainly the period of decline and disillusion. He described himself as the Last Man on the Orient Express when he took a trip to Bucharest in 1962.

"I saw no bemonocled diplomats, rajahs with retinue, Mata Haris. What had happened to the great, super-de-luxe Orient Express?" Wechsberg knew perfectly well what had happened to it, but he adds the comment of a Wagons-Lits official, who said "That is the paradox of our civilisation. We build faster trains and at the same time greater restrictions than before. *C'est idiot.* A way of life has come to an end, M'sieur. The Orient Express was part of that life."

The official added : "My Papa, God bless him, worked for the 'House' in those days" (Wagons-Lits staff often refer to the *Compagnie* as "La Maison"). "Papa's autograph book had the signatures of all the Kings and *milliardaires*. And the tips! Papa said that the Italian aristocrats, Russian Dukes and American expatriates were the best tippers. The French and German were not too bad. But the British, Swiss, and regular Americans were—thrifty."

On another trip, a dining-car waiter showed him a menu dating back to 1903. It began with foie gras, and continued with smoked salmon, oeufs à la gelée, sole Metternich, poulet en cocotte, dessert, cheese, and coffee. "And now we're serving just *zwiebelrostbraten*," he concluded. "Quite a come-down, isn't it?"

Wechsberg was also one of those hardy travellers who tried, like the *Life* magazine team, to get through the Iron Curtain without arrest in 1949. His route this time was the Orient Express from Paris to Warsaw. "Before the war," he comments, as the *New Yorker's* Reporter at Large (*New Yorker*, April 22, 1950), "Paris to Warsaw took 27 hours 17 minutes via Berlin. Now it was 42 hours 43 minutes via Prague, a more direct route." The delays? Call them diplomatic—or sheer bloody-mindedness on the part of Communist officials.

His car, No. 2, was labelled PARIS-STRASBOURG-STUTTGART-NURNBERG-CHEB-PRAHA- ZEBRZYDO-WICE ("I could foresee trouble at a place with a name like that") WARSZAWA. The chubby-faced French conductor told him that all berths were taken as far as Stuttgart, but when he saw that

Mr. Wechsberg's ticket went as far as Warsaw, he commented "Oh, la la! There'll be plenty of space at the end of the trip, I assure you."

Wechsberg couldn't help thinking of a friend who had told him, in ardent terms, that the Orient Express would be an exciting adventure. "Ever since I was a boy, it's had the reputation of being crawling with smugglers, *femmes fatales* and financiers, sounding as though they were drawn indiscriminately from Europe's police reports and the *Almanach de Gotha*. No doubt you've heard that everybody who rides on it has a mystery in his past and a dark purpose in his future. . . ."

How hard the illusion dies, and how persistent is its repetition! Wechsberg deduced that his friend had been seeing too many Hitchcock movies. He felt a momentary excitement on seeing a slender brunette, with a fur loosely draped over her shoulders, insisting that her trunk should accompany her into her compartment, and a man with "the jaunty, implacable air of a door-to-door salesman, who said, to no one in particular, 'Well, well, so this is the Orient Express, the Train of Mystery. . . .'" Later he met a French fellow-passenger, sighing, inevitably, for the old days. But at least there was a dining-car, because of the many Americans who, in that year, were travelling to Germany. "On the Arlberg," said the Frenchman, "they don't give a damn, because there are so few Americans. I used to travel on this train before the war. Some of the sleepers had showers, and the dining-cars took on the specialities of each country the train passed through." The menu, which consisted of Omelette à la Turcque, Escalope à la Milanaise, pommes mousselines, chouxfleurs Polonaises, and crème de Gruyère, he described as "a United Nations bistro".

When the slender brunette entered the dining-car, Wechsberg, all his romantic urges asserting themselves, decided she might be a spy. After a short scrutiny, the Frenchman joined the game of speculation as to which country she might be attached. "The British? The French? Not the Americans—they're too much like Boy Scouts to employ such girls. The Jugoslav Jugoslavs? The Cominform Jugoslavs? The Tito Bulgarians? I bet she gets off at Vienna or Prague. . . ."

In fact, as Wechsberg discovered later during a corridor conversation after the double Customs inspection at Strasbourg and Kehl (one on each side of that curious, lop-sided bridge over the Rhine), she came from Nuremberg, and was returning home from a visit to her brother in England. Far from being a spy, she was a music teacher, and was sort-of engaged to an American soldier. And she added her voice to the universal disillusion. "I was so excited about travelling on the Orient Express. It sounded so romantic and full of adventure. Now it's just like any other train. . . ." And now, obviously, she was just like any other woman to our Reporter at Large.

Lunch was provided in a Czechoslovak dining-car. There was much talk of money-changing for dollars by the staff, but very little food. At Schirnding, the exit-point from Germany, the truculent Customs officials were joined by a reluctant American M.P., who confided, "I'm from Hempstead, Long Island, and I always thought the Long Island Railroad was bad, but I'll take it over this line any time. . . . Everybody says this is the blue-plate special of Europe, but they can have it."

At Cheb there was an invasion of Czech officials. Finding that Joseph Wechsberg had on his American passport the fact that he was born in Czechoslovakia, they tipped all the contents of his suitcase on the floor, and tried to charge him with duty—payable in American money—on an excess number of razor-blades. When he offered each one of the officials a five-blade pack, gratis, nothing more was said. This, said the conductor later, was nothing. He recalled the time, on a journey in the opposite direction, out of Prague, when the passengers were almost entirely Czech, the entire train was suddenly searched, and fifteen hundred American dollars were found concealed in the *toilette*. The coaches were moved to a siding, and the passengers were subjected to cross-examination for sixteen hours—without the culprit being found.

So the Wechsberg journey dwindled until, on the entry into Poland at the border station of Bohumin, he was the only passenger. By chance his train stopped opposite the Warsaw-Rome Wagons-Lits train at one point, and from the throaty comments of the Polish conductor he gathered he was being congratulated. The Pole hadn't got any passengers at all.

Conductors, Wechsberg found, can be lonely people. His own

man confessed he got fed up with sitting at his little desk at the end of the corridor—the famous desk with the mirror above, the medicine-chest, and the stove at the feet. He told him that, while his son had decided to follow his father's profession, and was training to join the "House", his daughter was married, and lived in Syracuse, New York. He'd wanted to visit her—but how could he do that, on a wage of 30,000 francs* a month, with tips. Tips? No one tipped now. American officers gave him five cigarettes. Passengers from Eastern Europe merely tried to unload soft currency like Czech koruny, Polish zlotys, and Hungarian forints—no use to him at all. As he went to get Joseph Wechsberg a snack of garlic sausage, bread and vodka at a frontier station, he asked him one favour : that if he would meet his daughter in Syracuse, he would say all was going well. "Why destroy an illusion, M'sieur? Let her go on thinking that her Papa is an important man on an elegant, wonderful train—a real *train de mystère. . . .*"

*At that time about 1,200 francs to the pound sterling.

10

THEY MISSED THE ORIENT EXPRESS

Travellers' Tales: Postscript. The famous travellers—including Phileas Fogg —who did *not* go by Orient Express.

And what of those travellers who made their way eastward across Europe but *didn't* take the Orient Express? There is, of course, no compulsion to travel on the Continent's most famous train, but many people, at one time or another, have been tempted to do so.

It would be natural, one might think, for Jules Verne's global hero Phileas Fogg, of 7, Savile Row, Burlington Gardens, London, to have taken the Express as part of his journey round the world (*Around the World in 80 Days*. Sampson Low, London, 1874). But alas, M. Nagelmackers only founded his small *Compagnie Internationale* in Liége a year after the book was published, and it was another ten years before the celebrated inaugural trip across the Balkans was made.

Jules Verne was alive to such ventures in travel. Some years before he had been a passenger on board Isambard Kingdom Brunel's ill-fated vessel the *Great Eastern*, and out of this voyage from New York he wrote a book called *The Floating City*.

Phileas Fogg, described by his creator as "a bearded tranquil Byron, who might live on a thousand years without growing old", made an elaborate estimate of his eighty days for his sponsors, the London *Daily Telegraph*. The first leg, scheduled for seven days, was from London to Egypt, but the rail journey was French and Italian, via the Mont Cenis pass and through to Brindisi to catch the steamboat across the Mediterranean. Fogg left London carrying "a red-bound copy of Bradshaw's Continental Railway Steam Transit and General Guide".

Since there is something very Ruritanian about the whole ethos of the Orient Express, it is regrettable that the author of *The Prisoner of Zenda* did not send his hero from London by this route. Anthony Hope's bedizened, bemedalled adventure story made the very name "Ruritania" a part of the language, a symbol of all those corrupt but somehow romantic little kingdoms that formed the map of operetta. It was dramatised by Edward Rose, first produced at the St. James's in 1896, and revived several times. Its screen history has a pedigree almost as notable as that of the Rassendylls and Elphbergs themselves; Henry Ainley, Ronald Colman and Stewart Granger being among those who have taken the royal road to Strelsau.

In London, so the story goes, Rudolph Rassendyll, the red-haired cousin of King Rudolph the Fifth, was determined to go to his Coronation, in the capital Strelsau. He told his friends he was going for a holiday in the Tyrol and that he hoped this might form the material for a book—a reason given, by several authors in fact and fiction, for joining the Orient Express. He spends a day and a night at the Hotel Continental in Paris, and then takes a ticket to Dresden, which seems to be the closest real city to the fictitious frontier of Ruritania. Thereafter the adventures start, with the King a prisoner at Zenda, a small town fifty miles north of the capital, and Rudolph having to impersonate him at the Coronation, with the bonus of gazing into the luminous eyes of the betrothed, Princess Flavia. But Dresden, these days, is not on the romantic run to anywhere.

In 1870 a young man of 19, an Armenian called Kouyoumdjian, set out for Constantinople from the Bulgarian town of Rustchuk, on the Danube—the town where, thirteen years later, the V.I.P. travellers on the inaugural trip of the Orient Express left their comfortable train, to cross the river and be jolted along in Bulgarian six-wheel coaches to the Black Sea coast. Kouyoumdjian went by bullock cart to the Turkish capital, made some money there, returned and married a bright-eyed Armenian girl, by whom he had a son called Michael, in 1895

He became novelist Michael Arlen in 1922 when he took British citizenship and lived on to become the fashionable author of *The*

Green Hat and *These Charming People*, among other slightly satirical books about English society. He settled in both London and Southport, Lancashire, and drove a yellow Rolls-Royce which was longer than any other car in England, and he was probably the first man to have a car number-plate with his own initials— MA. But as far as one knows, he never went back to Rustchuk, nor did he ever use in his books the setting of the Balkans where he was born. A pity, perhaps. This sort of background would have suited a Wagons-Lits de Luxe—with a Madonna in a Green Hat.

That distinguished diplomat from the Court of St. James's, Sir Horace Rumbold, was appointed Queen Victoria's Ambassador in Athens in 1885 . But though the Orient Express was by now running regularly, it presumably wasn't expedient to send him by that route, which had only just been extended to Nis, the junction for the Athens line. He travelled, as did Phileas Fogg, on the train to Brindisi, but his Memoirs reveal that it was not a success.

"We provokingly began by missing the morning express for Paris at Charing Cross, and while waiting at the station for a later train to Dover, I was seized by a sudden attack of faintness and prostration, which prevented our proceeding on our journey before the afternoon. To complete our *contretemps* a butler, whom we had engaged only a few days before with the best of characters, showed such signs of intoxication on our arrival at the Lord Warden hotel, where we dined and awaited the night boat, that he had to be discharged and sent back to London there and then. . . . The same ill fate pursued us to Paris, where my wife was laid up for the best part of ten days. . . .

"We went on to Brindisi by the crowded, sluggish, ill-appointed night mail, having to turn out and change at Bologna at three in the morning. (Query : Why is it that travelling by rail through the glorious land of an eminently kindly, intelligent people is often made so singularly unpleasant by worn-out or insufficient rolling-stock and bad management, and by the too frequent want of civility by the Italian railway staff ?)". (*Final Recollections of a Diplomatist*. Arnold, London, 1905.)

Poor Sir Horace ! A diplomat may be the friend of Kings and

140

Archdukes, but until Mr. Nagelmackers and his Compagnie set an appropriate standard, they were at the mercy of local conditions.

One would have thought that a writer like S. J. Perelman, erratic traveller though he may be, might have opted for the Orient Express at one time during his two round-the-world trips for *Holiday* magazine. He is obviously addicted to the backwaters of Bangkok and other such outlandish places, and when he reaches near-civilisation he becomes peevish. The only European train journey I can discover is a highly unsatisfactory run from the Côte d'Azur to Paris on, presumably, the Blue Train.

At dinner-time in the Voiture Restaurant, this mild, self-deprecating, almost self-eliminating character suddenly lashes out on the subject of the Wagons-Lits dinner :

"The roast—a purely formal designation—was microscopic, the vegetables a travesty, the bread wellnigh inedible, sugar, butter and cream non-existent—and this aboard a luxury train which before the war had prided itself on its posh cuisine. . . ." (*Westward Ha!* Simon & Schuster, New York, 1947.)

Istanbul he visited on his second global orbit, in 1949, flying in aboard a decrepit plane belonging to Air India (which has long since prided itself on its Boeings). He arrived with his family, as near a total nervous wreck as if he'd come by train from Paris.

His wife was full of forebodings. "She denounced my irresponsibility in bringing two hapless infants into a strange town in the dead of night without a hotel reservation. 'I know this place,' she whimpered. 'It's full of Macedonian morphine peddlers and raddled soubrettes stealing submarine plans for Orson Welles." Her misgivings, it goes without saying, were totally unfounded. After only three hours of entreaty and bribery, we bivouacked in a crumbling old fly-trap reminiscent of a 47th Street theatrical hotel, rich with red plush and dusty palms. The lobby made up in atmosphere whatever comfort the rooms lacked; there was always a quorum of furtive-eyed raisin merchants from Smyrna whispering hypothetical deals, or buxom ladies of the town, redolent of attar and roses, rolling their liquid eyes in invitation. . . ."

Sightseeing the Perelmans found tedious until, after "leaving enough baksheesh in Santa Sophia to gild the transept" (ah, that's

141

more like my Perelman) they wandered into the Egyptian Bazaar and fell beneath its spell.

"The detritus of every civilisation since the tenth century clogs its miles of stalls; you can buy Saracen armour, early Victor talking-machines with brass horns, bejewelled Russian ikons, Boer War puttees, onyx boxes, primitive Negro statuary, electric vibrators, worthless oil stock, *ceintures de chasteté*, and furniture, rugs, lamps, tapestries, paintings and porcelains that would make the loose-wristed sodality of Third Avenue perish with desire." (*The Swiss Family Perelman*. Simon & Schuster, New York, 1949.)

Perelman was also attracted by the variety of kebabs to eat, and by the shortbread cakes topped with cream. Perhaps it is just as well that the Swiss Family Perelman headed for Italy by air. As a good international trencherman, S.J. wouldn't have liked that eighteen-hour gastronomic void in the middle of the Balkans.

11

A FAMOUS TRAIN IN FICTION

Thrills galore on the Orient—Maurice Dekobra and *The Madonna of the Sleeping Cars*—Graham Greene takes the *Stamboul Train*—Hercule Poirot finds *Murder on the Orient Express*—A Dutchman's tale of massacre in Macedonia—"The Lady Vanishes" as the wheels spin—Passengers at Victoria at 4.30 p.m.—Lawrence Durrell waits at Belgrade—James Bond travels from Turkey with Love and Death.

Istanbul's big covered market—the Egyptian Bazaar—isn't nearly as noisy as one would expect. The visitor is not subject to the strident, almost menacing assault of the Neapolitan marketeer, nor to the non-stop dancing, conjuring and story-telling of the market in Marrakesh. Many of the items in the windows have government prices on them—a thing unheard of in any *souk* or *medina* in North Africa. It takes a long time to get past the piles of carpets, the bewildering displays of antique weapons mixed up with "genuine" Byzantine ikons, and the load of junk and cheap hardware which proliferates in any bazaar. But at last you are out in the sunshine, beneath a tall minaret—the market has two mosques—and facing you, in a quiet square, is the book market.

It's difficult to believe how some of the English and American books got here. Stuffed in with the usual pornography are text books on solid geometry; a *Guide to Brighton,* dated 1924; copies of *Tanglewood Tales* and *Cranford* and *Tom Jones* alongside the works of Frank Harris; the poems of Longfellow and Keble's *Christian Year* lying on top of mounds of *National Geographical Magazines* and *Confidential*. These are merely the English language groups; other books abound in at least half a dozen other languages. Dust has settled on them all. There is little trading done. No one shouts the odds, or tries to sell you a battered *Carpet-baggers* in one hand and *Trigonometry for Schools* in the other.

143

But it was here that suddenly I caught a whiff of the chypre and *patchouli* of the 1920s as I came across a copy of the French novel which started the whole Orient Express mystique :

Maurice Dekobra

LA MADONE DES SLEEPINGS

Roman Cosmopolite 510 mille
Editions Baudinière, Paris 14.

The volume had belonged to a man with a Turkish name, who dated the fly-leaf 1928. I wondered if he had bought it at Paris Est, for the journey to Constantinople.

The original *Madone des Sleepings* burst on an astonished and pleasantly scandalised world in 1925. It was translated into twenty-seven languages, including Turkish, Estonian, Japanese, Persian, and Yiddish, and was made into a play and a film. The author led a life as cosmopolitan as his characters; newspaper correspondent in Scandinavia, Russia, Germany, England; lecturer at Berlin University, art critic in Vienna and New York, liaison officer during the Great War with the Indian and British armies. Dekobra became a keen orientalist and spent much time in Japan and China, and was once photographed, handsome and poker-faced, among the Geishas. He built a shrine in his Paris home, which may still exist.

Maurice Dekobra's background is not unlike Ian Fleming's. Both mingled professional journalistic skill with a bizarre, exotic, highly unlikely taste in women and places. Both were astonished at their success in this line of political spy-thriller laced with sex and good living and travel. Dekobra said of *La Madone* "If a tile had fallen on my head from a six-storey building, I could not have been more surprised."

Just as much was made of Dekobra's Madonna as is now made of the heroines in the James Bond thrillers. Wherever he went—London, New York, Berlin, Constantinople, Cairo, Shanghai—the book was discussed and her identity guessed at. But Dekobra asserted : "She is the true feminine puzzle, composed of innumerable portions of that great paradoxical goddess, gathered from the great European Expresses and ocean liners all over the world. When I think of her, I do not see one woman but ten."

Many more than ten women saw themselves as being like her.

The author, in his autobiography *Written with Lipstick,* protests his astonishment at receiving so many letters. He kept them in a special drawer under the inscription "The Tomb of the Unknown Woman". (*Written with Lipstick.* Hutchinson, London, 1956.)

From Vienna, an 18-year-old manicurist wrote "If you come to Vienna, I will manicure your hands. . . ." From Constantinople : "I am shy and timid, but if ever I met you I believe I should put out my lighted cigarette on your cheek. I am furious with you."

From Venice, an Italian girl addressed him as "Illustrious Signore". "I enclose my photo in bathing costume taken at the lido. Don't you think I am your Madonna? If I appeal to you, we will meet. . . ." And from Rumania : "Dear Maurice Dekobra, I am sending you on paper the imprint of my lips. . . ."

He tried another summing up on his Madonna. "She is an adventuress who travels by Pullman, seeking some hidden spot on the map of Love. An adventuress who is on the look-out for a throne or an operating table ; the arms of a lost lover or the fingers of a strangler. . . ."

Dekobra certainly devised an admirable formula for later writers. And yet *The Madonna of the Sleeping Cars* is not mainly about the Orient Express. As in Fleming's book, the girl who gets seduced by the hero Gérard en route is not the Madonna. The main plot is the smashing up of a Communist gang and the shooting of a villainous Madame Mouravieff, and only in the last few pages does Dekobra's heroine turn up at the Gare de l'Est for an unknown destination on the fabled train.

Who is she?

Dekobra's master-stroke is to make her a Scottish aristocrat. Just as Paris cannot resist Highland tartan skirts and coats, and cashmere twinsets, so she could not resist Winifred Grace Christabel Diana Wynham of Glensley Castle, daughter of the Duke of Inverness, educated at one Salisbury College and married, for a time in the war, to Lord Wynham, formerly British Ambassador to Russia.

A "tweedy" heroine, born in the Highlands. Yes, but also a ravishing blonde who had every desire to be ravished, a society girl whose picture was always in the society magazines, who was driven in a Rolls-Royce cabriolet, smoked perfumed cigarettes from a case of platinum and diamonds, and sat before her mauve pigskin toilet case, wearing raspberry coloured pyjamas, in a dressing-room of Nile green silk. (Her creator certainly knew how to blend his colours.)

Yet this same high-society belle dabbled in the new psychiatry, and startled fashionable London by a fantastic charity show, *Pagan Rhythms,* at which she danced at the Garrick Theatre in the nude, wearing only "a cache-sex no bigger than the hand of a sacristan, and held in place by an almost invisible garland of bindweed". By contrast, she claimed to have been an honorary Captain in a squad of policewomen, and a candidate in Elections in North Croydon.

Lady Diana was, in Dekobra's words, "the type of woman who would have brought tears to the eyes of John Ruskin. . . . High cheek-bones, sensual lips, and limpid, deceiving eyes which glowed behind long lashes." In our first glimpse of her, she is lying on a velvet couch, displaying her long legs, clad in cobweb-thin silk, but with her bosom concealed behind a copy of *The Times.* When we do see her full-length, her breasts beneath her negligée are like "two doves caught in a pink net". She has asked Gérard to call her psychiatrist.

Quite a girl, the Duke of Inverness's daughter, the Madonna of the Sleeping Cars. But I don't somehow think John Ruskin would have wept at the sight. I think he would have looked the other way.

The rest of Lady Diana's story, until the moment of her departure, is of little concern to lovers of the Orient Express. But the faithful Gérard, her secretary (he is, of course, secretly a Prince), is at one stage of the plot sent on an expedition to Constantinople, and during the journey he meets the sort of girl who is everyone's idea of a *femme fatale* of the Wagons-Lits—Klara is a German in the pay of the Soviet Union and Gérard meets her on the Berlin-Vienna Express. "An agreeable visage with vivid blue eyes which smiled from under a head of curly blonde hair. A mutinous nose above a sensual mouth and a mole on her left cheek-bone. Not badly shod, but with coarse silk stockings, and a string of imitation pearls. . . ." The flirtation with this damsel begins over glasses of Chartreuse "dancing merrily with the motion of the train", and blossoms at Vienna where there was a thirty-six hour wait for the

146

Orient Express. This is spent in bedroom 27 of the Hotel Bristol, which also has a Nile green décor.

He persuades Klara to travel with him to Constantinople (the route being that via Budapest, Brasov, Bucharest and Constanza, since at that time the Orient Express included the long sea-journey from the Rumanian port).

They spend three days in the old Turkish capital, with its "quill-like minarets pointing towards the zenith". His reaction, although he is accompanied by his "sweet Berlin flower" is not as lyrical as that of Stefan de Blowitz, but together they lose the notion of passing time, "inhaling old rose perfumes, the odours of raki and amber fragrance, recalling harems of days gone by. A lost couple, we wandered along the walls of *yalis* : bordered with the trees of Judaea : along the shores of the placid Bosphorus, in the golden quiet of twilight."

Finally, in the hotel bedroom, she admits to being a Soviet spy, and describes how she worked for the Bolsheviks in many parts of Europe, including London, where she posed as a German feminist and was interviewed by the socialist *Daily Herald*. Even the Sinn Feiners of Dublin come into her story. She was, in fact, signed up to spy on Gérard himself. "All those French imbeciles go crazy over pretty women, like frogs with a bit of red flannel." She begs him not to proceed to Batum. He insists, but he also forgives her, and as the boat steams away, he waves his handkerchief while "silently contemplating the delicate outline of my charming spy". Presumably Klara, who does not reappear in the story, is allowed to go on with the rest of her espionage.

Dekobra does not put a date on his story, but obviously post-revolutionary spying was a popular theme in the early twenties. From a railway point of view, Gérard seems to have experienced no trouble in getting around, and indeed the Orient Express—with its various permutations and variations of route—had been started the year after the Armistice of 1918. Then the plot thickens and the Communist and anti-Communist groups move into Scotland....

As soon as the spy, Madame Mouravieff, after taking a pot-shot at Lady Diana in her own ancestral castle at Glensley, is herself shot dead by another Russian faithful to the Madonna, the plot ceases to thicken and simmers down to the final departure of Lady Diana.

Gérard takes up the story :

"The Gare de l'Est. A little while before, at the Hotel Crillon, I had informed my wife that I had one more duty to perform. I did want to say goodbye to Lady Diana, who was leaving by the Orient Express, at exactly two o'clock, for an unknown destination.

"I was waiting for her on the platform. It was half past one. The early arrivals were wandering through the corridors of Wagons-Lits placarded Vienna, Belgrade, Bucharest, Constantinople. Suddenly I saw a little truck laden with two valises and a toilet case of mauve crocodile, which I recognised. I spied Lady Diana following the porter. She was a symphony in pearl grey, from her tiny hat, stabbed through with a diamond ornament, to the tips of her little shoes of alligator skin.

"Lady Diana, togged out for a long voyage, tripped lightly along the sunny platform. . . ."

She hailed a porter with the assurance of a seasoned traveller, gave him twenty francs, and added dashingly, "Play them on the races next Sunday." Standing near the locomotive, she reminisced with Gérard about the astonishing happenings of the past, and her plans for the future.

" 'It's best we part good friends,' she said. 'I will spend what money I have indulging my foremost passion which is travel. I will take up again my former errant existence, and be the slave only of my caprices. . . .

" '. . . I have a ticket for Constantinople. But I may step off at Vienna or Budapest. That depends absolutely on chance or on the colour of the eyes of my neighbour in the compartment. I have reserved rooms at the Imperial, on the Ring, and at the Hungaria, on the quay at Budapest. But I am just as likely to sleep in some horrible hotel in Josephstadt or in a palace on the hillside. . . . I'm giving myself exactly six weeks to discover the imbecile who will cater to my whims and ripen in my safe deposit some golden apples from the garden of the Hesperides. . . .' "

Given another kind of urge and itch, Lady Diana Wynham might have ended up a newspaper columnist.

148

"The hour of departure was imminent. Whistles were screeching and excited arms were tossing valises through the open windows. The car was swallowing baggage and vomiting the friends of travellers."

Let us leave the last words to the faithful, long-suffering Gérard.

"I can still see that beautiful face and those blonde curls between her hat and her flowing grey scarf. I can still see those great wet eyes, as sad as those of the virgins of Correggio. A mute farewell from the woman in quest of a Grail of certified cheques.

"The train started. The dear little grey-gloved hand still waved. My hat answered. For a long time I stood on the platform."

Lady Diana had said to him, "I'm sure that you've heard all about the hundreds of miles which I have covered on Continental railroads. A French humorist had the audacity to call me 'The Madonna of the Sleeping Cars'.... As a matter of fact, I have been in every European watering place : there is not a Customs officer who doesn't know the most sacred details of my lingerie. They say that to go away is to die a little, but it's my idea that to die would be to go too far, and that to travel is simply to change one's ideas."

"My eyes," wrote Gérard, Prince Seliman, "followed the rails along which the train had disappeared, the *train de luxe* bearing the 'Madonna of the Sleeping Cars' towards a new destiny."

In his "entertainment" based on the trip from Ostend to Istanbul via Subotica (*Stamboul Train*. Viking, New York, 1932), Graham Greene has achieved the most evocative and compelling tale in the Orient Express tradition. The book is all train, but unlike Agatha Christie's expert, detailed setting for a Poirot problem, *Stamboul Train* is there merely to be enjoyed, with shudders en route. You can hear the train noises and smell the train smells throughout, from the first hours on the ferry to Ostend ("the drenched deck, the smell of steam and oil and stale Bass from the bar, the shuffle of black silk, as the stewardess moved here and there carrying tin basins") to the dim lights and sudden death at Subotica, on the Hungarian frontier, and the last garish scene in a sleazy night-club in Istanbul.

This is one of Graham Greene's earliest novels, but it is one which sticks firmly in the memory. The creatures of his imagination on the Stamboul Train are not mere ciphers or caricatures. The author is as much concerned with human pity as with inhuman persecution, and though most of the passengers he portrays are repellent, they are not without salvation. "I can't get away from their damned faces," mutters the purser, as he watches them go ashore, and then he comes across the near-heroine, the dancing girl Carol Musker, from Nottingham.

"His mood relaxed a little at the unfamiliarity of the young face : this one had not complained. 'Don't you want a porter for your bag, miss?' 'I'd rather not,' she said, 'I can't understand what they say.' She wrinkled her mouth at him over the top of her cheap white mackintosh. 'Unless you'd like to carry it—Captain.' Her impudence delighted him. 'Ah, if I were a young man now you wouldn't be wanting a porter. . . . Going far?'

" 'All the way,' she said, gazing unhappily past the rails, the piles of luggage, the lit lamps in the restaurant-car, to the dark waiting coaches. 'Got a sleeper?' 'No.' 'You ought to 'ave a sleeper,' he said, 'going all the way like that. Three nights in a train. It's no joke. What do you want to go to Constantinople for anyway? Getting married?' 'Not that I know of.' She laughed a little through the melancholy of departure and the fear of strangers.

"She said goodbye and turned from him. Her mackintosh showed the thinness of her body, which even while stumbling through the rails and sleepers retained its self-consciousness. Her face, plain and piquant, her manner daring and depressed, lingered for a moment in his mind."

It takes a lot to impress a purser, if you're not a V.I.P. So Carol Musker joins passengers like Carleton Myatt, the young Jewish business type, Mr. Peters and his wife, and the notorious Dr. Czinner.

Myatt, a traveller in raisins, passes along the platform without a glance at the train, without finding the sign "Ostend-Cologne-Vienne-Belgrade-Istanbul" at all romantic.

"The route was familiar to him; the names travelled back at the level of his eyes, like the spires of minarets, cupolas or domes of the cities themselves, offering no permanent settlement to one of his race."

He wanted a single compartment, and by doubling the tip, he got one. Gradually and uneasily Graham Greene's characters settle down before the final horn is blown, and the train moves off.

"The driver turned his regulator full open, and the footplate shook with the weight of the coaches. Presently the engine settled smoothly to its work, the driver brought the cut-off back, and the last of the sun came out as the train passed through Bruges, the regulator closed, coasting with steam. The sunset lit up dripping walls, alleys with stagnant water radiant for a moment with liquid light. Somewhere within the dingy casing lay the ancient city, like a notorious jewel, too stared at, talked of, trafficked over. . . . The sparks of the express became visible, like hordes of scarlet beetles tempted into the air by night; they fell and smouldered by the track, touched leaves and twigs and turned to soot. A girl riding a cart-horse lifted her face and laughed; on the bank beside the line a man and woman lay embraced. Then darkness fell outside, and passengers through the glass could see only the transparent reflection of their own features. . . ."

This is the style of *Stamboul Train* at its best, a combination of expertise (Greene, like Ian Fleming, might well be a footplate man as well as an author) with the vivid sense of travel. He can even make the journey through Belgium sound adventurous.

"The great blast furnaces of Liège rose along the line like ancient castles burning in a border raid. The train lurched and the points clanged. Steel girders rose on either side, and very far below an empty street ran diagonally into the dark, and a lamp shone on the café door. . . .

"Newsboys shouted, and a line of stiff sedate men in black broadcloth and women in black veils waited along the platform, without interest, like a crowd of decorous strangers at a funeral. . . ."

The characters take shape as the train moves on. The lecherous Mr. Peters, who ignores his hiccupping wife and tries a little furtive caressing with Carol Musker: the author Quin Savory, who is collecting material for a novel as he travels on the Orient Express (a practice echoed by Eric Ambler's writer-detective in *The Mask of Demetrios*) and, joining the train at Cologne, the outrageous but somehow endearing Lesbian journalist, Mabel Warren, doting on her meek little protegée Janet Pardoe, and later to dote on Carol. They are all slightly larger—or smaller—than life, but certainly not unlike the sort of passengers the Orient Express would carry. Only the revolutionary, Dr. Czinner, under the alias of a schoolmaster, is destined for a violent death on the journey.

Carleton Myatt dines alone, and has the sense to realise—as James Bond would have done—that to order a Chambertin 1923 to drink with his veal may show good taste, but that no wine of that sort can really withstand the tremor of the train. After the meal he wanders down the corridor to the second-class, with its huddle of humanity, and there rescues Carol Musker from the attentions of Mr. Peters, and eventually gives her his first-class cabin for the night. Being chivalrous is one of the privileges of the first-class passenger, but, as in Myatt's case, the chivalry usually has its price, though in this case the down-trodden, defeatist Miss Musker willingly pays the debt to her temporary patron.

The arrival of "Dizzy" Mabel, drunk and protesting, with her little charge Janet, at the famous Cologne Hauptbahnhof livened up the journey considerably. Her job, briefly, was to get "sobstuff" from local sources; her beat was the Rhine; her tipple was gin. Unlike her illustrious journalistic predecessor, Stefan Opper de Blowitz, Mabel Warren had no ambition to interview Top People between stops; she set out, as journalists often do, to get what she could out of the passengers before the Orient Express reached Vienna. Being on a train certainly heightens one's sense of urgency, and obviously sets a deadline. All passengers are, in a way, captives. That is the best—and worst—of a long railway journey.

Throughout the journey, Graham Greene keeps up the "feel" of the landscape, and its effect on his characters as they wander in and out of each other's compartments with the sometimes purposeful, sometimes aimless *ennui* of railway travellers who cannot foresee the end of their journey. Mabel Warren tries to probe the secret of Dr. Czinner, the Jugoslav Socialist mystery-man masquerading as a teacher in an English school; Carol Musker, grateful for one warm night in the cabin-de-luxe, offers herself to Myatt for the second night.

"All that morning and all through lunch the snow continued to fall, lying deep at Passau on the roof of the Customs-shed, melted on the line by the steam from the engine into grey icy streams, and the Austrian officials picked their way in gum-boots and swore a little, searching the luggage perfunctorily. . . ."

There is, indeed, a murder at Vienna, but it doesn't take place on the train. The murderer, however, pinches Mabel Warren's handbag from the telephone booth on the station (she has been giving out the story, but is too inebriated to notice the loss at the time). Regretfully we lose her there for the moment, and Josef Grunlich, who shot the Assistant Station-Master in the back, gets a ticket on her money. While the lights of Vienna flash by, the author picks up snatches of disparate conversation in the *voiture-restaurant*.

" '. . . No, I won't have any more of this foreign beer. Ask them, haven't they got a Guinness. I'd just fancy a Guinness. . . .'

" '. . . . Of course, you are having a great sports revival in Germany. Splendid types of young men, one sees. But still it's not the same as cricket. Take Hobbs and Sutcliffe. . . .'

" 'Heller.' 'Don't swear, Jim.' 'I wasn't swearing. It's the beer. Try some of this. It's not so gassy. What you had before, they call Dunkel. . . .'

" '. . . Come back and talk a little after dinner. . . .'

" 'You won't be silly now, will you, Mr. Savory. . . ? '

" 'Don't promise . . . don't promise anything. . . . Tell me what you are going to do in Constantinople. . . .'

" '. . . . I have the greatest respect, of course, for the Roman Catholic Church. I am not bigoted. . . . As an example of organisation. . . .'

"All down the restaurant cars fell the sudden concerted silence which is said to mean that an angel passes overhead. But through the human silence the tumblers tingled on the table, the wheels thudded along the iron track, the windows shook and sparks flickered like match-heads through the darkness. . . ."

Q. C. Savory, the popular novelist, had dismissed Janet Pardoe from his mind, and as he watched the Danube flickering by a few hundred yards away, he tried to marshal his thoughts as in a railway marshalling yard.

"He wondered what terms he could use to describe the night. He could see tall trees fly backwards and telegraph poles which

153

caught the moonlight on their metal arms as they passed. ... I must show not all that I see but a few selected sharp points of vision. I must not mention the shadows across the snow, for their colour and shape are indefinite, but I may pick out the scarlet signal lamp shining against the white ground, the flame of the waiting-room fire in the country station, the bead of light on a barge beating back against the current. ..."

There are better descriptions by Graham Greene, author, than by the creature he had invented, the best-selling but very *parvenu* writer from Balham.

The silence during which all these thoughts are supposed to have taken place is broken by the waiters' cry of "Braised chicken, roast veal!"

"The angel had gone, and noisily and cheerfully, with the thud of wheels, the clatter of plates, voices talking and the tingle of mirrors, the express passed a long line of fir-trees and the flickering Danube. In the coach the pressure gauge rose, the driver turned the regulator open, and the speed of the train was increased by five miles an hour. ..."

From this moment on, the Graham Greene "entertainment" gathers momentum, and the life on the Stamboul train becomes less important. Dr. Czinner meets the murderer. Carol Musker and Carleton Myatt have understandable difficulty in making love as the train rumbles and lurches towards Belgrade: the snow thickens, and the guard gloomily reflects that three years ago the Orient Express was snowed up for forty-eight hours on one of the Balkan stretches of the line.

It is at the frontier station at Subotica that the drama reaches its climax with the death of Czinner, but the macabre scene does not take place on the train itself. Even for the peaceful, tourist travel-ler, these frontier stations like Subotica, Svilengrad, Pythion and Uzunkopru can conjure up the Greene-Fleming type of atmo-sphere. It always seems to be dead of night there. The buildings are often lit by oil or gas lamps. There is usually a long delay and mysterious comings-and-goings by sepulchral uniformed figures. These places are indeed a happy hunting-ground for the novelist. Yet the doomed Dr. Czinner shouted at his captors, "How old-fashioned you are with your frontiers and your patriotism. The

154

aeroplane doesn't know a frontier; even your financiers don't recognise frontiers. . . ."

After Czinner's death, Mabel Warren dramatically reappears, to claim Carol and take her back to Vienna as her "companion", Carleton Myatt reaches the Turkish capital, and as the book ends, he is making a bid for Janet Pardoe in the Pera Palace. The English troupe of dancers, which Carol should have joined, appear dressed as railway guards, and thump out a weary little ditty which might be Graham Greene's knell for the Orient Express.

> "Waiting at the station
> For a near relation,
> Puff, puff, puff, puff—
> The Istanbul train."

Real trainsmanship—or the art of going one better on the Wagons-Lits—will not stop at the dingy station of Sirkeci, on the European side of Istanbul. Though this is a terminus, it is also the springboard for the Taurus Express, through Asian Turkey to Aleppo, Mosul and Baghdad.

Agatha Christie, who as the wife of the archæologist Professor Mallowan, has often been with him on "digs" in that part of the Middle East, imagined her favourite detective Hercule Poirot involved in her *Murder on the Calais Coach* (Dodd, Mead, New York, 1934). But the thriller begins earlier:

"It was five o'clock on a winter's morning in Syria. Alongside the platform at Aleppo stood the train grandly designated in railway guides as the Taurus Express. It consisted of a kitchen car, a sleeping-car and two local coaches."

The Taurus Express is still grandly designated in the Wagons-Lits timetable, with a through sleeping-car to Baghdad on Thursdays. (Close examination of the "*Nature des Services*" reveals that the restaurant car today leaves the train before Aleppo.)

Many unseasoned travellers believe that the Orient Express connects directly with the Taurus. This is to overlook that there is no bridge between the European and Asian sides of Istanbul. Sirkeci station was the end of the line until the revolution of Mustapha Kemal. Then the Asian side was opened.

It was anxiety about making the connection at Haydaparsa which caused such distress to Agatha Christie's heroine, the otherwise cool and efficient Miss Debenham. The anxiety was understandable. There is no bridge over the Bosphorus, and no tunnel beneath (though this was once planned by the Germans). So Haydaparsa remains there, a railway station of some distinction, with its business facing east rather than west. For a moment let us consider its unique and pleasant situation. We know that Miss Debenham will catch the train at Sirkeci—and reap the consequences.

It is a relief to get out of the sticky, smoky Old City of Istanbul, and cross to Asia on one of the many ferries. You are greeted, moreover, with men selling French papers newly arrived, and glasses of freshly made tea.

The coastline of Istanbul looks magnificent from the ferry, stretching from the old Sultan's palace, Topkapi, with its long line of chimneys and walled seraglio, past the great Mosques, domes slumbering beneath those guided missiles, the minarets, past the Hilton Hotel, like an oblong box of luxury chocolates, to the later Royal Palace of Dolmabache, a sort of Quai d'Orsay on the sea-front.

Within about ten minutes the ferry nudges alongside the landing-stage at Uskudar, better known by its earlier name Scutari. You set foot—or wheels—on one of the oldest cities in the world. Once it was occupied by King Darius of Persia, by King Philip of Macedon, and by Constantine the Great. Today it is merely a suburb, with two mosques by the jetty, and trams as well as buses. These little box-like vehicles, trundling up the steep hill out of the town, bring an echo of San Francisco to the Bosphorus.

On the way to the station at Haydarpasa, you pass the building which was once the military hospital of Florence Nightingale. Strange to think that in this long, bleak, severe structure began the true legend of the Lady with the Lamp at Scutari, more than a hundred years ago. It has now reverted to its original use—a military barracks.

Of all railway stations in the Near East, perhaps in the world, Haydaparsa seems ideally placed. It is right on the sea-front, with a majestic panorama of Istanbul across the blue waters, ruffled now by fresh breeze. No smoke-cloud ever hangs over Haydaparsa. The secretary to the railway director, a beautiful dark-haired girl whose name means "Rose-Handed", learned her English at the American College in Istanbul, and agreed that working here, with the view over the Bosphorus, was better than in the main town. Yes, she said, the Taurus Express was' running very well. Many people used it—diplomats, business men, students even, because compared with air travel it was so cheap—"and many people has little money".

The Wagons-Lits sidings are a little way from the station, but it is obvious that this part of their service is progressing quite satisfactorily. The big brass plate on the office building proclaims the international character of the company. The Pullman-cars looked cleaner and better cared-for than much of the other rolling-stock on the Orient Express route.

For trainsmanship, then, you must know this ornate, remote, but breezy and sunlit station of Haydaparsa. The Dalziel dream of rounding the corner southwards through Beirut and Haifa never found fruition. He had about as much hope as Napoleon, storming his way up through Palestine towards his final defeat before the walls of Acre at the hands of the British and the Turks.

But the company persisted for as long as it could. After Aleppo, the train divided, and one section reached Tripoli (Syria) for a bus connection with Haifa. The most melancholy sight in Haifa today is the memorial to the Turkish Railways, whose trains reached the port regularly until the first world war, when they were apt to be frequently disrupted by Lawrence of Arabia. It has been left intact by both the British and the Israelis, and stands, adorned with elephants, on one of the main streets leading out of the city.

We left Hercule Poirot on the platform at Aleppo at five o'clock on a freezing Sunday morning. A French officer, whose duty it is to see him off after whatever delicate mission the detective has accomplished, assures him he will be in Stamboul on the Monday evening. He has somehow saved the honour of the French Army, and that is enough. The lieutenant hopes M. Poirot will not be snowed up in the Taurus Mountains.

Mary Debenham (Miss Christie's typically English heroine) looks out of her Wagon-Lit window, to see the French officer and the little muffled-up man with the enormous moustaches. Then they are *en voiture*. "Five o'clock," writes Miss Christie, "is an awkward time to board a train." But at least, four hours later, there is a breakfast car, where Poirot watches Miss Debenham talking with the English military sahib-type, Colonel Arbuthnot. After a chilly start, they are getting on very well together. Hercule Poirot says to himself, "The train, it is as dangerous as a sea voyage."

There is a slight accident—a small fire in the dining-car—which delays their arrival at Haydarpasa, and the desperate anxiety which this involves in the otherwise cool, collected Miss Debenham suggests that there is some over-riding reason why she must not miss the Orient Express connection in Stamboul. There is; and it is murder.

Poirot's presence on the Simplon-Orient (departure 9 p.m. from Sirkeci station) is purely fortuitous. He is accompanied by a director of the Wagons-Lits Company, who is mystified at not being able to get his companion a vacant berth, even though the conductor, he protests, always keep No. 16 vacant. For some mysterious reason—and it is in fact the main plot of *Murder on the Orient Express*—the Wagons-Lits are full. Room is found for Poirot eventually, and the train starts on its three-day journey bearing the destination plate

ISTANBOUL - TRIESTE - CALAIS

These were the lush days of the through coach to the Channel port. Miss Christie then settles down to organise her complex but highly entertaining story within the Wagon-Lit coach itself. It is placed, on the train, between the Athens-Paris coach and the Voiture-Restaurant, and so much depends on the behaviour of the travellers that she includes, in the book, an illustrated plan showing their exact disposition. Her book is perhaps the classic of the Orient Express thrillers, because throughout it is tied to the train, and reflects the author's intimate knowledge of the routine of the 1930s. Her book has not the "atmospheric" approach of Graham Greene. Without revealing the dénouement of a story which some may not have read, let us see how Miss Christie uses the Wagons-Lits background.

Poirot, secure in No. 7, upper berth, is astonished to see the Wagons-Lits conductor put up his luggage. "Unheard of!" he

exclaims, for in those days conductors were a race apart, the re-
cipients of confidences as well as tips; multi-lingual, helpful without being servile, and able to whistle up porters at will.

With his company director friend, Poirot dines excellently, at a
favoured table. Monsieur Bouc even becomes philosophical, towards the end of the meal, about "la vie du rail" on such a train.

" 'Ah,' he sighed, 'Had I the pen of a Balzac! I would depict
this scene.'

He waved a hand.

" 'It is an idea, that,' said Poirot.

" 'Ah, you agree? It has not been done, I think. And yet it lends
itself to romance, my friend. All around us are people, of all
classes, of all nationalities, of all ages. For three days these people,
these strangers to one another, are brought together. They eat and
sleep under one roof, they cannot get away from each other. At the
end of three days they part, they go their several ways, never,
perhaps, to see each other again.'

" 'And yet,' said Poirot, 'suppose an accident——'

" 'Ah no, my friend——'

" 'From your point of view it would be regrettable, I agree. But
nevertheless let us just for one moment suppose it. Then, perhaps,
all these here are linked together—by death.' "

Among the other passengers there is the hideous but aristocratic
Princess Dragomiroff, who is ordering mineral water and orange
juice for her compartment, and chicken cooked without sauces for
dinner. Presumably in those days the restaurant car would go
through Bulgaria into Jugoslavia unchanged.

Though all twelve passengers play an individual part in the
murder of the villain, Mr. Ratchett, alias Cassetti, this is no place
to recount their stories. The train runs into a snowdrift after Belgrade, between Vincovci and Brod, giving the talkative American
matron, Mrs. Hubbard, the chance to give everyone in earshot her
opinion of the less pleasing habits of the Turks in Smyrna, and of
the Orient Express itself—"these nasty trains, and all the outrages
I've heard of".

The outrage duly takes place, and M. Bouc and the Chef de
Train (he alone wears a blue uniform instead of the usual Wagons-
Lits brown) bring Poirot into the case. It is made more serious

because, Miss Christie notes, Jugoslavia is one of the few countries which does not put policemen on the train. Discovering that the dead man was a well-known criminal, M. Bouc declares "I cannot regret that he is dead—not at all! *Tout de même*, it is not necessary that he should be killed on the Orient Express. There are other places. . . ." When, later on, it becomes obvious that the murderer—or perhaps there were more than one—is still on the famous, vaunted international *train-de-luxe*, he feels like weeping.

But as the mystery unfolds, it is obvious that the snow-bound express is the perfect happy hunting-ground for Hercule Poirot. No one, as M. Bouc said on the journey out from Istanbul, can get away; the evidence remains in each compartment; witnesses, having nothing else to do, are at beck and call, and the restaurant-car doesn't merely sustain the characters with creature-comforts, but provides an excellent meeting place where Poirot can confront them with his findings. The Orient Express remains stationary and snow-bound throughout the rest of the book, but the author's uncanny skill in characterisation might make most readers feel that they, too, had been stranded in the Stamboul-Calais coach during all that time.

The Macedonian uprising of 1903, when the freedom-fighters or saboteurs (call them what you will, but the local name was *comitadjis*) fought for independence, was the setting for a Dutchman's historical novel published in the 1930s.

A. Den Doolard's book *Orient Express*—called *Express to the East* in the English translation by David Dejong (Arthur Barker, London, 1936.)—is much more concerned with the ravages of the Turks and Serbs, and the slow crushing of the Bulgar *comitadjis* than it is with the train. But still, in those troubled days, the Wagons-Lits cars got to the Greek and Turkish borders through a country in a state of anarchy. Twenty years before, the impressive inaugural trip had traversed the same route and those aboard had shaken their heads over the fate of this unhappy land—the most kicked-around country in Europe.

In his introduction, Den Doolard explains how he had tried to understand the contrasts in the area. "I had wandered for months through Macedonia, sometimes thirsty and penniless and dirty,

33. King of the Sleeping Cars: Maurice Dekobra, author of *The Madonna of the Sleeping Cars,* which has sold 750,000 copies since 1924 and largely established the romantic myth surrounding the Orient Express.

MAURICE DEKOBRA

LA MADONE
DES SLEEPINGS

ROMAN COSMOPOLITE

ÉDITIONS BAUDINIÈRE
27 *bis*, rue du Moulin-Vert, Paris

MAURICE DEKOBRA

LA MADONE
DES
SLEEPINGS

ROMAN

510ᵉ MILLE

ÉDITIONS BAUDINIÈRE
27 ᵇⁱˢ, Rue du Moulin-Vert
PARIS (14ᵉ)

---

34. *La Madone des Sleepings*: cover and pages from an early edition discovered by the author in the Egyptian Market, Istanbul, in 1964. It advertises another excursion into the Madonna's "*vie amoureuse*", this time in Italy.

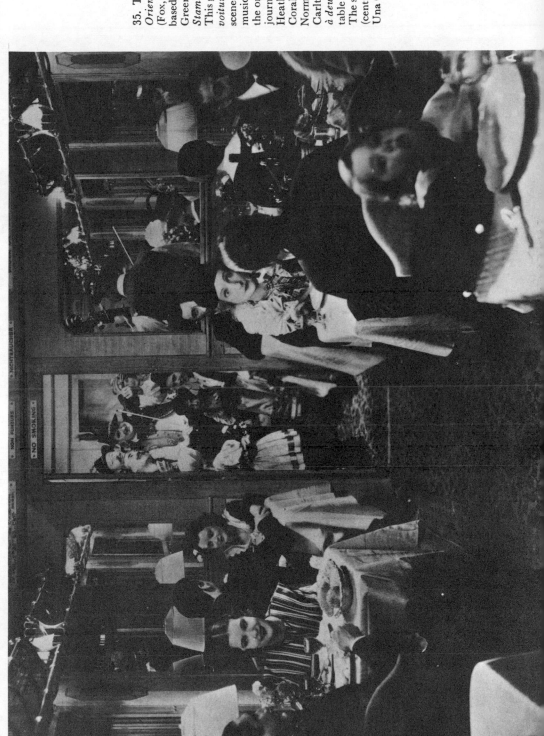

35. The film *Orient Express* (Fox, 1934) was based on Graham Greene's novel *Stamboul Train*. This gay *voiture-restaurant*, scene has gipsy musicians recalling the original journey of 1883. Heather Angel as Coral Musker and Norman Foster as Carlton Myatt dine *à deux* at the far table on the left. The startled lady (centre right) is Una O'Connor.

GRAHAM GREENE

Stamboul Train

AGATHA CHRISTIE

Murder on the Orient Express

38. *The Lady Vanishes*. A Gainsborough Film of 1938 and one of Alfred Hitchcock's greatest successes, it was based on the novel *The Wheel Spins* by Ethel Lina White. The action took place on a train reminiscent of the Orient Express, and in this tense scene Margaret Lockwood and Michael Redgrave try unsuccessfully to persuade a resolute Mary Clare and a vigilant Paul Lukas to admit that the Lady of the title ever existed at all. (Photograph by courtesy of the Rank Organisation).

39. The Gare de Lyon, Paris. Regularly on Thursdays and Sundays the Direct
Orient Express leaves here for Istanbul.

40. A first class ticket to Istanbul: exactly eighty-one years to the day after the inaugural trip of M. Nagelmackers and his V.I.P.'s the author left the Gare de Lyon on the Direct-Orient Express. His journey was hardly as eventful as James Bond's return from Istanbul in *From Russia With Love,* but the number of his ticket was, quite by chance, 00733.

41 and 42. Pre- and post-war Orient Expresses in Germany and France.

43, 44 and 45. Variations on the Orient Express route, which extend to the spelling of Istanbul.

46. Sirkeci Station, Istanbul: Turkish peasants photographed by the author
before the departure of the Orient Express.

47. The end of the line: the Bosphorus seen from the roofs of Topkapi Pa
in Istanbul, which is not without its own romantic and cinematic associati

sometimes drinking iced plum brandy in the luxurious Wagon-Restaurant of the Orient Express."

Gradually the train became a symbol in the author's mind, and whether it be true that the Macedonians made at least seven attempts to blow it up, the activities of the *comitadjis* would certainly allow for such guerilla warfare.

"If they pick the right day," Uncle Kosta says to his niece Milja, the heroine of the novel, "many a high-stationed gentleman will go up in the air with it, and when that happens they imagine that all of Europe will be concerned about Macedonia once more, and make it at last independent."

In the story the Brothers Kosta and Kroum Drangov, from the Macedonian village of Radovo, leave their fields where they've been harvesting (imagining each stalk they cut down to be a Turkish bashi-bazouk) and begin to work for the Secret Society of *comitadji*. There's already been much blowing-up of local railways by the Turks—"everywhere were rails twisted up like snakes that had been clubbed to death." And there is a great deal of atrocity and rape, and suicide in the traditional Macedonian style.

The girl Milja emerges as a key member of the *comitadji*, with a travelling job which is not unlike a political Madonna of the Sleeping Cars. Once her Uncle Kosta, who first saw the train twenty years before—in 1883, the year of its first trip—takes her near the railway track, and talks to her about this alien monster which glides swiftly through the countryside.

"It's an important line, Milja. Once a day a train passes which comes from Athens by way of Solun and goes to Belgrade, and then way off to the capital of France. The Orient Express, it is called. It's a train for rich people, you see. Everyone of any importance rides in it—ministers of state, wealthy merchants and the like, all the high Europeans, as I call them. Often I stand there watching it pass. We'll see it pretty soon, for it comes by in the late afternoon. The cars are painted blue with yellow stripes, and when they go by I say 'There rides money, Kosta, and power : but there does not ride happiness.' "

Milja replied "Uncle Kosta, it's a beautiful train. I should like to ride in it one day."

From that distance, she notices the polished rows of brass letters on the carriages, the proud symbol of the *Compagnie Inter-nationale*. Uncle Kosta, who knows his routes, tells her that at Nisch, one half of the train has gone eastward by way of Sofia, to Constantinople. "I suppose we'll never do more than look at it, Milja. That train isn't a toy for the likes of us to play with. . . ."

Milja eventually marries the chief of the *comitadji*, Ivan Todorov, one of the heroes of Macedonian history, and he persuades her to undertake secret missions for the cause—most of them along the route of the Orient Express. This is espionage in the old tradition. He gives her a new name—Marguerite Lagarde —and a cosmopolitan collection both of luggage labels and money. Her first mission is to Zagreb.

"You're not going by way of Bucharest, but directly to Belgrade. The Orient Express leaves at 2.30. Tomorrow morning at seven you'll be in Zagreb. There you'll take a taxi to the Cafe Kroso, where you'll order breakfast at once. Here's a recent number of *L'Illustration*. Take it out of your bag, which you'll have standing near you, and read it while you wait."

A stranger, he tells her, will come and offer her a cigarette, and later a thick letter in an envelope, which she must conceal in the magazine.

At 11.40 a.m. she is to catch the train to Sofia, for which she has a first-class ticket. During the three hours' stop in Belgrade, she is not to leave the station, but to dine in the restaurant, and order her meal in French—with perhaps a few words of Serbo-Croat. The night train, for which she has a Wagon-Lit cabin, leaves at a quarter to midnight.

"Orient Express at last," says Milja to herself, no doubt thinking back to the time when she saw what the *comitadjis* called "The Blue Train", with Uncle Kosta. "But alone, and without knowing why." The impact on the Macedonian girl is not a happy one.

"It was a long train journey back, again in an empty compartment with red cushions. She understood now why travelling in a de luxe train was conducive to loneliness. A bowing porter had walked ahead of her over a thick blue rug and had shut her into a red-lacquered closet, a little gleaming cell, one in a long row, which rocked quietly through the night. Above her narrow bed hung a covered light, which she did not know how to manipulate.

162

It was so hot in her luxurious closet that she rolled and tossed all night without getting a wink of sleep.

"A few men paced up and down the narrow corridor. They had watched her curiously and even suspiciously and had afterwards engaged in a whispered conversation with the brown porter. One of them later knocked on her door, but it had been fastened with chain and bolt."

This fastening is still standard equipment on the Wagons-Lits. But today the conductor would have objected to being called a "porter".

At twilight, near Nisch, she watches a peasant woman trudging across a field, and feels ashamed of herself in the role of a Wagons-Lits passenger.

"Here she sat, doing nothing but lean on soft pillows and stare outside, spending enough money to support this woman and her husband and her children for a whole week. . . . In the dining-car she had been scrutinised as if she were some odd animal just escaped from its cage. All that polite bowing and whispering, only because she had put money on the table—money for the polished and warmed monogrammed plate with its austere W.L., money for the silverware, for the polished windows which seemed too intricately fastened for any common mortal to raise, money for the electric fan (in 1903 ?) money for the rosewood woodwork. . . ."

In the dining-car, the other passengers, drinking a night-cap brandy, obviously didn't care. What were peasants to them? Merely movable pieces of landscape. Interesting to look at because of their colourful costumes. Then Milja went back to her sleeping-car "and happily, no brown servant appeared, to turn down her covers, shake her pillow, and then wait with beaming face for a tip."

Eventually she leaves her own private compartment and goes to sit in a third class carriage with Serbian peasants—the Serbs whom she has been brought up to hate. They accept her and give her cheese.

After this unwelcome journey, she is sent on more missions, to places like Varna and Bucharest, never knowing why. Her husband, the great Leader, is killed, and though the work of the *comitadjis* goes on, the secret society is split into two rival groups, one in Vienna, the other in Sofia. Milja belongs to the Viennese faction. She continues commuting for Communism, but eventually her train is wrecked—it seems by accident rather than design—and she is carried dead from the wreckage.

These Balkan people seem to have an obsession over the place of burial. Mutilation of corpses by the Turks, a common custom, may have had something to do with it. Uncle Kosta takes charge of the body, and buries it secretly at the edge of one of his fields.

"No one knew where Milja's grave was. But whenever Kosta ploughed in the spring, plodding patiently behind his two buffaloes, he thought of her. Twice daily the Orient Express thundered by. It appeared and vanished again, all in the space of ten seconds, and a moment later the smoke from its engine had drifted away over the barren hills. That train came from a strange world in which Milja had lived, a world of which he understood little more than did his black buffaloes, who snorted as they dragged the wooden plough through the crumbling earth."

Meanwhile, the "blue" train continued on its way unhindered, past the fields where Uncle Kosta and Ivan Todorov had fought and died. Since that time, even till today, there has been a stubborn reluctance on the part of Bulgaria to admit, or at least encourage, the passage of the luxury express. Evidence will be found from various chroniclers in this book. It is even apparent at the present time, when Bulgarians, for all their seemingly buoyant cheerfulness, still shout "capitalist!" at the two Wagons-Lits coaches which creep across their arid plains on the way to the land of the arch-enemy, the Ottoman Turk.

But Den Doolard finds a reconciliation.

"Macedonia, with its mad sun and its wild past, made me happy and also destroyed me. But all that love and hate had been wiped away; they had evaporated in the blue sky like the smoke of the Orient Express, like the flames of the watchfires on the Bulgarian borders, where I first learned about the *comitadjis*."

Alfred Hitchcock is a very endearing—and one might almost say, very enduring—example of a film director who gets his effect by building up tension, and blending it with the relief of occasional humour. He realised the value of confining his characters in a claustrophobic setting : it might have been anything from people

164

trapped in a lift to passengers involved in a trans-continental railway journey.

Ethel Lina White's mystery novel *The Wheel Spins* (Harper, New York, 1936) obviously appealed to him, and with the help of two British script-writers, Frank Launder and Sidney Gilliat, he set to work in 1938 on a distinguished film version which he called *The Lady Vanishes*. Despite the many alterations which his writers had to make before it became a typical Hitchcock story, the basic plot of *The Wheel Spins* gave the atmosphere he wanted, and he engaged Dame May Whitty to play the Lady, Michael Redgrave to play the junior lead, with bow-tie and wispy moustache, and Margaret Lockwood to play the heroine.

Miss White doesn't pretend that her train is the Orient Express as such (the Wagons-Lits connection is to be made at Trieste), but she has placed her temperamental heroine, Iris Carr, a pretty, rather spoiled orphan of independent means, in an unnamed Balkan country. She adds "all persons, events and places on the journey to Trieste are entirely fictitious", and in Alfred Hitchcock's hands, some of them are highly farcical, but this is all in the cause of cinema box-office appeal.

In the book, there two indomitably English spinsters, the Misses Flood-Porter, who always dress for dinner on the Continent, saying that "otherwise, we should feel we were letting England down". They are replaced in the film by two pukkah-sahib males from a vanished age. Their one interest (which cannot be satisfied in the far Balkans) is to know the state of play in a cricket-match between England and Australia in Manchester, which they discuss interminably and hope to see, not realising that abduction, attempted murder and espionage are likely to hinder the smooth running of the train. These characters, Caldicott and Charters, provided Naunton Wayne and the late Basil Radford with the opportunity to turn in two classic comedy performances; so successful indeed that they were called upon to repeat them in two other films—*Night Train to Munich* and *Crooks' Tour*.

To Iris Carr, on her holiday at a Ruritanian resort, the train had become a symbol. "In imagination, she saw it shooting through Europe, as though it were an explosive shuttle ripping through the scorched fabric of the map. . . . It caught up cities and

165

threaded them on a string. Illuminated names flashed before her eyes and were gone—Bucharest, Zagreb, Trieste, Milan, Basle, Calais. . . ."

This seems an improbable route, particularly as far as Basle is concerned, but Miss White, like other writers, has been impressed by the scenery of the Dragoman Pass in Bulgaria.

"The train treaded its way past piled-up chunks of disrupted landscape, like a Doré engraving of Dante's *Inferno*. Waterfalls slashed the walls of granite precipices with silver veining. Sometimes they passed arid patches, where dark pools, fringed with black-feathered rushes, lay in desolate hollows. . . ."

Iris Carr, at the outset of the novel, is recovering from a gay house-party at the resort, and from insinuations that she has been leading one of the husbands astray. Her comment—"As if I'd skid for a man who looks like Mickey Mouse!" has a pleasantly period flavour. She makes a disastrous start on the journey, catching sunstroke on the platform just before the train is due. In the film, she is struck on the head by a falling flower-box intended for the Vanishing Lady, Miss Froy.

This "tweedy spinster" appears in the book as an English governess going home on holiday. She tells Iris Carr that she speaks ten languages, also that : "If an international crisis arose in a railway carriage, and there were no interpreters, I could step into the breach and, perhaps, alter the destinies of the world. . . ."

Hitchcock's Miss Froy, however, is older and a fully-qualified British Secret Service agent, bringing a stolen code out of the Balkans. Both stories are complete with a sinister doctor and an invalid completely swathed in bandages, for whom Miss Froy is, of course, substituted, but in the book she is chosen, more or less by chance, as a dupe. In the film she is the real enemy.

The minor characters are those one might meet on any of these international expresses—a clergyman and his wife, a "honeymoon couple" who are obviously not married, a mysterious baroness, a rather casual, whimsical hero, and the train staff, every member of which is deeply involved in working for one side or the other. All this is the mixture as before. The element which binds the tale is Iris Carr's inability to get anyone to believe her story about Miss Froy's disappearance. Everyone has a different reason for lying.

166

It is a baffling situation for a girl recovering from sunstroke (or a blow on the head).

The arrival at Trieste is obviously to be the culmination of the plot. Iris gets worked up into one of her fevers.

"As her temperature rose, her head began to ache so furiously that it seemed to bang in a series of small explosions, which kept time with the frantic revolution of the wheels. 'You're *get*-ting near. You're *get*-ting near.' And then the rhythm changed, and began to chop out a devil's tattoo. 'Nearer-nearer-nearer-*nearer*-NEARER.' Nearer to Trieste. The express was in the relentless grip of the schedule. The pulsations of the engine throbbed through Iris like the shaken arteries of an overdriven heart. . . ."

It is possible to feel like that during an overnight journey to Trieste without having any spies or sinister doctors around!

Hitchcock, in the film, keeps up the *mitteleuropean* atmosphere, as recognisable as the flavour of a Balkan Sobranie cigarette. He gets away with his tension-and-humour blend, which includes an amusing fight in a *fourgon* baggage van full of animals, and amid the rough-and-tumble there are some pleasing glimpses of Miss Lockwood's legs. Otherwise, there is no "sex" in either story. One of Ethel Lina White's characters remarks: "Abandon is only permissible in a negligée, and definitely bad form on a train journey."

At no time, in *The Lady Vanishes,* is there any indication that the train has sleeping-cars, a fact which would be bound to emerge in the plot. But in one scene showing the train, there is a brief glimpse of the familiar Wagons-Lits coachwork. It is not often one can catch out Mr. Hitchcock.

Cecil Roberts is an English romantic novelist with a yen for travel. His most popular series began with the word "Gone"— which itself is a travel word. *Gone Rustic, Gone Rambling, Gone Sunwards,* and the author was described by one critic as "the inimitable Mr. Cecil Roberts . . . very entertaining on things seen and done in Florida, on millionaires, bananas, flamingoes, on Dr. Baekland, inventor of Bakelite, on the hundred and one things attracting his infinite and charming curiosity."

In his novel *Victoria Four-Thirty* (The Macmillan Co., New

167

York, 1937), Mr. Roberts is entertaining on the adventures of a number of travellers who catch, at 4.30 p.m. on platform 8 of this London station, the boat-train for Folkestone-Boulogne-Paris and the Arlberg-Orient Express.

This is the only popular work of fiction dealing specifically with this train, though Graham Greene's passengers bound for Stamboul from Ostend must have caught up with it before Vienna. As George Behrend points out, the Arlberg was the first through international Orient Express to be re-instated after the Second World War, but its origin dates back to the Treaty of Versailles in 1919, when it followed the Simplon-Orient as an alternative route, avoiding any passage through Germany. At first it went no farther than Vienna, but in 1932 it was extended to Bucharest, and was almost immediately given an extension to Athens, as an alternative to the Constantinople route, which still, in those days, ran to the Rumanian port of Constanza, with a thirteen-hour voyage down the Black Sea to the Bosphorus.

But *Victoria Four-Thirty* is not a book about railways. Just as Agatha Christie indulged herself in her detective-story simply by filling a Wagons-Lits coach full of suspects, Cecil Roberts turns a fanciful and not altogether implausible eye on a possible collection of very varied passengers, who are either involved with each other because of the train, or are impelled to catch the Arlberg-Orient for a number of very different reasons.

It is an old type of plot, but worked out in a way to hold attention en route.

The first character involved in Victoria Station on that day doesn't travel at all. He is Jim Brown, a railway porter, with his own understandably jealous thoughts.

"What a lot of miserable objects he carried luggage for—sleek, soft-voiced young men trailing behind old aunts, bored to death because they were travelling abroad. Why, the very labels excited him : Paris, Milan, Rome, Geneva, Vienna, Bucharest, Athens, Cairo, Baghdad. If his bag ever had one of those labels on it he'd run all the way down the platform instead of drawling—'Aw Portah !' or 'How frightfully crowded !' or 'Really, my dear, it's preposterous !' "

The actual passengers are introduced, with a background of

their reasons for being at Victoria on that day. They include a famous orchestral conductor, Herr Gollwitzer, travelling, as one might expect, to the Salzburg Festival. He goes to the renowned Thomas Cook office at the station, and would have been swamped by tourists (the month is August) were he not recognised as a V.I.P. and given special treatment. He at least knows the train well.

Nikolas Metaxa is a Greek restaurant proprietor from Soho, returning disappointed to Athens, via the Arlberg Express, second class. One third of his luggage consists of tins of food. There's a royal-diplomatic passenger, the Crown Prince of Slavonia, whose mythical father has been assassinated by a mythical Ruritanian Bomb. His main worry, as a typical schoolboy of thirteen, is that his pet rabbit has disappeared.

There's Mrs. Dorothy Blake, just married, and on her honeymoon via Wagons-Lits to Austria. This is pure saccharin romance of the 1930s, without a touch of Noel Coward satire or Somerset Maugham cynicism.

" 'You like my going-away dress?' she asked.

" 'You look marvellous—such a naughty little hat !'

" 'And a naughty little wife !'

" 'My angel !'

" 'Shall we always be as silly as this ?'

" 'Why not?' asked Derek.

" 'We couldn't go on like this, or we'd pop.'

" 'Then let's, till we do !' answered Derek. 'Hullo, here's Victoria. Darling, we're on our honeymoon ! Can you believe it ?'

" 'Hardly.' "

The car drew up to the kerb. A porter appeared. Derek helped out his wife.

" 'The four-thirty Folkestone-Boulogne boat train,' he said to the young porter. . . ."

It wasn't Jim Brown, the porter in the book, but he was watching and envying.

"Jim wondered where they were going for the honeymoon. A label hanging from the dressing-case satisfied his curiousity. Mrs. D. Blake, passenger to Hotel Anton, Kitzbuhel, Austria."

For himself, he said, he'd choose Lugano. Out of all the places named on his passengers' luggage, that's where he would take his girl-friend Lizzie—to Lugano, where they would have a bedroom "high upon the mountain side, overlooking a blue lake and a range of snow-capped mountains, exactly as the hotel label promised. . . ."

Then Cecil Roberts includes an author, Henry Fanning, who has been recommended to have a break somewhere, to find an idea for a new book. The choice is Vienna, and Henry is obviously escaping from a possessive wife who still, after twenty years of marriage, calls him "Daddy". This revolting title is kept up till the moment of his reluctant departure. He is in search of a plot for another book.

" 'You'll meet someone,' says his wife Alice, 'a Prime Minister or an Ambassador—or a lady with a salon may annex you and ask you to dine.'

" 'But I'm looking for a plot!'

" 'You're as likely to find it,' replies Alice, 'at a good dinner table as in a cheap restaurant.'

Herr Emil Gerhardt of Berlin is a German film star with a trace of Jewish blood who, in the mid-1930s, is not welcome in the country where he was once an idol. The author shows an appreciation of the gradual stranglehold of Nazism here. Gerhardt gets to Vienna, where a film part is supposed to be waiting for him, but meanwhile the director he seeks has been taken to a place which, in those years, we just heard of as a "Concentration Camp." It seemed an odd title then.

Sister Teresa of Transylvania is a nun returning via Bucharest (change trains, in those days, at Vienna). She also has her part to play in the book, but it is an unexpected one. At the onset she is contentedly ordering tea and buttered toast in the Pullman car between London and Folkestone.

There are characters a-plenty (or how else would Mr. Roberts make his train journey so rewarding?). Mr. Percy Bowley of Derby, an engineer fleeing the country and his relations with £500 in Bank of England notes, General Zoronoff, once a high officer in the Russian Imperial Army, now a chauffeur-guide employed by Thomas Cook's, to drive two American ladies, in Salzburg for the Festival, over the Grossglockner pass to Venice.

Then there is a Turk, Alexander Bekir, who is going to his native Salonika. (The division of the train is at Nish in Jugoslavia,

but Mr. Roberts takes the Athens route with his remaining passengers.) There is a dim Dr. Wyfold, of Wargrave in the Home
Counties, trying to trace his son Reggie, who has gone native in
Austria; and a very pregnant Austrian girl, Elise Vogel of Feld-
kirch, for whom the Arlberg-Orient Express accelerates the birth
of the child she is carrying, the casual donation of a Count from St.
Cyr, a "suave young blade".

This is all great fun for Cecil Roberts, and it is also fun for his
readers. Given the predilections and exaggerations, these could in
fact be real passengers on the Arlberg-Orient Express in the heyday of the thirties. The first half of the book is called "THEY SET
OUT," the latter part, "THEY ARRIVE"—and it's as simple as
that. The honeymoon couple are less adventurous than James
Bond, who enjoyed his Russian girl on the Simplon-Orient. Mr.
and Mrs. Blake have communicating doors, but all they exchange
is a chaste salute, with all the admirable reticence and understanding of the British middle-class.

Mr. Fanning the novelist finds his inspiration by meeting a girl
on the train who fell in love with an Austrian ski instructor (surely
a situation so obvious it was not necessary to leave London to find
it). Elise Vogel's baby is born on the train, and Herr Gollwitzer
and Sister Teresa come in useful here. Emil Gerhardt, the partly-
Jewish actor, gasses himself in Vienna rather than face Nazi in-
vestigation, and after the train has divided at Nish, we are left with
Mr. Bekir, en route for Salonika, and his favourite minarets, re-
minders of Turkish rule in Macedonia before the Greeks moved in.
The final passenger is the Greek, Nikolas Metaxa.

So the Arlberg-Orient finishes its journey to Athens.

"All night, after leaving Salonica it chuffed along southwards
hugging the flat plain by the Gulf. It passed the foot of Mount
Olympus and, turning inland, went down the Vale of Tempe,
sung of by the poets of Ancient Greece."

Lawrence Durrell is a writer with an international reputation
and a knowledge of backgrounds as discriminating as, that of, say
Rose Macaulay. The Mediterranean in his milieu. *Prospero's Cell*
explored Corfu; *Bitter Lemons* gave a penetrating insight on that
beautiful but tragic island of Cyprus. The quartet of novels under

171

the generic code-name "Alexandria" ranged far and wide. But his sketches of Diplomatic Life (*Esprit de Corps*. E. P. Dutton, New York, 1957) make up a real collector's piece.

It is inscribed to Members of the Chancery of His Majesty's Embassy in Belgrade, 1951. Durrell was obviously one of the company, but this is no mere record of diplomatic happenings; rather a series of light-hearted accounts relating to minor diplomatic disasters, with the Orient Express always in the background. By this route alone, it seems, did the odd assortment of characters arrive in the Jugoslav capital. Durrell's colleague Antrobus, a man "portentous, always dropping into a whisper, clicking his tongue, making a po-face, pursing his lips, turning the palms of his hands outwards and making 'what would you' gestures"—Antrobus is the one who sums up the Esprit de l'Express.

" 'Every nation,' said Antrobus, 'has its particular *idée fixe*. For the Jugoslavs it is trains. Nothing can compare for breathtaking romance with the railway trains. Railway engines have to be put under armed guard when not in motion or they would be poked to pieces by the enquiring peasantry. No other object arouses the concupiscence of the Serb like a train. They drool over it, old boy, positively drool. *Ils bavent.*'

" 'You twig this the minute you alight from the Orient Express at Belgrade because there is something queer about the station building itself. It leans to one side. It is neatly cracked from platform level to clock-tower. Moreover, there are several distinct sets of ruts in the concrete of the platform which are highly suggestive. The first porter you engage will clear up the mystery. Apparently every fifteenth train or so leaps the barriers, grinds across the freight section and buries itself in the booking office. No one is ever hurt and the whole town joyfully bands together to dig the engine out. Everyone is rather proud of this particular idiosyncrasy. It is part of the Serbian way of life. . . .' "

Perhaps no writer of thrillers would be more fitted to include the Orient Express in one of his books than Ian Fleming. As a world traveller, boulevardier, gourmet, and newspaperman in real life, his job as author was to supply an eager reading public with adventures more and more fabulous. It's no wonder that, in

From Russia with Love (Macmillan, New York, 1957), his bitter-sweet hero, James Bond, after fighting Communist espionage in Turkey, should at last board the Orient Express for the penultimate adventures.

Tatiana the beautiful blond spy, whose favourite costume for Bond was a black velvet ribbon around her neck, black stockings and nothing else, didn't want to take the Spektor—the Thing—back to England on a plane. " 'We will take the train, this Orient Express," she told him. "It leaves at nine tonight. Do you think I haven't been thinking this thing out? We will be over the frontier at dawn . . . I will travel with you as your wife . . . I shall like that. In one of those coupés I have read about. They must be very comfortable. Like a tiny house on wheels. During the day we will talk and read and at night you will stand in the corridor outside our house and guard it.' "

Like hell, thought Bond. She wants to make love to me for four nights en route, then she'll be safe when we get to London. But she obviously will have agents on the train.

As readers of the book and viewers of the film will remember, Bond took the chance, against his better judgment, and his creator certainly knew the whole pattern and routine of the Istanbul-Paris run on the Simplon-Orient line.

"The great trains are going out all over Europe, one by one, but still, three times a week, the Orient Express thunders superbly over the glittering steel track between Istanbul and Paris. . . . Under the arc-lights, the long-chassied German locomotive panted quietly with the laboured breath of a dragon dying of asthma. Each heavy breath seemed certain to be the last. Then came another. Wisps of steam rose from the couplings between the carriages and died quickly in the warm August air. The Orient Express was the only live train in the ugly, cheaply architectured burrow that is Istanbul's main station. The trains on the other lines were engineless and unattended—waiting for tomorrow. Only Track No. 3, and its platform, throbbed with the tragic poetry of departure. . . ."

De Blowitz would have liked that last phrase, and indeed the whole setting. He would have realised that part of Fleming's gift is to mingle journalistic reality with horrific fantasy.

173

"The heavy bronze cipher on the side of the dark blue coach said 'COMPAGNIE INTERNATIONALE DES WAGONS-LITS ET DES GRANDS EXPRESS EUROPEENS'. Above the cipher, fitted into metal slots, was a flat iron sign that announced, in block capitals on white, ORIENT EXPRESS, and underneath, in three lines :

ISTANBUL	THESSALONIKI	BEOGRAD
VENEZIA	MILAN	
LAUSANNE	PARIS	

"James Bond gazed vaguely at one of the most romantic signs in the world." What secretly worried him—and must presumably have struck Ian Fleming at one time—was that Milan was not spelled MILANO.

As the world knows, the girl nearly missed the train, a thing the Madonna would never have done. The engine's safety-valve let off the excess steam. Passengers, mostly taking the local Thessaloniki line for Greece, screeched their farewells, and the brown-uniformed Wagons-Lits attendant intoned his customary "*En voiture, s'il vous plaît*". But she was there, in the last carriage, and they made their celebrated rendevous in the central coupé, at No. 7 and No. 8, to be joined later by the faithful Kerim.

What follows is strictly from Fleming's vivid imagination. It is presumably possible that all these shennanigans could have gone on without the railway authorities stopping the train entirely, but we must accept the story for the exciting to-and-fro it is. At least the casualties were less than those encompassed by the elaborate plot of Agatha Christie on the same run. Of the three Soviet agents on the train, one was disposed of by having his ticket taken from him while on the train. Bond returned to No. 7 and his girl, but to a scene less passionate than a real Orient Madonna could have wished, for he had problems. The Turkish frontier led to Greece. "No love lost between Greece and England. Then Yugoslavia—whose side was Tito on? Probably both."

The train reached the frontier station at Uzunkopru. "Some goods-trucks, led by a straining engine, filed by. The silhouette of sheds showed briefly. With a jolt and a screech of couplings, the Orient Express took the points and swerved away from the through line. Four sets of rails with grass growing between them showed outside the window, and the empty length of the down platform. A cock crowed. The express slowed down to walking speed and finally, with a sigh of hydraulic brakes and a noisy whoosh of let-off steam, ground to a stop. The girl stirred in her sleep. Bond softly shifted her head on the pillow and got up and slipped out of the door."

Fleming knew his wayside Balkan stations, with their low platforms, dour buildings and unshaven officials, standing about and not even trying to look important. He knew also that the Wagons-Lits conductor's job, in however remote an area, is to proceed ahead of the Customs officers, rousing his charges in advance. During all this time at the Turkish Frontier two of the Soviet agents were arrested.

"The engine whistled, a new kind of whistle, the brave shrill blast of a Greek engine-driver. The door of the Wagons-Lits carriage clanged shut. The plain-clothes man and the second policeman appeared walking over to the station. The guard at the back of the train looked at his watch and held out his flag. There was a jerk and a diminishing crescendo of explosive puffs from the engine and the front section of the Orient Express began to move. The section that would be taking the northern route through the Iron Curtain—through Dragoman on the Bulgarian frontier, only fifty miles away—was left beside the dusty platform, waiting."

There is a realistic tang for any reader at this moment in the story.

"[Bond] watched the dead, dusty platform, with its chickens and the small black figure of the guard, until the long train took the points and jerked harshly on to the single main line. He looked away across the ugly, parched countryside towards the golden guinea sun climbing out of the Turkish plain. It was going to be a beautiful day. . . ."

A beautiful day—if James Bond had merely been a passenger on the Simplon-Orient, uncluttered by a glamorous girl-spy, a pathological killer, a secret agent and a doomed Turk.

"A painless visit from the Greek Customs . . . and then the berths were folded away as the train hurried south towards the Gulf of Enez at the head of the Aegean. Outside, there was extra light and colour. The men at the little stations and in the fields

175

were handsome. Sunflowers, maize, vines and racks of tobacco were ripening in the sun. . . ."

Kerim Bey, the Turk, had said, "There is always excitement on the Orient Express," and his creator saw to it that excitement galore should continue until the Simplon Tunnel and beyond. The Wagons-Lits conductor had been amply bribed, on the understanding that the hunt was on for a smuggling gang, taking Turkish opium to Paris. Dinner was taken, just as the train pulled into the "hideous" modern station of Thessaloniki, and that night Kerim, "the man who carried the sun with him", was murdered. At Belgrade, where the Orient Express arrived later, there was an eight-hour wait for the Bulgarian section of the train to join them. The shadow of SMERSH, the secret society, fell across the proceedings, but there was to be no lack of subsequent excitement on the final journey towards Paris.

The Express left at nine o'clock on its run down the valley of the Sava, reaching Zagreb at dawn. Then "they hammered into the mountains of Slovenia where the apple trees and the chalets were almost Austrian. The train laboured its way towards Ljubljana. The girl awoke. They had breakfast of fried eggs and hard brown bread and coffee that was mostly chicory. The restaurant car was full of cheerful English and American tourists from the Adriatic coast. . . ."

After Jugoslavia, the joy of Italy at the frontier station of Poggioreale. "The first smell of the soft life with the happy jabbering of Italian officials and the carefree upturned faces of the station crowd. The new diesel-electric engine gave a slap-happy whistle" (Fleming is good at recognising his changes of locomotive) "the meadow of brown hands fluttered, and they were loping easily down into Venezia Giulia, towards the distant sparkle of Trieste and the gay blue of the Adriatic. . . ."

At Trieste the final hazard began as the hired killer Nash joined the train. The actual shooting of Bond was to be done as the train entered the Simplon Tunnel, and devotees of Ian Fleming who ever travel that route will no doubt feel the heightened tension as the Orient Express draws near.

But first there is good food from the Wagon-Restaurant, lovemaking in No. 7 between Trieste and Venice, and silence until the

176

tinkling of the dinner-bell near Verona. For those who are genuinely married, or who have girl friends who are not necessarily Soviet spies, presumably these amorous afternoons on the Orient Express can be very pleasant. Certainly the conductors are known to exercise every discretion towards clients they trust and like. The subsequent shooting-match between Bond and the agent Nash is hokum in Fleming's own particular style, and Bond leaves the Orient Express at Dijon at five-thirty in the morning. It is hardly a romantic departure, but the details of the whole journey from Istanbul have been faithfully recorded.

"At last they were down the steps and on to the hard, motionless platform. A blue-smocked porter took their luggage. . . . Only a handful in the third class, who had ridden 'hard' through the night saw a young man help a young girl away from the dusty carriage with the romantic names on its side towards the drab door that said 'SORTIE'. . . ."

In his final exultation over the trapped Bond, the killer Nash had summed up the elements which, in the minds of thriller-writers and their public, make such a train as the Orient Express the perfect background to the plot.

" 'Old man, the story's got everything. Orient Express. Beautiful Russian spy murdered in Simplon Tunnel. Filthy pictures. Secret cipher machine. Handsome British spy with career ruined murders her and commits suicide. Sex, spies, luxury train. . . . Old man, it'll run for months!' "

When *From Russia with Love* was first published the Simplon-Orient had, in fact, five years to run. At midnight on May 26, 1962, it officially ceased to exist. But this, as in so many other routes of the *Compagnie Internationale,* was merely a case of "*Le train est mort: vive le train!*" for, as described elsewhere, the Simplon was replaced by the Direct Orient, which still runs a connection twice weekly between Paris and Istanbul. There were many sentimental valedictions for the Simplon-Orient, but in the same salamander-like fashion, the double name arose on two separate trains, the Simplon Express (Paris-Venice) and the Orient-Express (Paris-Stuttgart-Munich-Vienna). The Wagons-Lits Company was not going to abandon its romantic names without a struggle.

177

12

A LITTLE WORLD ON WHEELS

The Author Joins the Direct Orient Express in Paris on the anniversary of the Inaugural Trip—Rigours and rewards of the 1,800-mile journey via Lausanne, Milan, Trieste, Zagreb, Belgrade, Dimitrovgrad, Pythion, Uzunkopru and Istanbul (Sirkeci Station).

Eighty-one years, to the day, after the inaugural trip of M. Nagelmackers and his V.I.P.'s, the Direct-Orient Express is ready to leave. Not for Constantinople, but for Istanbul. Not from the Gare de l'Est but from the Gare de Lyon. Not at seven-thirty in the evening, but at ten minutes to midnight.

The transit passengers from Calais have been shunted across Paris from the Gare du Nord. There is the usual confusion about changing trains in Paris. Two Liverpool women, bound inexplicably for Ankara, second class without sleepers, are already apprehensive—as well they might be. An amiable Turkish business man is alone relaxed. "It's a long journey," he says, "but I come this way because I want to stay alive." Perhaps Turks remember that the inaugural flight to London by Turkish Airways ended in disaster in an English wood, one of the few survivors being Prime Minister Menderes—and he survived only to be hanged by the Turks themselves shortly afterwards.

To most travellers, the Gare de Lyon means the south, the Midi, the Blue Train, the Rome Express, the Simplon Express. Before nationalisation, the letters of the company P.L.M.—Paris—Lyons —Méditerranée—held a unique attraction.

But this Direct Orient, a comparatively new route combining the old Simplon-Orient with the remains of the original Orient, will go nowhere near the sea except at Venice. It travels twice a week, Thursdays and Sundays. The handsome time-table of

Wagons-Lits—blue and gold, the traditional colour of the sleeping cars—devotes two pages to this and the sister expresses, the Jugoslavia and the Balkan. Towards the end of the journey the little Customs-houses sprout thick on the page—four between Belgrade and Istanbul. What the novice wouldn't notice in the documentation is just where the crossed knives and forks come, indicating a meal. But I have been warned.

There are only two through coaches to the Golden Horn; one a sleeping-car, the other a day-coach, divided into half first class, half second. Every seat is taken : the luggage is piled to the roof : the corridor is already ominously full of hangers-on. On each carriage the sort of sign James Bond found so romantic :

PARIS—LAUSANNE—MILANO— VENEZIA—BEOGRAD—SOFIA— ISTANBUL

Bond was puzzled because, on his trip, Milano was spelt "Milan". I am puzzled because one carriage spells Istanbul with an "n", and the other with an "m". These are the sort of minor details which stick in the mind even amid the welter of farewells and shouting and station announcements. The front half of the train seems bound for Switzerland only : two sleepers for Neuchatel and Interlaken, and in these there are vacancies. There is also, somewhere along the dark row of sleeping-cars, the slip-coach for Athens. Indeed, the one possible contender for the title of Madonna of the Sleeping-cars, 1965, a dark-haired beauty lugging an outsize suitcase is, alas, bound for Athens, and hurries towards the head of the train.

Final Announcements : the great moment is here. Children are held perilously out of doors and windows. We are at one with Carlton Myatt and Coral Musker and Hercule Poirot and Opper de Blowitz and Miss Froy and Lady Diana Wynham. A French group outside one of the rear coaches sings "Auld Lang Syne"—in French. Without a whistle, we are off on the eighteen-hundred mile trip, away from the wavings and the weepings, and about to enter that strange, private existence which is a long railway journey.

Voiture No. 7, the sleeping-car, contains two first-class single compartments, several doubles, and a "compartiment special", in which a family shares a group of four compartments. Agatha Christie's ground-plan might come in useful here, but there are no sinister or seductive characters so far. I've met a garrulous retired textile manufacturer who has lived most of his life in Puerto Rico and is heading eventually for Manila; an Australian nurse bound for Beirut, who wanted to see Istanbul first; a young, willowy Bulgarian girl, a student at Sofia University, back after two months in England; and an English student of archaeology who hopes to work his way round through Baghdad and Basra to Jordan.

The Direct Orient Express is obviously not top priority as far as rolling stock is concerned. The *Compagnie Internationale* time-table contains a colour supplement showing their latest types— LX16, LX20, YT, YU, and Z—a "Z" car which is a modernised form of the present Y car, in which I am sleeping.

Compartment No. 3 in Voiture 7, is to be my bed-sitting-room for three days and nights. It was built in the Charente—that part of France which incongruously produces both railway carriages and those small, sweet Charentais melons. The bed, covered with a tartan rug, is comfortable, the linen crisp and clean. Plenty of room for luggage, but nowhere to hang any clothes. No fold-away bedside table for early morning tea or coffee (not that any was ever forthcoming, despite the publicity photographs). Nowhere to hang your watch. On the return journey via the Balkan Express—old German carriages—there was a hook and padded base to hang a fob-watch, such as is always provided in first-class sleepers on British Railways.

Familiar objects for any Englishman who has travelled on his domestic lines are the heavy, thick decanter containing drinking water, and the chamber-pot in equally thick porcelain. They are traditional, although on the Orient Express there is no notice, English-style, saying: "This utensil is not to be used for solid matter." As for the alarm, there's a notice which reads, in four languages, "In case of danger, pull down the ring. Any abuses will be punished."

There are two towels about the size of pocket-handkerchiefs but soap is provided, and wrapped. The water runs hot, but the cold tap runs twice as freely. Above the tiddley—tiddley—tiddley sound of a French train at speed, you feel : "Well, this is my home. I'd better get used to it." And then you reflect that this cabine-de-luxe is costing as much as the first-class fare itself, and you say : "I must get the best out of it."

Sleeping in trains evokes a sharp mixture of opinion among travellers. There are those who claim that the rhythm of the train —de Blowitz's "*berceuse* of the wheels"—encourages slumber. Certainly on main-line European expresses, the long length of rail induces a kind of dream-like, floating feeling which is in itself a sedative. It is when the track is old, and in short sections; when the locomotive is steam and has to be watered; when the railway officials, all hackles and umbrage, shout beneath the windows in strange, harsh languages : these are the ingredients for insomnia. Perhaps, too, the very fact that one is embarking along the fabulous route to the Bosphorus is an encouragement to peer out curiously at every stop.

Lausanne is the first appreciable one. Ten to seven in the morning, a grey, quiet morning, with the neat, box-like Swiss houses set against mountains speckled with snow. Very few people about. But at Vevey the commuters are out in force : serious-looking business types with mufflers, schoolboys with brief-cases, little secretaries scampering down the platform, each with a bright umbrella. Vevey. Chocolate, of course, a red wrapper for plain, a violet wrapper for milk. And Charlie Chaplin lives here, but it's too early to expect to see him about.

The sun strengthens, the little bell rings for breakfast. All is very civilised. For two and a half Swiss francs there's café complet and a Perrier—but no croissants. The run to Brig is uneventful, the Customs formalities very brisk, but it seems impossible that this voiture-restaurant, this very life-line for the creature comforts, should now disappear, just as *la vie du rail* is becoming a pleasant experience. God knows when we shall see another (actually it is to be at Belgrade).

Iselle, and then the Simplon Tunnel. Ian Fleming took Bond in the opposite direction, but as the train comes out from the Simplon into blinding sunshine, I reflect that it was here that Nash, the killer, shot at Bond in the centre coupe of voiture No. 7. I am in

181

voiture No. 7 of the Direct-Orient and my rail ticket is No. 00733. If things go on like this, I shall begin to believe that Bond's journey really happened.

Domodossola is a jerk back to reality. The corridors are suddenly full of uniformed officials wearing dark glasses, and are just as suddenly empty again. A youth in a white coat hauls a trolley of refreshments and says he will take any money. Any money? *Ecco,* he admits, I don't take Turkish money. Then we are off into Italy. But already it's becoming obvious that this Orient is to be no real Express, no *rapido,* no *blitz*-train. It even stops at Stresa, where, presumably, it stopped in 1933, but then the Simplon-Orient must have been bringing delegates to the famous Stresa Conference, one of Mussolini's diplomatic extravaganzas.

Lake Maggiore unfolds like a travel brochure, in glowing colour with a backdrop of majestic mountains. There's a dramatic, aggressive quality about many of the expensive villas round the lake, in sharp contrast to the tiny coves with their brightly-painted fishing boats. Into Milan, exactly as advertised, at 12.20. It wasn't only Mussolini who got the Italian trains to run on time. There isn't time to see much of this gargantuan, echoing station, though there's time to change money, and lay in a couple of litres of chianti against the threat of Balkan austerity. The wise traveller on the Direct Orient stocks up at Milan as if for a siege of indefinite period. Incongruously, the main vendor on the platform is a seller of dolls—enormous ones, almost life-size. With overcrowding like it is on the Orient, it's surprising to find that he's made one or two sales. You might just as well buy extra passengers, when no more are needed.

Milan is the last gesture of civilisation and creature comforts before the Direct Orient leaves for the long trek through the rest of Europe. The Wagons-Lits timetable, if you examine the "*Nature de Services*" closely, admits that there are no crossed knives and forks until Belgrade. But one doesn't necessarily spend the time en route in reading the small print, to discover what are the small concessions. Although the Jugoslav border, at Poggioreale del Corso, is not reached till nearly nine hours after the departure from Milan, the Italian railway authorities obviously don't consider the Orient merits anything more than a tray of cold food,

182

called a Plateau Express, dumped in your *cabine-de-luxe* by two uniformed youngsters. On inspection, it consists of a plastic, airline-type tray containing a large, uninviting slice of meat, a slice of ham, a tired artichoke, a sliver of cheese, and a pear with the shape and hardness of a hand-grenade. To cut the meat, there's a plastic knife which snaps at the first contact. I throw the whole tray out of the window, but am eventually faced with a bill for 1,500 lire. The gesture seemed worth it. Italian Railways have obviously written off the Orient Express line, which was once their special pride and joy.

Trieste, like Brig, has always been a trouble-spot. Once it had been the Austro-Hungarian Empire's outlet to the sea, and when it passed to the Italians after 1918, an eternity of bitterness began, first with Austria and then, from 1945, with Jugoslavia. As far as the Simplon-Orient Express is concerned, it became the eastern terminus as long ago as 1912, six years after the Simplon Tunnel was opened. As far as the passengers of the sixties are concerned, it is still a trouble spot. The new Jugoslav Wagons-Lits conductor, wearing a brown jacket, not the dirty blue pullover of the man on the first leg of the journey, was unable to promise any food until Belgrade next morning.

At the refreshment bar on the station, they wouldn't take any money but Italian. Not even dollars, or traveller's cheques. "Go and change it," said the Trieste woman severely, "at the Cambio." But it was by then twenty past eight, and the Cambio was closed. Defeat once again. Resignation. Return to voiture No. 7.

An elderly Turkish lady with a lean, wise, interesting face said she and her husband were going back home to Istanbul after several months' holiday in Western Europe. Why go by train? "Oh well, my husband likes it that way, so I go along with him." She admitted that the service was disgraceful, that the old days of Wagons-Lits courtesy as well as comfort seemed to have disappeared. But she shrugged her shoulders. They were going home, she and her husband: that was the main thing, and the door closed quietly on them both.

An indignation meeting with the man from Puerto Rico, the young archaeologist (Marlborough and Trinity College, Dublin), the nurse from Queensland, the beautiful Bulgarian girl, and

183

myself, got us nowhere. We began, for the first and not the last time, to feel like refugees.

The frontier stations between Italy and Jugoslavia on this route are Poggioreale del Corso and Sezana. At Poggio a real row developed. Nobody on the train knew what it was about, but it held everything up for half an hour. Italian officials, sporting dazzling white gloves, argued with their sombre Jugoslav opposite numbers. The only man to benefit from this brawl was an ice-cream vendor, who, creeping unobtrusively along the platform, was doing a roaring trade. To us, he seemed more important than the station-master or all the Customs men combined, but he was finally hustled out of the way by the officials with the white gloves and the dark glasses.

Passports were collected by a Jugoslav girl, who swept, broad-hipped and challenging, down the platform, and swung herself up to the door of our coach. Not a Bond agent: not even a Graham Greene lesbian. Just a passport collector. It's no good imagining things—they're not happening. Customs takes no time at all. At last, the whistle. The guard holds up the stick known in most continental countries as a "poached egg" (a red circle on a white ground) and the Orient Express trundles out, nearly an hour late, towards Ljubljana, Zagreb, and Belgrade. The first steam locomotive can be heard, hissing away on a siding. We are on our way in primitive country, in primitive conditions.

First impression of Jugoslavia is exactly what one had expected. For the men, the peaked cap. For the women, the head-scarf. Instead of lorries, horse carts. Instead of tractors, the horse plough and later the oxen. On the farms, a multitude of geese, with goose-girls chivvying them around.

They all might have been extras in a film—they and the groups of smartly-dressed military types with dark glasses who hopped on and off the train when we stopped at Vincovci. Near here, I seem to remember, the train in Agatha Christie's *Murder on the Orient Express* was held up in a snow-drift, giving Hercule Poirot plenty of time to conduct his delicate enquiries. But now the Jugs are brisk: we're behind schedule for Belgrade. Whistle and off.

Belgrade, the "White City", doesn't look its best from the railway. There are some fine new skyscrapers, but the land outside the town is dry and arid, almost like a desert. At the station, there's the usual rush for the man with the trolley, and for the fountains, to refill the water-bottles after the night. Our conductor, a rather inarticulate but smiling character, promises a restaurant-car—the best promise he could make. The women from Liverpool are wandering, like two Lady Macbeths, from compartment to compartment, asking about food. Being on this train, I realise, is like being in hospital, where patients live mainly for their meals and creature-comforts.

By the time we leave Belgrade, the corridor of the day coach and an Athens coach beyond that, are jammed with peasants, picturesque but unsavoury, and the Lady Macbeths have climbed back to their seats, thankful to regain them. To reach the restaurant-car, we have almost literally to fight our way, climbing over leathern-faced old women, children with pasty faces and huge dark eyes, and grizzled shepherds clutching bundles. Even if you were travelling first-class (without sleeper) you could not escape this mob outside your door.

The restaurant, with white-coated stewards admitting only bona-fide Wagons-Lits passengers, is a temporary oasis of civilisation. But very temporary. As with the Swiss car whipped off at Brig (however long ago was that?) the Jugoslav one is due to disappear, along the Greek line, through the earthquake-ridden town of Skopje, at a quarter past one. For the Sophia and Istanbul passengers, therefore, breakfast is at ten o'clock, lunch at noon. Beyond that? The head waiter shrugs his shoulders : after all, he is not a Bulgarian.

The meals are comparatively cheap, nothing like French or Swiss prices. The American from Puerto Rico looks at the dinars he gets for change. "This is Mickey Mouse money," he says. "Whatever I give them, I always seem to get the same amount back." This at lunch, after a second assault-course through the shouting, sweating mob in the corridor. "They'd make nice *Life* pictures," is the American's comment, "but boy, you need to be a hurdle-jumper to get past."

For hours the landscape rolled past, a flat pattern of maize fields, with mounds of turnips stacked by each wayside stop. Bunches of paprika ripened outside the farmhouse windows. Then

185

the steam-hauled Express began to wind through that extra-ordinary gorge, the Dragoman Pass. Here the volcanic rocks, worn into strange shapes by the river, and by the wind which is said to blow incessantly, tower up to a thousand feet or more. There is no sign of life or habitation down by the green waters. Hemmed in by the rocks, the locomotive emits a blood-curdling succession of shrieks and howls. The driver must have fun playing variations on his whistle, while the noise of the wheels on rails gives another clattering echo.

It's a relief when the country levels out, and we approach the Bulgarian border at Dimitrovgrad. Since the dining-car disappeared at a place called Crveni Krst, I have the assurance of the conductor that he will "get me something" before he hands over to his Bulgarian colleague.

By coincidence, we pull up at a station before Dimitrovgrad exactly opposite the Direct Orient Express returning from Istanbul to Paris : the signboards are the same as ours. The passengers are only twenty-four hours out of Istanbul, anyhow, and look cheerful. We must look pretty desperate by now. There's a carriage labelled SOPHIA-WARZAWA, with two very pretty girls leaning out of one of the windows. Girls like that are always going in another direction. These two, bronzed and smiling, have probably been on holiday in Bulgaria's Golden Sands resort near Varna.

There are few formalities at Dimitrovgrad, but enough time for the conductor to forage for "something". He climbs aboard again, with, wrapped in newspaper, half a sausage, five hard-boiled eggs, a piece of stinking cheese, two maize loaves, a bottle of Bulgarian wine and one of mineral water. For this he charges the equivalent of about three dollars. It will have to do for all of us, though the Australian nurse has nursed a half-litre of chianti all the way from Venice. I then ask, "How am I to cut all this food up?" The conductor's round face creases itself into an expression of bewilderment. Then he smiles : the Bulgarian conductor will see to this if I ask him. He accepts a tip with good grace, and disappears. I put the odorous bundle away in my bed-sitter, and await our arrival in Dragoman.

The name puzzled me. I first encountered it in Cairo. A Dragoman was a guide : any sort of guide. But it was definitely a

Muslim word. How, then, can it be the name of a west Bulgarian frontier station? I ask Lilian, the Bulgarian student, who is looking very excited—the station-master of Dragoman is her uncle—but she doesn't know. We have all had talks with Lilian, and asked her how things are in her country, and whether she's really a good Communist. She has admitted certain doubts, but points out very fairly that if previous regulations hadn't been relaxed, she wouldn't have been able to spend several weeks in England and France.

Her uncle supplies the answer from the platform. Certainly the name Dragoman is of Muslim origin. But have I forgotten that Bulgaria was under Turkish rule for five hundred years? I remember the *comitadjis* of the Macedonian war, and the attempts to blow up the Capitalist Orient Express: the atrocity stories related to Stefan de Blowitz in 1883: yes, Bulgaria is indeed the most kicked-around country in Europe.

I ask the station-master about the handsome war-memorial on the platform. Lilian hastens to explain: it isn't a war-memorial, it's a Revolution memorial. "From that day in 1944, September the 9th," she says, "the history of our country really begins."

A little over an hour later we are entering Sofia. "I am sorry, it is not a beautiful station," says Lilian. "This is the one they should have bombed in the war, but they bombed the other one."

In the gathering dusk it is like any other station. But a great surge of humanity moves across the low, open platform towards the train. Surely they don't think there's room to accommodate them within our two poor, battered Wagons-Lits coaches? I misjudge the situation. These Bulgarians are without luggage. They are here to welcome back their teacher and fellow-student with cheers and shouts and flowers. Lilian is almost weeping. It's obviously a great moment. Her father climbs aboard, handsome, grey-haired, shaking hands with everyone and speaking excellent French. So, with a greeting as fervent as anything Miss Bulgaria, or an Olympic Gold Medallist could desire, she disappears with the crowd.

It is a wonderfully cheerful contrast to the sustained misery of the previous twenty-four hours. The American textile man and I decide to storm the station buffet in search of slivovitz. The build-

ing is noisy and boisterous. It's Saturday evening, and many of the
young men are soldiers, taking their girl-friends out. When it
comes to paying for our drinks (with one eye cocked on the train,
since it has a habit of disappearing as soon as it arrives) we have, of
course, no Bulgarian leva. The handsome, barrel-shaped waitress
scornfully waves aside our offer of dollars or pounds sterling. It
really shakes my American companion to have his greenbacks
referred to as "capitalist money". There's nothing for it but to try
out a sheaf of Jugoslav dinars. She looks at them with contempt
until the amount is so great that not even the most patriotic Bulgarian could turn them down. She stuffs the dinars up her mutton-
chop sleeve, and nods.

We have paid about four dollars for drinks worth about a tenth
of that. But we have been in a Bulgarian buffet in Sofia, and we
scramble back on to the train like naughty schoolboys.

The Wagons-Lits attendant has made up the bed in No. 3. This
ritual is something which was kept up throughout the journey by
each conductor. Whatever the other shortcomings, the linen was
changed each day; crisp and fresh, with the antimacassar placed
in position at ten in the morning. You might starve, but at least
you'd die with your sheets clean. In French, I manage to explain
about my picnic supper, and the difficulty of dealing with it. The
Bulgarian conductor looks sympathetic and disappears into his
compartment at the end of the coach. He reappears with a pen-
knife, which he wipes on his trousers as he offers it to me.

Thus is supper dished out to the American and myself by the
*Compagnie Internationale des Wagons-Lits et des Grands Express
Européens.* How Grand can an Express be, and how Direct can an
Orient be?

What's it like to be a Bulgarian? I found myself asking this
question as we pulled into Plovdiv (once Philippopolis, the
Thracian town of Philip of Macedon, the Roman Triniontium, of
Marcus Aurelius and Trajan). The platform seemed as crowded as
at Sofia, and at ten o'clock at night they were invading the local
trains, mercifully leaving the Orient Express alone. Everything
was very gay and cheerful : they obviously enjoy Saturday nights
in Bulgaria, and there's a sort of noisy bravado in their greetings.
Good Communists, presumably. The American was hopping mad

when a Bulgarian, foiled in his attempt to get into our coach, shook his fist and shouted, in English, "Capitalists!" Of course we are, or we wouldn't be here in our Wagons-Lits *voiture,* sealed off and starving. So I hope *he's* a good Communist. The American fumes: "I don't believe in co-existence. That God-damned bastard called me a Capitalist! We've got to get even with them. We'll have to kill an awful lot of people . . ." and the rest is just a weary muttering.

The handsome, red-and-white, Russian-built diesel locomotive, which took us from Sofia to Plovdiv, disappears, as all diesels do on this journey, and we are back on steam again. I'm determined to stay awake as long as I can, and allowing for cat-naps between the clean sheets, I must see the frontier stations of Svilengrad and Pythion. We actually go through a corner of Greece on the journey, but there's no Greek Customs. This is the neck of the woods fought over with such bitterness through so many decades.

Bulgaria itself, apart from the occupation by the Turks, was occupied by the Russians in 1878, and by the British, Italians and French African troops in 1918. But Macedonia had Greek domination to deal with as well. "Come over into Macedonia and help us," would have been a vain call in those days. No one helped this wretched part of the Balkan world.

Svilengrad is very much a Graham Greene place. The station-master stands in a little wooden office, lit by an oil lamp. Grouped round him are several dim figures in greatcoats. Another official arrives out of the darkness with a noisy acetylene flare. All compare notes, or regulations, or whatever the foolscap pages are, beneath the golden glow. I wouldn't have been surprised to learn that the Orient Express had just run over Anna Karenina. It's that sort of setting. The night is warm and smoky, with a smell of railways about it. This is the sort of place that doesn't exist during the day. In all the time-tables I've seen quoting Svilengrad, the arrival seems always to be in the small hours.

The dawn is just lifting when we arrive at Pythion, on the Turkish border, at about five a.m. Dragoman was a Muslim name: surely Pythion, like Marathon, is a Greek name, dating back to the rule of the hated Greeks in Macedonia? There is utter silence everywhere: in fact, it must have been the silence that

189

woke me. No longer is there the panting of the Westinghouse brake, that obligato of the night : no banshee wail from any whistle. The dirty, scruffy station looks completely deserted, until a figure in a greatcoat, carrying a lamp, clumps down the platform and disappears into some office.

Then another babble of voices, and a *ting-ting* which might indicate "train entering section". As the cocks crow and the light strengthens, an engine whistle wails, there's a trembling on the rails. What eventually arrives is not a train, but a single locomotive, bearing the Turkish crescent, hauling a fourgon or baggage wagon. This little equipage squeals to a stop, and disgorges what must obviously be the Turkish Customs and Security officials. I'm too tired to watch further. Anyhow, according to my time-table, we're nearly an hour behind schedule. Perhaps we never recovered from that argument at Poggioreale. . . .

The next awakening is only about half an hour later, at Uzunkopru. There it is, the name on the wooden building, the fabled name, at twenty to seven on a golden morning. There's a buvette, and a little office (shut, of course) which says, in English, TOURIST INFORMATION OFFICE (I merely wanted to be informed about future eating arrangements, if any). The frontier guards and Customs men are drinking tea in the buffet doorway, out of small glasses. Then suddenly a guardian angel appears in our corridor, with tiny cups of Turkish coffee, bitter rather than sweet, and loaded with dregs, but a welcome assault on the taste-buds of the tongue, and there is nothing to pay. "Welcome to Turkey," says the conductor with a beam. "You will come with me to the dining-car soon after we are leaving."

Uzunkopru . . . where those two Russian spies belonging to SMERSH were taken off the train in the Ian Fleming novel, false passports and all. It all looks so pleasant and peaceful now. The tinny jangle of Turkish music comes from a radio inside the bar. Small boys are holding up water melons the size of footballs for the travellers who have survived the third night on the rails. Mounds of turnips at the end of the platform. A row of ox-carts ready for loading. A minaret gleaming in the distance : our first minaret. Today is Sunday, but this is Muslim country, so there's no significance in that.

190

As the train trundles off into arid, featureless country which might be anywhere, the occupants of *voiture* No. 7, including the American, the Australian nurse and the archæologist, are invited to push their way past the mounds of luggage and the squatting peasants, towards the now almost mythical vehicle, the dining-car. Turkish Customs officials are engaged in what looks like a hand-to-hand struggle with local passengers, but we, hollow-eyed, grey with fatigue, bristling of chin and dry of tongue, stumble past without question.

There it is—a small Turkish buffet car dating back, surely, to the days of Edmond About and M. Nagelmackers and the inaugural trip of 1883. There are remnants of tattered splendour about it : inlaid panelling in what was once an artistic de-sign of contrasting mahogany and walnut; mirrors on the walls, chased with designs, two chandeliers in greenish metal, lit by single naked electric bulbs, a raised bar along the centre of the car, giving a strangely wild-west-saloon atmosphere to the whole place.

At that hour and after that degree of privation, it seems like fairyland. There's a small kitchen at one end which might have been a Turkish field-kitchen during the Siege of Vienna in the seventeenth century, but at least some kind of food is coming from it.

A cheerful, smiling young Turk offers us glasses of tea—aro-matic, astringent, reviving. He puts a lavish mixture on the centre counter : cream cheese, pats of butter (we last saw butter back in Italy), plates of black olives, gherkins, sardines, hard cheese and a dish of what I assume is the famous rose-petal jam. We clutch and swallow indiscriminately. He then produces several bottles of beer, and from the far end I can see that one Customs officer is being served with a steaming dish of kebab. This is perhaps more than a delicate stomach can absorb so early in the morning, but we're told that another session can be arranged after the Customs men have been their rounds. We stagger back to voiture No. 7, and there's no Customs delay for us at all.

The countryside between the border and Istanbul is a startling contrast. At one stage it looks like a scene from the Bible, with shepherds watching their flocks (by day) and a general air of primitive, desiccated misery. Then there are miles of green,

191

wooded hills and glades, like the hinterland of the Thames Valley or Wimbledon Common, or Hampstead Heath. Then bleakness descends, and presents a background as bare as the landscape of the moon.

We make another foray to the little buffet car which so bravely carries the notice WELCOME TO TURKEY in three languages —English, French and German. There's sausage and ham and bottles of Turkish wine, warm and brackish and of doubtful origin, but at this stage we'll take anything, and it all seems very cheap.

Some of the delay in schedule is caught up when, at a station not far from Istanbul, the line becomes electrified (for the first time, I estimate, since Venice—or was it Milan?). The appearance of the Orient Express is an opportunity for week-end sightseers to wave as it passes. The rump of this once-famous train, now shrunk to three coaches, one fourgon, and several goods trucks which have been ignominiously attached to the rear—the last indignity a noble train could suffer.

But now, the trucks are detached. A few teenage girls and their boy-friends come close to the carriage windows and talk to us in English. Our young archeaologist singles out a dark-haired beauty and challenges her to climb aboard and come to Istanbul with us. At the drop of a Turkish scimitar, I think she'd have done so, but the boy-friends think otherwise.

Now the pace of the train increases. The Sea of Marmara sweeps majestically into view, and the first bathing beaches. A glance at the map shows how much of a seaside city Istanbul is, open to the water on three sides. Early maps and charts of Constantinople show that this has been so through the centuries. As one seventeenth century traveller wrote: "The harbour of Constantinople is the most spacious, the finest, and the most advantageously situated in the world."

The entry into the city by rail is probably as impressive as the journey from the Black Sea down the Bosphorus, the route of that inaugural trip back in the eighties. The train passes the old city walls which stretch in picturesque ruin right from the Fort of the Seven Towers on the Sea of Marmara, to Eyup, the village of Pierre Loti, overlooking the sluggish Golden Horn. From here onwards the line runs close to the sea, and one after another the great mosques appear, with their minarets which Johnny Morris likened to guided missiles.

The final curve, after St. Sophia, is round Seraglio Point, under the walls of Topkapi Palace, the home of the Sultans from the 15th Century onwards, until it became a museum. The walls of the Seraglio, the old Harem, are clearly visible. De Blowitz observed them on his return journey. Sirkeci Station lies just short of the Galata Bridge, connecting the old town with the new. We can hardly believe that this is journey's end, amid all the seething crowd and shouting under a blinding sun. There is a rush of relatives, some smart-looking, some broad-faced peasants in head-scarves. By a miracle a young and pretty representative of the Turkish Tourist Board recognises me, perhaps from the lamentable photograph on my Basin (Press) card, which was sent to Istanbul several weeks before. I offer my ticket 00733 with regret (but am allowed to keep it as a souvenir) and am whisked away in a Government car. This is a very different reception from the one given to the travellers of 1883, the "sixth rate Tattersall's" described by the *Times* correspondent.

It is all here : the Galata Bridge, the Genoese Galata Tower, the Bosphorus with the ferries crossing to Asia. From the balcony of my hotel room, high above the blue waters, there is a view which seems to erase all the trials of the journey. There is even an immense United States aircraft carrier, firmly anchored in the middle of the Straits, reminder that Turkey is an allied country, and the third largest contributor of troops and funds to the North Atlantic Treaty Organisation.

13

JOURNEY'S END

A walk around the "sad, severe, gorgeous" city—Topkapi Palace and Santa Sophia—Modern Turkish life—Lady Mary Wortley Montagu and the Turkish Bath—Reflections on Orient Expresses—The Lure of Istanbul—Goodbye to the Bosphorus.

Istanbul, in the words of James Morris, one of the best and most sensitive of travel-writers, is a "sad, severe, gorgeous" city. Sad, perhaps, because the Ottomans lost an Empire which at one time stretched westward to the gates of Vienna, and eastward to the Egyptian desert, or perhaps because Constantinople was the last capital of the great Roman Empire before falling to the Turks, and everything about Istanbul is designed on a scale befitting the capital of an Empire. Severe, because life has always seemed cheap to the Turks. They have made magnificent soldiers, but have been indifferent philosophers and still more indifferent humanitarians. The legends of cruelty behind the sunlit walls of the Seraglio at Topkapi are legion : the tales of weighted corpses on the bed of the Bosphorus multiply. Gorgeous, because, in its setting, Istanbul can challenge any other city in the world.

The prospect of a taste of the casbah, a whiff of Asia, a pause at the cross-roads of two continents, is surely the promise which has brought so many travellers on the long and tedious railway journey from Paris. There's the unspoken thought that a mild form of danger lurks here, that law and order, as we know them in the democracies, could somehow be set aside. There's a perverse pleasure in shuddering about atrocities, and in brooding over the appalling lives of the Pashas, Great Eunuchs, Grand Viziers, Sultans, Sultanas and other high-and-mighty who gave Constantinople a world-wide reputation for colourful corruption. The tame life of Europe has been left behind.

194

The seventeenth century English traveller Edward Browne summed up this change in the eastward journey.

"A man seems to take leave of our world when he hath passed a day's journey from Rab (Gyor): and, before he comes to Buda, seems to enter upon a new stage of the world, quite different from that of western countries: for he then bids adieu to hair on the head, bands, cuffs, hats, gloves, beds, beer: and enters upon habits, manners and a course of life which, with no great variety but under some conformity, extends into China and the utmost parts of Asia. . . ." (Quoted in *The Siege of Vienna* by John Stoye. Holt, New York, 1965.)

It is also, perhaps, for Christians, the change to a Muslim country: the elaborate ritual of muezzin and minaret (which, in modern Istanbul, amid the frenzy of the traffic, seems to have as little impact on the ordinary man's life as church-going does in New York or London). Holy Friday was always the day when the Sultan appeared in public, at the mosque. Even the tetchy, terrified Abdul Hamid kept his Friday ritual—which is why Stefan de Blowitz got his interview. Today, with a republic run by a General, and with the impact of Ataturk imprinted on the nation's mind and language, this is all of less importance. But it is all valuable as a means of persuading a British or American tourist that Istanbul and the Bosphorus should be part of his Grand Tour.

The other element is, of course, the position of women in a country like Turkey. Polygamy and the subjection of the allegedly weaker sex is something which interests female writers as well as male. In Turkey, they ranged from the eccentric Lady Hester Stanhope, who maintained her extraordinary existence in a remote ruined monastery, dressing like a man ("sometimes as Chief of Albanians, sometimes as a Syrian soldier, sometimes as a Bedouin Arab, and at other times like the son of a Pasha") to Rose Macaulay, whose *Towers of Trebizond* is one of the most tender and yet caustic books on Turkey, and whose Aunt Dot went travelling into Arabia, not by the Taurus Express, but by camel.

Another celebrated resident of Constantinople was Lady Mary Wortley Montagu, wife of Edward, appointed Ambassador to the Sublime Porte in 1717. Her letters to Alexander Pope and other English worthies could almost qualify her as the Madame de

Sevigné of the Turkish capital, but eventually she tired both of Turkey and of her husband, and went to live in Italy. My own favourite piece among her Constantinople commentaries is her visit to a female Turkish bath.

"Designing to go *incognito,* I hired a Turkish coach. These *voitures* are not at all like ours, but much more convenient for the country, the heat being so great that glasses would be very troublesome. . . . I went to the bagnio about ten o'clock. It was already full of women. It is built of stone, in the shape of a dome, with no windows but in the roof, which gives light enough. . . . I was in my travelling habit, which is a riding dress, and certainly appeared very extraordinary to them. Yet there was not one of them that shewed the least surprise or impertinent curiosity, but received me with all the obliging civility possible. I know no European court where the ladies would have behaved themselves in so polite a manner to a stranger."

The portress stood at the door, and everyone apparently was expected to give her a crown, or ten shillings. "This," said Lady Mary "seemed a great deal to me".

In the first room "there were four fountains of cold water, running on the floor in channels for that purpose, which carried the streams into the next room, with the same sort of marble sofas, but so hot with streams of sulphur proceeding from the adjoining baths, it was impossible to stay there with one's cloaths on. . . ."

Inside "there were many fine women naked, in different postures, some in conversation, some working, others drinking sherbert or coffee, or just lying negligently on their cushions."

Attending them were their slaves, "without any distinction of rank by their dress, all being in the state of nature, that is, in plain English, stark naked, without any beauty or defect concealed. Yet there was not the least wanton smile or immodest gesture among them. They walked and moved with the same majestic grace which Milton describes of our General Mother. . . ."

"In short, it is the women's coffee-house, where all the news of the town is told, scandal invented, etc. They generally take this diversion once a week, and stay there at least four or five hours, without getting cold by coming out of the hot bath into the cold room, which was very surprising to me. . . ."

Lady Mary also pursued the story of the antics of the Whirling Dervishes (souvenirs of which can be bought in the more garish stores of the Egyptian Bazaar). They still perform today, but rather self-consciously, and the whole operation needs a lot of organising. In Lady Mary's time their devotions appeared to her "as whimsical as any at Rome". Every Tuesday and Friday they appeared, and each was personally blessed by the Sheikh before beginning his celebrated rotation. The whole ceremony is, surely, part of the early sun-worship tradition. The point about the Dervishes is that as in Lady Mary's time, they do continue until exhausted, or in a sort of trance. "They did not become giddy," reports the Ambassador's observant wife, "which is not to be wondered at, when it is considered, they are all used to it from their infancy, most of them being devoted to this way of life from their birth."

It is said that the Sheikh himself took part in the dance if there were any signs of danger or distress. At the end of the ceremony, all gave the familiar acknowledgment: "There is no God but God."

No one arriving at Sirkeci Station after the journey from Paris would want to take the next train back. Istanbul is a goal, a terminus, a place every traveller—whether he's flown in from Paris in four hours, or trundled through the Balkans in seventy-two hours—must look at, must try to assess and assimilate.

Being bewitched by the light on the Bosphorus at sundown is one thing. That is the travel brochure come true. Getting accustomed to Istanbul in the 1960s is another.

It's a sprawling town, with no pattern to it other than the three towns which contain it : the Old City, with the mosques and the Seraglio and the bazaar : the New City, Pera, with the Hilton Hotel and the airline offices and Taksim Square and the night-clubs and all the featureless shop-window stuff of any city in the Middle East or Southern Europe : and the Asian town across the Bosphorus, Uskudar (known in British history as Scutari), with the trams going slowly up the steep hills, with Florence Nightingale's old hospital and the pleasant heathland overlooking the whole majestic setting of the city.

It doesn't take long to get to know Istanbul, superficially. Even a short drive around reminds you that it's a seaside town (New York may have its Coney Island handy, but you have to go fifty miles out of London to find beaches like those on the Sea of Marmara, close to the heart of Istanbul).

Then we delve into history. It may be the incredible, echoing water cisterns built underground by the Emperor Justinian nearly fifteen hundred years ago—and made use of prominently in the James Bond film *From Russia, with Love*. It may be the mosques. Take your pick out of five hundred. Suleiman the Magnificent? Santa Sophia, the biggest of them all? The Blue Mosque of Sultan Ahmed—recent, but redolent with colour and ceramics?

Suleiman's Mosque has probably the best situation, reflecting the magnificence of the Ottoman Empire which stretched at that time from the outskirts of Vienna to Egypt and Persia. Santa Sophia will be, for many, the great let-down. It has everything in antiquity to recommend it. The Emperor Constantine built his first Christian church here about three hundred years after the Crucifixion. Justinian, in A.D. 532, had marble and porphyry sent to Constantinople, so that he could build a place bigger than Solomon's Temple in Jerusalem—an unworthy Christian ambition, maybe, but one he seems to have achieved. It was opened as a Christian church five years later, but nine hundred years passed before the Turks, taking the city in 1453, converted it into a mosque. Today, it is a museum, and a dusty, noisy museum at that. It's as if St. Paul's Cathedral in London (the nave of Santa Sophia is about the same size) had been turned over as a shrine for British Railways. The main reason for converting it—or, one might say, un-converting it—into a museum is that the most precious Christian frescoes and mosaics in the world have been discovered there, and, with the aid of various American institutes, are being revealed year by year. With all these mosques in Istanbul, the Turks have been wise to sacrifice one to the cause of international culture and tourism. The mosaics are staggering in their impact, glittering with pure gold, and with those challenging bright-eyed Byzantine faces. Jesus is there, and Mary, and the Archangel Gabriel. The place echoes with the buzz of school-parties and the hammering of working-parties, discovering more mosaics. It is all enormous and very grubby—in fact rather like a religious railway station.

The Blue Mosque of Sultan Ahmed is in direct contrast. Here is a mosque in use, which means shoes removed, and carpets laid down, and a general air of activity. The blue colour scheme is as good as you'd expect from such a comparatively late work (seventeenth century) but most of it has been painted on, and isn't ceramic work, as one might expect it to be. There are, however, some magnificent tiles, and the dome is one of the largest in the world, over a hundred feet in diameter.

The temptation, in Istanbul, is to quote Omar Khayyam, who wrote of Isfahan :

> "Think, in this battered caravanserai
> Whose portals are alternate Night and Day
> How Sultan after Sultan with his Pomp
> Abode his Hour or two, and went his way."

As with the Sultans of Persia, so with the Sultans of Turkey. The Imperial Palace and Seraglio of Topkapi is, like the Shwe Dagon Temple in Rangoon or the Temple of the Emerald Buddha in Bangkok, a place no traveller will ever forget. It has been a museum for more than a century, and there is peace and quiet here, high above the din of the market and the traffic heading for Galata Bridge. The long, quaint line of chimneys in the royal kitchens are a mere memory of the gigantic feasts laid on by Sultans in their pomp. Hibiscus and poinsettia glow in the central garden. The men on duty inside the Imperial Treasury are sad, indifferent types, though fully armed. Ever since Eric Ambler wrote his thriller about a robbery at Topkapi, *Light of Day*, they have presumably been aware of the value of the gold and jewels under their care. I was told that some of these immense rubies and emeralds are, in fact, imitations, for reasons of security, but they are so large and ostentatious that I don't mind. How big can a precious stone be before it ceases to look precious? Surely the setting of the jewel is the important thing, like the Black Prince's ruby set in the Royal Crown of England. Lumps of green or red stone are, in themselves, ugly and unromantic—though no doubt useful as an investment.

199

The treasure rooms of Topkapi also reveal a monotony of gems. It seems that Sultans would order everything to be bejewelled: writing-cases, books, hookahs, pistols, bird cages—all are studded with rubies and emeralds. In the Tutankhamen museum in Cairo you get tired of the sight of gold, but it is often worked in artistically with *lapis lazuli*. The treasures of Topkapi are the vulgar products of men without taste.

There is one room here which very vividly portrays "Sultan after Sultan in his pomp". The ceremonial robes of every ruler from Mohammed II in the fifteenth century are displayed in glass cases, and every robe is of a different colour or design. There must have been a long tradition among tailors with the Imperial warrant, to see that no fashion was ever repeated. On the walls are the official portraits of the Sultans. Abdul Hamid II, who received the *Times* representative from the Orient Express, and lived on, remarkably, to die a peaceful death in exile in 1918, stares stonily from the picture frame. Near him is his uniform, with the coat lined in crimson silk.

Not all Sultans died so peacefully. One was garrotted on the city walls, and his tunic, cut in the effort to save his life, is there in its original state, with a large, faded bloodstain down one side. Another cheerful exhibit is the blood-stained robe of Sultan Abdul Azazin, who committed suicide by cutting the veins in his wrists with scissors. The Museum authorities have included the scissors themselves in the glass case.

The vast kitchens are now used to house the most remarkable collection in Topkapi, more to be admired than the twenty-million dollar jewelled throne or all the daggers and pendants and bracelets: the porcelain, which comes mainly from China and Japan, and is the biggest and most valuable collection of its kind in the world. Tenth century, Sung dynasty; fourteenth century, Yuan dynasty; fifteenth and sixteenth centuries, Ming dynasty. All beautifuly simple in design and colour. Everything priceless. All given as presentations to the Sultans. There is, in fact, so much of this porcelain that only a proportion can be exhibited.

At one time about five thousand people lived within the walls of the Seraglio. It was a town within a town. Later the Sultans lived in the ornate but reasonably modest Dolmabache Palace on the banks of the Bosphorus, with the one exception of Abdul Hamid II, who lived out his life in mortal fear in the Yilditz Palace. There are so many legends and tales about Topkapi Palace that we must call a halt, and remember that, while the Turks do not in any way attempt to whitewash the misdeeds of their Sultans—and indeed realise that their lavish excesses are one reason why tourists come to Topkapi—they are themselves in an entirely different category, a modest, abstemious, almost shy people, who have accepted the westernising influence of Kemal Ataturk without a murmur, but who also apparently approved of the imprisonment and slaughter of the entire Menderes regime.

What is the real lure of Istanbul? Has it still the attraction which led travellers to old Constantinople? It is, to be sure, the only city in the world which is astride two continents. At dusk, when the myriad lights wink out from Asia, beyond Leander's Tower, the city has a magic of its own. But there's a grey cloud of industrial smoke hanging round the Golden Horn, and the din in Taksim Square, where the commuters are queueing up for the long-distance Dolmus taxis, is tremendous : no muezzin could be heard by the Faithful at this hour. The wretched, animal-like *hamals*, the porters who carry such fantastic loads are still pounding their way up the hill from the Old City. No, Istanbul is not really a romantic city. It combines the qualities of Liverpool and Naples.

Yet there must be some lure about standing on the edge of Asia, some atmosphere which has brought Western travellers on the Orient Express for more than eighty years, in all manner of comfort and discomfort. Travelling by train has its disadvantages; in fact, to describe the Direct Orient or Istanbul Express as an Express is a falsehood. It is an interminable stopping-train, as several travellers have pointed out. The only reason for going on it (apart perhaps from an aversion to air travel) is to get a glimpse of life in the countries through which you pass—that, and the genuine economy of travelling the hard way. Only the Wagons-Lits supplements bring the price into line with air-tickets.

201

No doubt the policy of the *Compagnie Internationale* will continue to exploit the precious word "Orient" in their schedules (though the present "Orient Express" is in fact merely a train as far as Vienna). The original idea of M. Nagelmackers and Lord Dalziel was to provide a *train-de-luxe* service which would isolate the supplement-paying passengers from any contact with local conditions, and to speed them through countries and past frontiers with the greatest expedition and the minimum of interruption. It was once a status-symbol to have a sheaf of Wagons-Lits tickets; it is so no longer. An age has passed. Bulgaria, one of the more mysterious countries visited by the train, is developing a big tourist trade round the Black Sea resorts near Varna, where de Blowitz and his colleagues had such a miserable time. But it is mainly being being organised by air.

To struggle through to the Sea of Marmara by way of all those countries is at least a rewarding experience. As R. L. Stevenson wrote, on a train journey "the thoughts alight, as the humour moves them, at unfrequented stations". The Orient Express should be preserved for two types; the student, for whom it is cheap, and the sentimentalist, for whom it is fun, and something of an education. Between the Gare de Lyon and the Seraglio is the whole span of Europe. No wonder the thriller writers found the route such a profitable subject, substituting danger and desire for what is merely, these days, disillusion and delay.

The train—and the place. These are the twin elements which have given the Orient Express a unique reputation in the minds of travellers, as well as readers. On the night before your departure back to Western Europe, there could be a jumble of fact-and-fiction memories. On a tour of the town, down by the Yilditz Palace, you might think not only of Sultan Abdul Hamid creeping nightly from room to room, followed by his eunuchs, but of the portly, ridiculous figure of Stefan Opper de Blowitz, dangling his short legs over the window sill, to catch the attention of the "Shadow of God upon Earth". The tall, moustachioed Nagelmackers is busy working out the cost of his epic journey, and checking up on the return tickets. At the Pera Palace Hotel, Carleton Myatt and Janet Pardoe are furtively holding hands under the restaurant table; a little French detective called Poirot

has just checked in, only to be told that he must be at Sirkeci
Station, off Seraglio Point, to catch the night Orient Express.
The English Players under Edward Stirling are to perform *The
Second Mrs. Tanqueray* at the local theatre: perhaps Lady
Diana Wynham has sent her chauffeur out to buy seats. Maybe
James Bond is checking his own reservations with Kerim Bey, the
Turk who said: "There is always excitement on the Orient
Express." Perhaps S. J. Perelman is wishing he hadn't booked his
air-tickets to Rome after all. He might have caught up with
Joseph Wechsberg and learned all about the fabulous Wagons-
Lits conductors.

Bond, anyhow, has sampled the cocktails in the Istanbul
Hilton; and in the little villages along the Bosphorus, people are
sitting out in the cafés, drinking tea from samovars, and watching the ships go by. The muezzin, unheeded, cries, "There is no
God but God", as the cavalcade of coaches passes by to the State
Ball, and the British Ambassador prepares to receive a sun-
tanned, exhausted wearer of the Silver Greyhound, the Queen's
Messenger. In the city, Lady Mary Wortley Montagu casts an
appraising eye over the nubile odalisques in the women's Turkish
bath; the reporter Johnny Morris watches, fascinated, as the
letter-writers ply their peculiar trade in the Egyptian bazaar.

It is a wrench to leave Istanbul because, inevitably, you leave
without discovering its secret. And you leave either at high noon,
on the Direct Orient to Paris, or at 3.20 in the afternoon for
Munich on the Istanbul Express. At both times, the station is as
crowded as a cattle market, and as noisy. Sounds ricochet from
the ugly station walls. The platform is seething with people of all
types—the solid peasant women seeing their sons off to work in
Germany or Jugoslavia, the students whose friends are taking a
course in a Western University, the elegant blonde who brings
her black poodle along, to wish her gentleman friend farewell.

This is more than the mere departure of a train. Every time the
Orient leaves Sirkeci, it is an event and an occasion. For many, it
is a changing-point in life, a new career, a decision taken, a
journey to another home. This is what gives the scene its essential
pathos, amid all the din, and the scurrying to fill water-bottles at
the station fountain. Several of the coaches are local—one is

merely going as far as Uzunkopru—but the magic name-boards which fascinated James Bond are there on two of them, ending with the word PARIS.

The Wagons-Lits conductor consults his list, and prepares to put his house in order. Yes, he assures a sceptical passenger, there is a restaurant car as far as the border. After that? He shrugs his shoulders; it is not his responsibility. But in Turkey, Madame, you will be comfortable, and well fed. There is kebab for lunch, a pleasant reminder of your stay.

The din increases, as if everyone on the station knows that the moment of departure has arrived. At midday, the two clock hands are one. There's an outbreak of whistling, a shuddering of carriages, and a slow, almost imperceptible movement forward.

Then the extraordinary sound which accompanies the departure. It is half roar, half sigh. The Orient Express glides out of the station's humid shade into the brilliant sunshine, sidling past the old Seraglio walls towards the first of many frontiers.

INDEX

INDEX

INDEX

INDEX

INDEX